Moscow and the New Left

Klaus Mehnert

MOSCOW AND THE NEW LEFT

Translated by
HELMUT FISCHER from the German
and
LUTHER WILSON from the Russian

UNIVERSITY OF CALIFORNIA PRESS

Berkeley · Los Angeles · London

0 0 7 7 6 8

HX
314
.Z7 M4313
1975

Title of the German original: *Moskau und die Neue Linke*;
published by Deutsche Verlags-Anstalt, Stuttgart, Germany

University of California Press
Berkeley and Los Angeles, California
University of California Press, Ltd.
London, England

Printed in the United States of America

To my friends
among the intelligentsia
in West and East.
They have more in common
than they think.

Klaus Mehnert

CONTENTS

PREFACE

This book is a sequel to my earlier *Peking and the New Left* (1969), which, however, discussed mainly Peking's own New Left, the Red Guards. The present volume examines Moscow's attitude toward the New Left outside the Soviet orbit. I am pleased to have both studies published by the University of California, the school I attended forty-seven years ago.

The New Left, in its by now classical form, had its heyday in the sixties, and came to an end toward the ebb of the American engagement in Vietnam. In this book, the term New Left encompasses all those revolutionary movements and groups in the West which desired to change the world and its life style radically, according to socialist principles but by methods and aims very different from those of the old left, led by Moscow. This New Left includes the rebellious Parisian students of May, 1968, the American and the German SDS (the initials are the same, the meanings somewhat different), the anarchists, Trotskyites, and Maoists (outside China), and the politically relevant groups among the hippies.

No systemization of the New Left's countless shifting trends and currents has been attempted here; Moscow too rarely differentiates among them. The reader can find an official Soviet interpretation of the New Left in the next-to-last document of this book. One thing is clear: leftists who do not fit into current Soviet tactics are denigrated by the Soviet leadership, and called "leftists" in quotation marks. Only unswerving followers of the Moscow line may call themselves plain leftists. My practice, on the contrary, is to use quotation marks only when quoting from Soviet sources. For me the New Left is left.

What, then, is the New Left for the Soviet leaders—an ally, rival, or an enemy? What is their attitude toward radical movements on the left which adamantly refuse Moscow's dogma tĺat socialism, by definition, can only be Soviet socialism, as interpreted and practiced by the USSR? Is it irrelevant for the "socialist Soviet Union" what happens ideologically in the "capitalist West," is the Soviet Union immune to movements in West-

ern industrial society, among them the unrest of youth, or do such movements manage to penetrate the thought curtain along the Soviet border?

To seek answers to these questions seemed valuable, for they could
show, applied to an interesting model, the New Left, how Moscow reacts
to unexpected events abroad, and whether its thinking has managed to
mature beyond simplistic, black-and-white propaganda toward greater so-
phistication. The answers to these questions might also indicate whether
Soviet readers, from their publications, learn more than clichés about intellectual developments outside their country, and perhaps even whether such
information, through a kind of osmosis, can exert an influence on them.

Apart from conversations with Soviet citizens, Soviet publications are
the chief basis of this study. In addition to all books and pamphlets available, I used primarily twenty-five Moscow periodicals (generally for the
five years from 1968 on, in some instances beginning with 1960). Thus I
found some four hundred relevant articles, which, together with the books
and pamphlets, add up to about 3,000 magazine pages. Articles in the daily
press are not included in these figures; these were investigated only for
periods of unusual tension, like May and June 1968 during the Paris uprising.

For the Western reader and researcher it is awkward that, with few exceptions, Soviet writers have not yet learned to cite chapter and verse for
their quotations. They refer to books used without indicating where and
when these were published, they cite authors as witnesses without giving
their initials, when referring to articles they seldom mention the year of
publication, let alone the exact date. Indexes are rare.

This book, by giving detailed bibliographical data, tries to enable the
reader to check all the material employed. Where only one article by an
author was used, only his name is given in parenthesis (e.g. Afanas'yev);
if more than one article, the key word of each title is added (e.g. Kon,
"Reflections"). One short chapter ("Materials") discusses the periodicals
examined, another ("Authors") tells the reader about the most important
writers cited. Excerpts from twenty-five articles are printed as documents
in the appendix, along with some relevant quotations from Lenin and
from official statements.

Most of the book was written from September 1972 to June 1973, while
I was the guest of Columbia University's Research Institute on Communist Affairs. My sincere thanks to my host Zbigniew Brzezinski, the Institute's director, and his staff and my colleagues, especially Marshall and
Colette Shulman, and students in New York for their stimulating ideas
and fellowship during many informative discussions. My thanks, also, to

the staff of Columbia's Russian Institute, Library of the School of International Affairs, and Butler Library.

My thanks to Max Knight of the University of California Press for his great help, and my appreciation for the work of the translators, Helmut Fischer (from the German text) and Luther Wilson (from the Russian). Mr. Wilson has followed the transliteration system of the United States Board on Geographic Names, with the modification that names ending in *iy* are rendered with a plain *y*. Ellipses in Russian originals are given as dots . . . , omissions by the author as [. . .].

In the present book the author participates as a third party in the debate between Moscow and the New Left. Knowing both parties and their dialogue from the beginning, though aligned with neither side, I am concerned with their future and that of the world in general. Thus I hope that this book—my share, so to speak, in a three-way dialogue—may contribute to a new, emerging style of debate suitable to our age, an age of peaceful coexistence, yet one in which (as the Soviet leaders tell us unceasingly) the "ideological struggle" cannot be dispensed with.

The echo from Moscow to the German edition, to be sure, has not been especially encouraging. E. Ambartsumov, three of whose articles are mentioned in this book, published an ill-tempered review of more than 3,000 words in *Literaturnaya Gazeta* (6, 1974, 14). Among his dislikes is my chapter on Lenin. The Moscow dogmatists, I realize, prefer a monopoly on interpreting Lenin, but like it or not, they must grant to foreign observers the right to check the words of the master before examining the writings of his lesser disciples. If Ambartsumov found factual errors, he does not disclose them, nor does he contribute any pertinent statements by Lenin which I might have overlooked.

On the one hand, Ambartsumov detects contradictions between the book's assertion that Moscow for many years had overlooked the New Left and, on the other hand, my repeated reference to statements by Soviet writers who did in fact discuss the New Left. It is easy, of course, for Soviet authors to criticize a foreign book because no reader of their reviews will ever read the book. (None of the fifteen copies of the German edition which I sent to friends in Moscow reached them.) Hence readers of Ambartsumov will never know that what he calls a contradiction is merely the result of lapse of time: Until 1968 the New Left was indeed overlooked, after the Paris revolt of that year it was noted and gradually understood. Is it a contradiction if, in reporting a process, its first phase is seen to differ from the second, as the egg differs from the chicken?

Any favorable remarks which I make about Soviet authors (and there are quite a few) do not fit into the Soviet picture of the biased Western observer; each time, therefore, Ambartsumov jubilantly declares that I was "forced to admit" this or that. Forced by whom, Mr. Ambartsumov? Even now it is inconceivable to him and some of his colleagues that as a rule Western scholars study problems to discover the facts, not to prove a point.

According to Ambartsumov, I am constitutionally incapable of grasping Soviet realities because my German grandfather once owned a chocolate factory in Moscow. To say that my grandfather, who died in 1907, and his factory (incidentally still the best in the USSR, under the new name Red October) have determined my *Weltanschauung,* approaches the worst kind of primitive Marxism. But if grandfathers are indeed important, what about a study concerning the grandfathers of current Moscow ideologues? How many such grandfathers were red-blooded proletarians? Surely Ambartsumov's were not.

The attack against the book shows how unhappy Moscow is about the New Left's peculiar ways, and about foreign authors describing Moscow's slowness of reaction to it. Obviously Ambartsumov, originally not a bad writer, after some troubles during recent years hopes to ingratiate himself with his superiors by his review. I wish him well. But he did not proceed very skillfully:

He thought it witty to compare me with Gulliver's Laputians, one of whose "Eyes turned inward, and the other directly up to the Zenith." Very well. But he forgot that the inhabitants of Laputa also have other characteristics: Their clothes are, as Jonathan Swift tells us, "very ill made, and quite out of Shape," their "Houses are very ill built, the Walls bevil," "They long to see the world" although permission "is not easy to be obtained," and they even demand "great Immunitys, the Choice of their own Governor, and other like Exorbitances," for which, of course, they are severely punished. These and many other Laputian features resemble conditions less in the West than in a country much closer to Mr. Ambartsumov, and much more familiar to him.

It might have been wiser for him not to quote the fancies of Jonathan Swift, but to stick to verifiable facts, as we shall now proceed to do.

Berkeley (California) and
Schömberg (West Germany)   K.M.

I

THUS SPAKE LENIN

"[. . .] there is no more precarious moment for a government in a revolutionary period than the beginning of concessions, the beginning of vacillation" (V. I. Lenin, March 1, 1903, "The Autocracy is Wavering," from *Collected Works,* English translation of the 4th Russian edition, VI, 351).

In the Soviet Union, anyone writing on any subject uses Lenin as a means of orientation. From Lenin he adopts the system of coordinates into which he fits his subject. Thus, in articles or books that deal with more than impressions of the New Left, quotations and categories derived from Lenin are seldom absent; this practice also applies to works about youth. Some articles are based entirely on Lenin, for example L. Spiridonov's "V. I. Lenin on the Role and Place of Students in the Revolutionary Movement."

Lenin has written a great deal on leftists. When they rejected his leadership he placed the word in quotation marks, a practice still observed today, even by the Chinese, when speaking of leftist anti-Maoists. Lenin's continuing concern was to distinguish his own left from the "left" that rivaled him, and to smash that "left" ideologically; hence his works, according to the index to the fourth edition, contain references to "leftists" on as many as 850 pages. This does not include the many references to leftists without quotation marks.

One of Lenin's writings is concerned entirely with this subject: *"Left-Wing" Communism—An Infantile Disorder* (1920). Here he rages against the "leftists'" lack of a sense of reality; for three chapters (VI–VIII) he demands their readiness for compromise, for cooperation with even the "most reactionary" labor unions and parliaments. He sees them entirely as rebels without plan, as victims of anarchy because of a lack of a clear ideology, as "petty-bourgeois gone wild." They are characterized as such even

1

today, as by the historian K. Varlamov in his article "Lenin Against Petty Bourgeois Revolutionarism."

Lenin also speaks of youth, though more rarely and with noticeably less interest. In his works concerning youth (also published as special editions in many languages), young people preoccupy him little; he has not much to say about the problems, psychology, or behavior of youth. He does not see generations, only classes; hence youth also interests him primarily from the viewpoint of its deployment in the class struggle.

Most of his writings on youth thus relate specifically to revolutionary, at any rate revolutionizable youth. His remarks concerning "youth in the revolution and in the revolutionary movement" appear, according to the index, on only 81 pages of his works; furthermore, they are unequally distributed. In the five volumes containing the writings of the years 1901 to 1905 this subject is referred to on 52 pages, the remaining thirty volumes contain references on a mere 29. After the failure of the revolution of 1905 Lenin lost interest in revolutionary youth.

Understandably Lenin occupied himself almost exclusively with Russian youth, not youth in general. But his picture of revolutionary Russian youth early in the century resembles that of the youth of the sixties in the rest of the world, despite the basic changes that have occurred in the position of Russia, the West, and the world in the intervening years.

ON THE COURSE OF DISTURBANCES

The unrest of Russian students of his time emerges in Lenin's publications of the years 1901 to 1905, for the first time in January 1901 (see the document, "Student Unrest 1901"). (The parenthetical numbers in this chapter refer to the bibliography's numbered list of Lenin's writings; some documents can be found in the appendix.)

The disputes begin, first, with small academic arguments centering on the person of a professor (Lenin, No. 1), on permission for a memorial service for a leftist author, dead for forty years (Lenin, No. 2), on an unauthorized demonstration in honor of a liberal writer (Lenin, No. 2), on greater academic freedom (Lenin, No. 14).

Second: The authorities react clumsily. At one point they give in, then again arrest protesting students (Lenin, Nos. 1, 4); they permit the students some self-government, then revoke it (Lenin, No. 4); they "flirt" with the students, then again use force (Lenin, No. 4).

Lenin, I might add, held a low opinion of such indecisive politics, even in the interests of the tsarist regime. His attitude can be formulated in this way: If someone in power begins to yield, he shovels his own grave. "There is no more precarious moment for a government in a revolutionary period than the beginning of concessions, the beginning of vacillation." Explaining, he adds: "The [Russian] government wanted to make concessions on the student question—and made a laughing-stock of itself, advancing the revolutionisation of the students by seven-league strides" (Lenin, No. 5). Even today Lenin's successors take his teaching to heart.

Third: The authorities and conservative public opinion brand the students rowdies and treat them accordingly, thus provoking them to yet more battle and driving them into the arms of revolution (Lenin, No. 1).

Fourth: The protest spreads from academic questions to general political questions (Lenin, No. 2); Lenin's first significant call was for the transition from academic battle to political battle. The students were not to limit themselves to the battle for academic, that is, student freedom, but to fight for the freedom of the entire people, for political freedom (Lenin, No. 3). This remark in particular is often quoted by Soviet authors writing on the New Left today.

Fifth: Students and workers join in the struggle against the regime (Lenin, No. 12). For Lenin this point was decisive. Its realization presupposed that the students move from the narrow frame of higher education into the general political arena.

Lenin's descriptions, of course, were at the same time attempts to influence the students. From reports of Russia reaching him during his exile he selected whatever news fit into his conceptions, and which, in his writings, could serve as models for the further nurturing of the Russian Revolution. But he was not satisfied with describing models. He posed demands: in his articles, which were distributed in the Russian underground, and in his letters to the comrades back home.

Nor did he shy from giving the students direct instructions for battle. The first were harmless: the throwing of stink bombs (Lenin, No. 1); later they went further: explosives were to be prepared, police stations blasted, opponents killed. All must learn, he said, the revolutionary style of battle, "if it is only by beating up policemen: a score or so victims will be more than compensated for by the fact that this will train hundreds of experienced fighters, who tomorrow will be leading hundreds of thousands" (Lenin, No. 14).

In his writings of those years Lenin continuously warned radical youth about the liberals who were objects of his special hate. He scorned them as *"khodul'nyye lyudishky,"* or "manikins on stilts" (Lenin, No. 14); he mocked their timidity (Lenin, No. 15), their scurrying back and forth between the revolutionary students and reactionary authorities (Lenin, No. 11). He warned youth of "false friends," of the pseudo-revolutionaries, in other words of the "leftists" in quotation marks.

WARNING OF COMPETITION FROM THE LEFT

The words of his warnings resemble those that we will hear, six decades later, from his successors concerning "false friends" like Herbert Marcuse, in fact to such an extent that quotation is instructive:

> [All student groups and study circles are advised] that they should beware of those false friends of the youth who divert them from a thorough revolutionary training through recourse to empty revolutionary or idealistic phrase-mongering and philistine complaints about the harm and uselessness of sharp polemics between the revolutionary and the opposition movement [that is, the other "leftist" groups], for as matter of fact these false friends are only spreading an unprincipled and unserious attitude towards revolutionary work [. . .] (Lenin, No. 7).

The aim of these warnings about "false friends" emerges in the following lines of the same document, a resolution drafted by Lenin for the Second Party Congress (1903). Its title, "On the Attitude Towards the Student Youth": "[All student groups are advised] that they should endeavour, when undertaking practical activities, to establish prior contact with the Social-Democratic [in later usage, Bolshevist] organisations, so as to have the benefit of their advice and, as far as possible, to avoid serious mistakes at the very outset of their work" (Lenin, No. 7).

Lenin tried unceasingly to keep revolutionary students from these "false friends" and draw them into his own camp. This was the central theme of his essay, "The Tasks of the Revolutionary Youth" (Lenin, No. 9), appearing in issue 2-3 of the Russian periodical *Student* (Zurich, 1903). It is a typical product of Lenin's pen, full of excessive, voluble polemics against revolutionary rivals. His thesis is expressed in fourteen pages but might have been stated in four. But at the time, and even many years later, Lenin found himself in a continuing debate with many groups and splinter groups of the left.

The sense of his statements, however, is clear: There was no revolutionary youth as such; only Lenin's organization, at that time a small rivulet alongside the rapidly growing revolutionary stream, was truly revolutionary. As he writes himself, he and his followers were called "fanatics of division and dissension," but this did not disturb him. His aim, after all, was not to join the various revolutionary groups into one movement, but the exact opposite, the extraction and organization of a small, conspiratorial, reliable party elite. Or better: an underground organization, because the word "party" implies the idea of public existence. Furthermore, according to Lenin, youth was not to choose the revolutionary current as a whole, but only one party, naturally his. The claim that it was possible to stand above narrow parties was nothing more, for him, than the "hypocritical cant of the ruling classes." For Lenin it was clear: Whoever was not for him, was against him. The Social Revolutionaries, for example, who strongly influenced academic youth, he called a "subdivision of the bourgeois democrats"; soon after his victory of 1917 he destroyed them. In the final analysis, for Lenin there existed only his own organization; all remaining groups, in his eyes, were wrong and enemies.

During his entire political career Lenin, the revolutionary of a primarily agricultural country, preached that only the industrial proletariat was capable of revolution. How, then, would he fit revolutionary students into his thinking? By drawing up two theses.

One thesis stated, without detailed substantiation, that it was reasonable for students—who were mostly of bourgeois, partly of aristocratic origins —to convert to socialism. The socialism of course was the Leninist kind. Using the German word, Lenin declared that only *Superkluge* ("super smarts") thought this inconceivable (Lenin, No. 8). The question of why the sons of the upper class, the young people with "white [coat] linings" (Lenin, No. 1) should one day turn against the interests of their class, Lenin did not examine. On this point, in fact, Soviet authors writing on today's New Left are uninstructed; and as we shall see, they find it difficult to develop plausible reasons of their own.

Lenin wanted the workers to be led by professional revolutionaries, a decisive maxim in his strategy of revolution. Hence he declared that a student, too, could become such a professional. "Regardless of whether student or worker, he can make himself into a professional revolutionary," said Lenin's pamphlet, *What Is to Be Done?* (Lenin, No. 3). Conversely a revolution-minded student was useless, unless he joined Lenin's ranks and made revolution his profession. Unless he did he was worse than a dabbler, since he endangered others. (Lenin, No. 3, IVa, "What is Primitiveness?")

In sum, despite his bourgeois or even petty-bourgeois origin, a student could become a qualified revolutionary, but only by joining Lenin. All other revolutionary groups were "leftists" who had to be fought and, after the victory, destroyed.

After the overthrow of the revolution of 1905, revolutionary student youth disappeared for eleven years from Lenin's horizon. He discussed various questions concerning youth—military service, child labor, sex—but not the role of academic youth in the revolution. There were three exceptions.

First, in 1908 Lenin published his essay, "The Student Movement and the Present Political Situation." He spoke of the "eternal struggle in autocratic Russia against the student organisations," lamented the abortive revolution, the lulling to sleep of revolutionary forces, and the return to prerevolutionary conditions ("Back to the old days! Back to prerevolutionary Russia!"). And he regretted "that even the most active elements of the student body rigidly adhere to pure academism" (Lenin, No. 15).

Second, toward the end of 1912 Lenin wrote a note not published until forty-two years later. In it he made the remark, probably suggesting a mood of resignation, that "the power of organisations is not determined by the number of members, but by their influence on the masses." He believed even then that "he could venture the apparent paradox: the number of members in an organisation should not exceed a minimum *so that* its influence on the masses would remain broad *and firm!*" (Lenin, No. 16).

Third, at the beginning of World War I, Lenin commented in a brief essay on a pamphlet, in German, of an international youth organization (Lenin, No. 19). Although it lacked "theoretical clarity and consistency," he did not expect these qualities in a work composed by young people; for, he admitted, youth was "seething, turbulent, inquiring." Part of this essay is included in the appendix, as the document "Youth—'Seething' and 'Inquiring'." This is essentially the only place in Lenin's works where he talks of specific characteristics of youth. The essay, by the way, is often mentioned even today by Soviet authors who, when discussing the unrest of Western youth, refer to Lenin to protect themselves.

About the same time, in his correspondence, Lenin discussed another theme which indirectly might be called revolutionary. This was the sexual revolution, as we would call it today. Inessa Armand, his French devotee and associate on questions of women and youth, sent him the plan for a book during the first winter of the war. The book, on women's problems, would also deal with the "freedom of love." Though it was never written,

Lenin commented on the plan in two letters to her (a letter from her intervened between his two). In view of the significance of "sexual liberation" for the New Left of our time, Lenin's unequivocal position is significant (see the document "Free Love—Free of What?"); his response also characterizes Lenin the man. In her memoirs the German Communist Klara Zetkin reports that Lenin discussed the question of love and marriage with her as well.

Lenin has not explained the reasons for his disinterest in academic youth after 1905. But they can be inferred from his disappointment on the course of the revolution of 1905, and from his studies on the development of Russia. In 1913 Lenin found statistics in a Russian periodical on the proportionate share of crimes, by the various social groups, against the tsarist state. Between 1884 and 1908, he read, the percentage of students and academics involved in such crimes had receded from 53.3 to 22.9 percent; that of peasants, on the other hand, had increased from 7.1 to 24.2 percent; and the share of people working in commerce and industry had increased from 15.1 to 47.7 percent (Lenin, No. 17). The readiness for revolutionary action, Lenin must have noted, had decreased among intellectuals, increased among peasants and workers.

In a lecture in January 1917 before young workers in Zurich, Lenin analyzed the phases of the Russian revolution (see the document, "Only the Proletariat . . ."). In the first phase, especially 1825, the aristocracy had carried the revolution; in the second phase, Lenin noted, essentially up to the assassination of Tsar Alexander II in 1881, it was carried by the intellectuals of the bourgeoisie; finally, in the third, especially in 1905, by the proletariat. In the first phase, he added, the revolution had been led by officers, yet in the third it was they who had brutally suppressed it (Lenin, No. 20). We can add what Lenin in his lecture could not yet know—that in the fourth phase, finally, during the February and the October revolutions of 1917, the young bourgeoisie, then for the most part in uniform at the front, was in the camp of the monarchists or liberals; only few followed the leadership of Lenin. Academic youth was no longer the "vanguard of all the democratic forces," to use Lenin's words of praise as late as during the first revolution of 1905 (Lenin, Nos. 11, 12, 14).

After the 1917 October Revolution, Lenin needed the country's youth first of all as fighters in the civil war, then as diligent students who were to acquire the know-how of the sons of the bourgoisie; the latter for the most part had fallen at the front, were imprisoned, had emigrated, had also been reduced to ineffectiveness as a class. He cared nothing for a youth that was critical or rebellious. Lenin's one major address to youth, at the Komsomol Congress of 1920, wholly stressed the motto, Learn! (Lenin, No. 22). And in these years he turned just once to the youth of the rest of the world, in a message to the Third World Congress of the Communist Youth International, held at the end of 1922 in Moscow (Lenin, No. 23). It too contained a summons, Learn! Its length: six lines.*

* As regards the quotations from Lenin in this chapter, whenever possible I have substituted the corresponding passages and references from the standard English translation of the 4th Russian edition. The many quotations in the remainder of the text are mostly from Russian originals unavailable in English; some are from American, or other foreign sources; because of the complexity of finding and translating the corresponding quotations from many scattered sources, I have translated them directly from the author's German whenever a Soviet translation from Russian into English was not readily available. The author has checked my translations of them and of the entire text, and provided translations, from the Russian, of the remaining chapter epigraphs. Luther Wilson has checked my English transcriptions of Russian names and phrases in the text. *Trans.*

II

OVERLOOKED (1960-1967)

Lenin on "revolutionary-democratic groups" outside his party: "It would be sheer pedantry for us simply to dismiss these groups, or to 'overlook' their formation and their tremendous importance for the struggle for freedom. It would be unpardonable doctrinairism" (From *Proletary*, No. 4, July 17, 1905, contained in *Collected Works*, English translation of the 4th Russian edition, VIII, 509).

"Empty faces—without vague wishes, without dreams, without discontents, without the yeast that ought to ferment the blood of youth; [. . .] without ideals, without beliefs" (Konstantinovsky, 1967).

"In the USA more than five million young people who have graduated from high school cannot find work" (Reshetov, "The 'Open' Generation," 1967).

As a good student of Marx, Lenin continually emphasized the leadership role of the proletariat during the transition to socialism and communism. But in preparing for the revolution in a country like Russia, which stood barely at the threshold of industrialization and fit badly into the Marxist scheme, Lenin had to undertake some corrections. Among these was his teaching, developed especially in *What Is to Be Done?* (1902), that the leadership of the revolution must not be entrusted to the proletariat, which was chiefly interested in bettering its own economic situation, not in the revolution as such, and which thought in economic terms—hence Lenin's battle against "economism"—not in political terms.

Instead the leadership role must be in the hands of a small group, a combat unit of conspirators, the Bolsheviks. The Bolsheviks, in today's usage Communists, was the name given, after the division of Russia's social-democratic party in 1903, to the left wing grouped around Lenin; however, Lenin himself continued to call his group the "Russian Social-Democrats." The members of his combat unit did not need to be proletarians, and were not except in isolated cases. Most came from the intelligentsia, to a great extent the Jewish intelligentsia, since the tsarist state oppressed the Jews in particular; or, like Lenin himself, they came from the lesser aristocracy or the bourgeoisie. In turn-of-the-century Russia, students came almost exclusively from non-proletarian circles; this did not stop Lenin from seeing them as potential allies.

In the years until the overthrow of the revolution of 1905, years in which the proletariat and the Bolsheviks were still weak, Lenin, as explained in the previous chapter, took the unrest at the universities very seriously. Naturally he called on the students to join the workers, but even so the disturbances pleased him. Lenin's writings at the beginning of the century imply the following about student unrest: Student unrest was good, it had to be exploited, even when not of proletarian origin, and as a last resort even when not subordinate to the Bolshevik Party—which, in any case, existed then only in its beginnings.

How did the disciples of Lenin react when, 60 years later, student unrest erupted?

There has always been student unrest, but in our time it gained new significance. In 1960, for the first time since the May 1919 disturbances in China, students made history. Through hectic marathon demonstrations, Japanese students prevented the state visit of the most powerful man in the world, President Eisenhower, in their country; their fellow students in Korea brought on the fall of Syngman Rhee, the old and rigid "Father of the Country." My 1960 stay in the Far East, in Japan and Korea as well, prompted my own interest in this new form of student unrest. (Like most observers I viewed June 1953 in East Berlin and fall 1956 in Poland and Hungary as peculiarities of the Eastern bloc.) In the same year, 1960, the American student movement began with the sit-ins in the South.

Soon university unrest became evident in other countries, in the Federal Republic of Germany, especially in Berlin, as well. The first climax occurred in early summer 1967, with the riots at the Shah's visit and the death of the student Benno Ohnesorg. Although radical groups existed on the right, the unrest of the sixties was shaped by the left: the New Left, as it came to be called after Charles Wright Mills' "Letter to the New Left" in the fall of 1960.

The West saw the rapid germination of an extensive literature—essays, pamphlets, periodicals, books—in which the New Left debated with itself or was discussed by others, by sociologists, psychologists, philosophers, educators. By the end of 1967 many extensive and inclusive investigations

existed. As early as the beginning of 1966, Milorad Drachkovitch provided
a comprehensive overview in *Western Politica* (I, 1966, 3–21); Susanne
Kleemann, in her study of student unrest, listed for America alone 350
essays and books which appeared before the end of 1967. Herbert Marcuse
had become widely known as a teacher, even as the guru of the New Left.
Proponents and opponents agreed that, for the first time in a long time,
something of note was happening in the non-Communist left. But until
the end of 1967 or early 1968, the Soviet Union, which otherwise treats
every strike and demonstration copiously in its press, hardly noticed.

Let us look first at essays for the period treated in this chapter, essays in
two periodicals which had the most interest, relatively, in the youthful unrest of the following years. The two are: *Molodoy Kommunist* (*The
Young Communist*, henceforth abbreviated *MK*), and *Mirovaya Ekonomika i Mezhdunarodnyye Otnosheniya* (*World Economy and International Relations*, to be abbreviated *MEiMO*).

At first one might think that the organ of the Communist Youth Organization (Komsomol) had early recognized the significance of the New
Left; in the eight years from 1960 to 1967 it published a total of 21 essays
on youth questions in non-Communist countries. But on closer inspection
most of these contributions yield little. Some were pure travel reportage
(Burkov and Kashlev wrote on the United States); others reported on
isolated problems of youth (Yaroshevsky and Pumpyansky on juvenile
crime, Spitsyn on youth gangs, Petrov on sex); a third group discussed
foreign countries in general (Rakhovetsky on Japan, Karushin on England, Tur's "Light Against Darkness" on West Germany). But mostly
such reportage was written as if there had never been a New Left. The
concept "New Left" did surface for the first time in Karushin's report on
England, but without any details. Karushin simply mentioned the movement briefly in the context of his major theme, which was the protest of
many Britons against the atom bomb and NATO.

The new development is felt earliest in the contributions of foreign authors. In 1960, the year of the demonstrations against Eisenhower's visit,
the Japanese commentator Ono included the students of his country em-
phatically in the "first ranks of the fighters." Ross gave equal status to
America's Communist youth and "other groups of progressive youth." The
Secretary of the French Communist Party Central Committee, Leroy,
dropped an accusation apparent to meticulous readers of *Molodoy Kommunist*, an accusation which would become increasingly significant: radical Western youth's susceptibility to the notion that Soviet Communism

was obsolete. Daymond informed the same readers on the new institution, the teach-in.

Throughout these eight years Soviet authors provided readers of *Molodoy Kommunist* with only four essays in which hints of a New Left could be discovered. The essays were by Mokhnachev, Gur'yev, Rukhovich, and Reshetov.

A CONFUSED PICTURE

Mokhnachev, although speaking only of Latin America, first noted in March 1960 the significance of students in the revolutionary movement, especially in countries with few industrial workers. According to him, the student movement there assumed "a place of honor in the people's struggle for democratic rights and freedoms," and "often [appeared] as the major organizing force of the democratic mass movement." This first Soviet description of the Leftist student movement of the sixties is the most positive and most Leninist.

Two years later, in an essay titled "Uncle Sam's Stepsons," Gur'yev predicted that the road which the rebellious among American youth had taken, "will lead inevitably to the struggle against the omnipotence of the monopolies, and to a true democratization of the internal and external life of their country." The young generation, then, would no longer be America's problem, but America's pride.

Since Mokhnachev as well as Gur'yev reached these conclusions in passing, basically only two essays remain which, between 1960 and 1967, treated the phenomenon of the New Left, though without addressing it by that name.

In May 1961 *Molodoy Kommunist* published an eight-page essay by Rukhovich, under the long-winded title "The Bourgeois Propaganda Myth about the 'Spiritual Crisis' of Contemporary Youth." Its thoughts:

Bourgeois propaganda, in the service of capital, sought to persuade Western youth of its demoralization and utter political disinterest. But a "spiritual crisis" of youth did not exist in actuality; therefore the reasons which supposedly contributed to the development of such a crisis could not exist. Nor was it true that "scientific-technological progress," in other words the mechanization of life, led to spiritual crisis; and affluence could not be blamed, since it benefitted only a small part of the population, and the worker's integration into the bourgeoisie was inconceivable; nor was Kinsey correct in saying that the crisis was due to youthful sexuality.

Rather, Western reactionary forces had invented the myth of a spiritual crisis, in order to effect the actual demoralization and depoliticization of youth, to make it defenseless and exploit it even more shamelessly.

As major support of this thesis Rukhovich invoked the Vatican's *Osservatore Romano*. There he claimed to have found the following quotation (he does not cite the date or even the year; if a reader should find the reference, I would welcome the information):

> We must set in motion all means of weaning [*otvodit*] youth away from politics. Entice it toward amusements, sports, toward love and games of chance [*asartnyye igry*]—in short toward everything except politics, which leads straightway [*pryamyokhon'ko*] into the arms of the Communists.

The Soviet author drew the conclusion:

> To divert youth from social and economic questions, from the struggle for their rights and interests, the apologists of capitalism [helped by a slandering of youth] seek to incite children against father, father against children, in order to foment the war of all against all, and to lessen and weaken youth's participation in the political life of society.

But all this would lead to nothing, he continued. Today's young people were active fighters for the overthrow of the bourgeois world. There was no crisis of youth, only a crisis of capitalism.

At this point many things get mixed up for Rukhovich, not surprising in view of his various, chronologically diffuse evidence. Among others he calls the Frenchman Duvivier responsible for the myth of youth's spiritual crisis, also Kinsey and another American, L. Lundberg, the Germans Helmut Schelsky and Karl Bednarik, and the Swiss A. Seiler, Lorenz Stucki, and Wilhelm Röpke. Duvivier's *Where Goes Today's Youth?* appeared in 1946, Kinsey's work between 1948 and 1953, Bednarik's *Today's Young Worker—a New Type* in 1953, Schelsky's *Skeptical Generation* in 1957. The articles of the three Swiss authors above (from the *Schweizer Rundschau*) also date from earlier years.

Rukhovich evidently read these books and articles at random and therefore did not realize that Western youth, after the end of World War II, underwent several phases. At first it actually was skeptical and apolitical; only at the turn of the fifties into the sixties did it begin to politicize.

Anyone who knows the Soviet journalist's difficulties in obtaining current sociological data from foreign countries, especially in 1961, will judge Rukhovich less harshly than he would a Western author. In fact it is to

Rukhovich's credit that he concerned himself, as early as 1961, with Western investigations on the subject of youth, that he made his readers aware
—although in confused form, and although questioning their significance
—of problems of which they were hardly conscious, problems of scientific-
technological progress, of affluence, of proliferating interest in sex. And it
is to his credit that, while not naming his sources, he anticipates some of
the basic traits that would characterize youth in the sixties. Of course he
does not refer to the New Left as such. His vocabulary does not extend
beyond the Beatniks, who belong to the previous decade.

THE FIRST HINTS

Six years passed before *Molodoy Kommunist* again thought it worthwhile
to discuss Western student unrest. In March 1967 the periodical published
an article titled "The 'Open' Generation." That, declared its author
Reshetov, was what most foreign sociologists called the younger generation because it was "open to ideas." To prove youth's readiness to swerve
from established pathways, Reshetov mentioned its protest against the
Vietnam War and racial discrimination, and as examples of the form of
their protest he cited the hippies and the "mods." (See the document
"First Hint.")

According to Western sociologists, reported Reshetov, the reason for
youth's protest movement was its satiety (*peresyshchennost*); since it had
everything, it sought outlets for its energies. Reshetov called this explanation an "absurdity." Conversely he reported in detail on the economic distress of Western youth and students, viewing it as the real cause of the
unrest. Thus he followed the traditional Soviet analysis, according to
which political unrest must have its primary roots in the unsatisfactory
economic position of those concerned. This kind of simplistic Marxist argumentation, encountered even today, has greatly contributed to Moscow's
delay in understanding the New Left.

Only at the end of his article, and significantly by referring to Western
authors, does Reshetov briefly mention other possible reasons for the
behavior of youth: the "scientific-technological revolution," which like
the first industrial revolution produced far-reaching political consequences,
and the lack of a philosophy convincing to youth.

The same Reshetov published another essay three months later. But the
assumption that he would further develop his earlier ideas proved false.
Under the equivocal title, "The Prophets Retire," he described—rather
one-sidedly—the efforts of Western authorities to educate their youth to-

ward anti-Communism, and toward a belief in the internal harmony of Western society; he, in turn, emphasized the social conflicts by which it is shaken. (Yet a year later, when tensions caused the explosion in France, it was the Communists who shrank from the consequences of revolution.)

"Never has Communism been as attractive as today," Reshetov finally quoted a Western periodical, striking a chord which even now resonates throughout Soviet journalism: the equating of Communism with Soviet Communism. This equation is essentially correct for the first period after the October Revolution, but hardly for the sixties, in which most young revolutionaries associated the word "Communism" with Mao and Marcuse, with Castro and Ché Guevara, but hardly with Khrushchev or even Brezhnev.

Therefore we can confirm: In the years before 1968, *Molodoy Kommunist,* the periodical suited before any other to observe, to understand, and to interpret the radicalization of youth in the non-Communist world, this periodical treated that theme only tangentially, only twice by referring to it as a problem, and even then showed little understanding of the nature and causes of the unrest.

A look at *MEiMO,* the second periodical important to our question, underscores this judgment. *MEiMO* (Moscow's standard abbreviation) is published by the Institute for World Economy and International Relations of the Soviet Academy of Sciences in Moscow; it is reputedly the most serious foreign affairs organ of the country. Since 1968 this periodical, as we shall see, has commented extensively on the New Left, and from then on has considered the New Left its appropriate subject matter. Yet before that it devoted not a single essay to the movement.

From 1960 through 1967 *MEiMO* published a series of contributions on countries in which youthful unrest was in full gear, yet without mentioning this unrest: for example on Japan, on Latin America, on Italy. Discussion of the New Left would have been possible, as well, in articles treating the Western petty bourgeoisie, the bourgeoisie's role in the national liberation movement, bourgeois ideology, the class struggle in foreign countries, or, in an article by Arab-Ogly, "pseudo-revolutionary myth-making" in the West.

Nothing like that. The article describing the fight in Japan against the security pact with the United States mentioned the students who played important roles in the struggle, but in few words and after the workers and employees; and Arab-Ogly, by myth-makers, did not mean Herbert Marcuse or Daniel Bell, but struggled with authors like Arnold Toynbee and James Burnham, whose *Managerial Revolution* had appeared a quar-

ter century before. The new revolutionary events in the West were treated
entirely in the traditional "class struggle" manner: Everything depended
on the proletariat, and the proletariat was inexorably on the road to power.

MEiMO's specialty is the observation of countries abroad, and, through
association with the institute of the same name, it commands a large staff
of assistants. Yet in the entire eight years it published just one essay that
hints of the New Left, Modrzhinskaya's November 1966 article on America. The writer stayed with the Soviet women's delegation in the United
States, where she experienced the fight against the Vietnam War. She correctly noted a leftist tendency among American intellectuals, and sensed
that this tendency was difficult to reconcile with the Soviet scheme of
thought. Hence she warned of treating opponents on the left "without
appropriate differentiation like any homogeneous [*odnolikiy*] mass," and
called for a dialogue of Soviet Marxism "with the critically disposed intelligentsia" of America. But Modrzhinskaya was the only one.

At the beginning of 1968, on the eve of the events in Paris, *MEiMO*
finally published an introductory history of the New Left, Churbanov's
"The New Left Movement," which provides an accurate picture of its
development. Excerpts in the document "A Brief History" provide a brief
summary on the New Left's first years for anyone not familiar with its
development. Churbanov's dispassioned tone is probably due to the fact
that neither he nor the editors foresaw what would soon happen in France.

MEAGER YIELD

In the eight years from 1960 through 1967, in which the New Left moved
onto the world stage, *Molodoy Kommunist* and *MEiMO* should have been
the first periodicals to recognize and analyze the phenomenon. But although they published 192 issues, of 124 and 160 pages respectively for
27,000 total pages, the two periodicals barely hinted at the new youthful
unrest. And if rare hints were dropped, it was by means of worn catch-
words and without understanding of the true context.

The unrest of youth did not arise and develop behind closed doors; in
fact it received unusual publicity in the West and elicited a flood of publications, from reportage to thorough analyses. Hence Moscow's neglect
of the movement was not due to a lack of information, but must have been
caused by an inability to understand, or even take seriously, unexpected
developments which did not fit into a primitively Marxist frame of reference.

Because my systematic checking of these two most appropriate periodicals, from 1960 through 1967, resulted in such meager yields, I undertook only spot checks for other periodicals, which yielded even less. Though it appears in many languages, the weekly *Novoye Vremya* (henceforth cited as *NT* after the English language edition *New Times*) has done little for the recognition of the phenomenon New Left; in part this is due to the usual brevity of the articles in *New Times*. In 1967, for example, A. and P. Tur described Munich hippies as being "in sharp contrast to the city's affluence"; Konstantinovsky reported on aimless youth in Vienna, a youth "without vague wishes, without dreams, without discontents, without the yeast that ought to ferment the blood of youth; [. . .] without ideals, without beliefs"; Romanzov called the convention of a short-lived organization in Chicago "an important event"; and Herbert Aptheker depicted the peace movement, "spontaneous, increasingly militant," in the United States. All these are snapshots and not always to the point, like the logic that the Viennese hippies were atoning for the sins of their Nazi fathers.

Only one article has come to my attention—written by a woman—which gave the Soviet reader an idea of what occurred among some of the West's students. Probably not by accident the article appeared in June 1967 in the best periodical, *Novyy Mir* (*New World*), then still edited by Aleksandr Tvardovsky, under the unassuming heading "From Foreign Periodicals."

Its author Orlova had read a series of pertinent articles in the American press, as well as Paul Jacobs and Saul Landau's *The New Radicals* (New York, 1966). On the whole her picture of rebellious youth was accurate and sympathetic, although she was a bit confused by the peculiar mixture of romantic and revolutionary spirit which she found. She called the movement "amorphous, hazy," "without any theory, without understanding, without respect for history," "without ideology," "skeptical about Marxism," but also "noble" and the "hope and future" of America. Of course she then quoted Bettina Aptheker: Everything depended on young people's recognition of the authority of the American Communist Party. In order to make the movement comprehensible to her readers, Orlova compared its members to the *narodniki* of 19th Century Russia, saying, in other words, that they felt a romantic kinship with the masses of the people and tried, by half-measures, to better their social conditions.

All in all the yield is meager until the beginning of 1968. It remains to be pondered, in a later context, how the "capital of world revolution" could ignore the rise of a revolutionary movement which embraced the entire world.

III

THE SHOCK OF PARIS (1968)

" 'Unexpected'—this word was used more frequently than others to characterize the French events" (*LG* 27, 1968, 14).

"For the adventures of the ultra-revolutionaries [i.e. of the New Left] in May 1968, the French Left paid with its electoral defeat in June" (*Pravda,* July 2, 1968, p. 5).

In 1968, the year of the May uprising in France, even Moscow finally awoke, but slowly and at first only in the daily press, represented in the following discussion by the party organ *Pravda* and the Komsomol's *Komsomol'skaya Pravda.*

The unrest at the University of Nanterre outside Paris, and at the Sorbonne in Paris, was ignored by both newspapers until the middle of May. But probably the judgment of the leadership in Moscow coincided with that of the French party organ *L'Humanité,* when the latter, in the first days of May, called the rebelling students "political adventurers" and servants of de Gaulle and monopolist capital. When ten thousand students or more had demonstrated May 5 on the Boulevard St. Germaine, hundreds of students had been arrested, and hundreds of students and policemen had been injured, *L'Humanité* (and with it the French Communist Party) briefly changed its position and promised to support the students' demands.

Pravda waited until May 12 to begin its reports, *Komsomol'skaya Pravda* two days more. Both took up *L'Humanité's* new slogan: The workers sympathized with the students. But the two papers devoted only modest coverage to the events. As late as May 14 *Pravda* wrote more comprehensively on the battle against the emergency powers acts in West Germany, and the Vietnam peace negotiations just beginning in Paris ranked before the street fights on the Left Bank.

Pravda carried the first major article (six columns) under a characteristic heading that emphasized the proletarian aspect: "The Strikes are Spreading." Its author, B. Kotov, in the weeks that followed generally reported for his paper from Paris. *Komsomol'skaya Pravda* also emphasized, throughout, the role of the industrial workers. The titles: "Two Millions Strike" (*Pravda,* May 20, 1968), "The Wave of Strikes Rises" (*Pravda,* May 21), "France Strikes" (*Koms. Pr.,* May 21), "Seven Millions Strike" (*Pravda,* May 22), "The Class Struggle Front Widens (*Pravda,* May 26, 1968).

Meanwhile the attitude toward the radical students had become unfriendly again. The French workers were praised for rebuffing Cohn-Bendit, the "freshly minted leader of a little band of crazy Parisian students," at their factory gates, when he "ran [to them] from Paris," "a political provocateur" with his "extremist slogans and his anti-Communist ranting" (*Pravda,* May 21, 1968).

On May 22 *Komsomol'skaya Pravda* brought the first major report; titled "France: Student—68," it finally placed the students at center stage. Its author, Alice Renold, a student at the Institute for Foreign Languages in Moscow and perhaps a French Communist, represented the Marxist line in its primitive form. She emphasized the economic distress of the students and advised Parisian youth that the proletariat, not they, were the vanguard of progress. No mention of the other contributing factors to the May unrest.

The party centers in Paris and Moscow were equally concerned that the extremism of the radical students played into the hands of French conservative forces. "Every provocation pleases the authorities" (*Pravda,* May 24, 1968). Kotov called the students splitters of the left (*Pravda,* May 24, 1968). On the *workers'* side, he reported, there had "not [been even] the smallest incidents," on the *students'* side, however, mass riots, bloody confrontations with the police, barricades, tear gas, dozens of wounded. Among the student demonstrators he claimed to have discovered "bands of provocateurs," among them "not a few fascist-like rogues of the extreme right student movement," a "windfall [*nakhodka*] for those who wished to scare the country with 'looming anarchy' and bloodletting" (*Pravda,* May 26, 1968). In contrast *Komsomol'skaya Pravda* (May 24, 1968) accepted *L'Humanité's* report that Roger Garaudy, soon after suspended from the Communist Party, had commented positively on the students.

Both papers reported on the French Communist Party's appeal to the intellectuals, to join the workers who had also struck for them, but under no circumstances to join the anarchists, who only incited the population's enmity against the working class (May 28, 1968). A day later they reported on a warning of the French Communist Politburo against leftist groups who did not want to work with the French Communist Party. On May 29 *Pravda* carried Yuri Zhukov's venomous attack on Herbert Marcuse and his "werewolves"; this attack, until then Moscow's sharpest against the New Left, will deserve further mention.

To the extent that President de Gaulle became involved, especially after his visit of General Massu in Baden-Baden, the Moscow press began to play down the unrest. The titles of articles became mechanical and meaningless: "The Factory Workers of France Continue the Battle" (*Pravda*, May 31, 1968), "The Battle Intensifies" (*Pravda*, June 1, 1968), "The Road of Battle" (*Pravda*, June 2, 1968). The French Communist Party's readiness for new elections instead of street battles was hinted at (*Pravda*, May 31, 1968). "France Prepares for Elections," finally announced a laconic *Komsomol'skaya Pravda* (June 5, 1968).

The election and the run-off were a sharp disappointment. De Gaulle's party won handily. *Pravda* diagnosed a shift to the right, with the students to blame. Their anarchistic behavior had enabled monopolist capital to disseminate among the people a fear of civil war, and thus induce a conservative reaction during the elections. On July 2 Kotov summaried in *Pravda*: "For the adventures of the ultra-revolutionaries [his designation for the New Left] in May 1968, the French Left [meaning the French Communist Party especially] paid with its electoral defeat in June."

What actually happened in May and June in Paris, what relationship had actually developed between the French Communist Party and the French New Left—these questions lie beyond the concerns of this study. On that subject dozens of books, hundreds, perhaps thousands of articles have been written in the West. Richard Johnson's book is especially revealing. An American student in Paris during the events described, he reports, clearly and to the point, although with perceptible sympathy for the New Left, the development of the relationship between the students and the Communist Party of France.

MARCUSE HERE, MARCUSE THERE

For Moscow's attitude toward the New Left the May 1968 events in Paris were decisive. But the effect of the shock was so great that much time would pass before serious analyses were published in the Soviet Union. Nothing showed the extent of the shock as clearly as Zhukov's *Pravda* article of May 30. Until further developments, he set the operative tone.

Yuri Zhukov is the most prominent Soviet journalist commenting on the New Left up to now, and as we shall see, commenting in lively fashion. Since 1947, with some interruptions, Zhukov has been associated with *Pravda,* with five years as foreign affairs editor. He is also a Soviet representative in the World Peace Council, member of the Foreign Affairs Committee of the Supreme Soviet, recipient of the Lenin Prize and the Order of the Red Banner. His article is reprinted with minor cuts in the appendix (see the document "The Three M's"); it is especially instructive.

The article's irritated, even furious tone gives evidence of Moscow's mood at the time. For the first time it also acquainted the Soviet reader more closely with Herbert Marcuse, the man with whom Soviet journalism would deal frequently in the years to come. For Zhukov, Marcuse is the guilty party, and of course it is always useful to know the guilty party's name. The first paragraph, which mentions Marcuse's name seven times right off, sounds like "Figaro here, Figaro there": Marcuse is everywhere. Even the article's title, "Werewolves," is indicative. To characterize Marcuse's followers appropriately, Zhukov resorts to the vocabulary of the horror film.

Zhukov's eruption is exceptional and therefore especially interesting. Soon a dignified reserve again descended over Soviet journalism. The party's leading theoretical monthly, *Kommunist,* was silent, although it before any others was particularly suited to illuminate the events in France, and to work out a plausible line for the remaining Soviet periodicals. The leading article in its May issue, which appeared at the beginning of June (no. 8, 1968, imprimatur May 31), took a position only in this sense: Like its title, it called "the working class . . . the leading force in the struggle for socialism and Communism," and therefore, without expressly saying so, it denied the students any claim to even a secondary leadership role. To understand how the leading ideological organ of Soviet Communism, in an editorial, treated an important sociological question—calling on the Marx of yore, and on ossified theoretical positions to support the leadership role of workers in the industrial states of 1968—to understand this the reader must read the decisive paragraphs himself (Document, "The Proletariat Must Lead!").

The journal of Soviet philosophers, *Voprosy Filosofii,* was equally silent, though its ideological bent should have involved it quickly with the New Left. *Voprosy Filosofii* extricated itself by printing in its June issue an American's article on the American New Left, an article it had commissioned long before. It is true, however, that the journal's editors had invited an American speaker for such a lecture as early as the beginning of 1967, and had afterwards asked him to write the corresponding article. (Parsons never answered my letters in which I asked for some information concerning his invitation.) Hence the editors had a manuscript in storage, "The Philosophy of Life of Americans and the New Lefts," with which to react indirectly to events in France.

Its author, Professor Howard L. Parsons from the Department of Philosophy at the University of Bridgeport, belongs to the left wing of American intellectuals. In the essay's first half Parsons described the American "philosophy of life," which he called anti-intellectual, pragmatic, hedonist, politically indifferent, and anarchist; he devoted the second half to the New Left which was nurtured in this soil, and which he called a "mixture of progressive and anarchistic philosophies." He mentioned several of the movement's spiritual progenitors, though not Marcuse, noted strong influences from eccentric Bohemian elements (hair style, dress, manners, sexual peculiarities, alcohol abuse), and spoke of an "orgy of political protests."

The manifold New Left groups, according to Parsons, shared these traits: a belief in democracy (for most, democracy "in the traditional middle class sense"); a rejection of the American system, of authoritarianism, of political parties (including leftist parties), and of adults ("Trust no one over 35"); a feeling of solidarity with the poor and oppressed, especially with blacks. Parsons saw the New Left's protest as primarily "moral and activist," not "intellectual and ideological."

Parsons is sympathetic to the Soviet system, as emerges in his undated work on Soviet ethics. Therefore he could tell readers of *Voprosy Filosofii* some things which, until then, they had not encountered in print, for example the significance "of the events of 1956" for the birth of the New Left. Every reader of the journal must have known that he meant events in Poland and Hungary. And where, in listing the goals against which the New Left fought in America, Parsons named "conformity, corruption, loss of the sense of responsibility," he helped his Soviet readers understand some of the otherwise unexplained behavior of the New Left in Paris.

The same cannot be said of an article in the May issue of the young people's periodical, *Yunost'* (*Youth*). Commissioned for the 150th anniversary of Karl Marx's birth, the article served as filler for a missing report on the Paris uprising. In "Marx and Youth" its author, Boris Yakovlev, wanted to show that "Marx dearly loved youth." His evidence of course is lacking. In Marx's extensive correspondence he managed to find four sympathetic comments on young people: a Russian, a German, and two Englishmen ("nice young fellow," "clear, critical mind," "rough, good natured, not too bright," "good dissertation"). In lieu of more evidence Yakovlev presented quotations that portray the youthful Marx as an idealist, and the older Marx as a loving husband. We are also told whom Marx opposed, or would oppose today: the Maoists, whom he would scorn as "pseudo-Communist egalitarians"; the Chinese people's communes, which had been his target when he attacked "barracks-Communism"; and all who took love and marriage lightly.

So passed the summer of 1968, without analysis of Parisian events in pertinent Soviet publications, certainly without conclusions drawn from such analyses. Two articles deserve mention, one by Molchanov in the weekly *Literaturnaya Gazeta* in early July, and one by Rubinsky in *MEiMO* a month later.

Literaturnaya Gazeta, the liveliest Soviet periodical and perhaps the most open to new developments of any, dared to pass judgment as early as July 3, long before the official line was clear. The key word which preceded Molchanov's article, and which forms an epigraph to this chapter, was "unexpected." Unexpectedly—for Moscow as well, and especially for Moscow—events had erupted in May, and so unexpectedly for Molchanov that weeks later he still did not undertake analysis of their causes. His one lame attempt to explain the background of the Parisian May was incongruous with the significance of those weeks. He hinted that the whole thing might have been provoked by the powerful French monopolist capitalists, using the New Left to scare the French petty bourgeoisie with looming anarchy and Communism, and so stabilize the existing regime. Molchanov's picture of this petty bourgeoisie is not flattering, and he forgets that it also applies to many French workers:

> A good-natured clown with beret and dark jacket that won't close over the belly, who spends his free time in the café behind a bottle of wine, tosses down the next glass, and accompanies this with highly radical remarks. Because his heart is naturally on the left, but his wallet, his wallet he carries on the right. . . . He is for order above all, although he usually votes for the left. When things reach the point of barricades his horror is so great that he sees nothing, only the necessity of preserving his apparent affluence and his peaceful existence.

Molchanov openly admitted that the election results bitterly disappointed the Communists. "Alas [*uvy*]," he wrote, "their opponents not only preserved their majority, but even extended it."

Rubinsky was much more cautious. His traditional report did not match his stirring title, "Storm Over France." As appropriate for Soviet authors, the article began with economic arguments, with the supposedly negative effects of the Common Market on France, and with the exploitation of the workers. Then Rubinsky described the protest of academic youth against the faults of French higher education, a protest which gradually extended against society in general. During this protest, he wrote, it had become clear that most French students were oriented toward the left.

So far, so good. Now comes the unavoidable *odnako:* however. However, the collapse of traditional morality among the French middle classes, from which most students came, and the questioning of prevailing, including academic values, and the insights into the bankruptcy of bourgeois civilization, all these had provided "a favorable soil for political extremism in the academic milieu." From this soil derived the

> loud, though short-lived success of the anarchist, Trotskyite, and even "Maoist" groups, which demanded the destruction of all forms of governmental and political organizations because they viewed them as the source of social injustice and spiritual repression. The primary means of the struggle, so preached the "ultra-leftists," was blind force, which in their opinion would artificially induce a revolutionary situation.

There followed a somber description, familiar to us from reports in the daily press, of youthful misdeeds, especially those of Cohn-Bendit, which —again this expression—"worked into the hands of reaction."

Against this gloomy background the French Communist Party shines all the more brightly. The conclusion of Rubinsky's article, "The Vanguard in Battle," was essentially devoted to its praise.

Led by the French Communist Party, the workers had "escorted [the pushy 'ultra-Leftist' students] politely, but firmly, beyond the factory gates." Certainly there had been bloody clashes between *workers* and police, as well, but the responsibility for them, argued the Soviet article, fell "squarely on the authorities" (during clashes between *students* and police, the students had been called the provocateurs). The workers had achieved a notable increase in wages and had "returned to work with their heads raised high." Unfortunately they had been unable to secure these successes politically, because the elections had resulted in a shift to the right; and for this, in the eyes of both the French and Russian Communists, the New Left was to blame.

Inostrannaya Literatura (*Foreign Literature*) commented on France in only part of a survey. Under the heading "Glosses on Foreign Papers and

Periodicals," Breytburd first discussed the May events in France. He called his contribution "Asphalt and Cobblestones," an allusion to the fact that Paris had paved its cobblestone boulevards with asphalt to hinder the erection of barricades. But he also mentioned youthful unrest in other countries, relying on essays by Hans Magnus Enzensberger and the Persian B. Nirumand in the *Kursbuch*, the West German left wing review, and on contributions by Italian authors, among them Luigi Longo and Alberto Moravia.

Though *Inostrannaya Literatura* is primarily oriented toward foreign literature, careful readers discovered some new facts. Namely, the unrest among youth was an "exceedingly complex" and worldwide phenomenon; among countries affected the author named West Germany, France, Italy, Spain, Portugal, the USA, Mexico, Brazil, though not Japan. In addition, he reported, rebelling youth searched for a counter culture; it stood for direct democracy, and thus opposed elected but autonomous institutions, centers of leadership, and established leaders; it did not trust official Communist parties and believed that there were Communists outside the party; it felt that the orthodox Communist parties had been "taken unawares" by the emergence of the New Left, and even, in Longo's words, believed that the French student movement had explosively ignited "a people's movement of unheard of extent," with the Italian movement forming an "element of the entire Italian revolutionary" movement.

The Soviet reader was unaccustomed to such information. For the rest, of course, he found himself quickly in familiar territory. Breytburd told him that the carriers of this stirring movement were inspired by "anarchist, nihilist, Bakunian, Nechayevian, Pekingese ideas," that they were "childishly naive," "ultraleftist and neo-Trotskyite." The Russian for "left" is *levyy*, or *levatskiy* ("leftist"); Breytburd even used *ultralevatskiy*.

JUGGLING THE HOT POTATO

In the last months of 1968, the year so important for Soviet Communism, there were only four other articles on the New Left in the periodicals I investigated. But instead of looking into the events of Paris, they all skirted the issue. The articles appeared in the organs of the Foreign Ministry, the Armed Forces, the Party, and the Komsomol.

International Affairs, which echoes the opinions of the Foreign Ministry, collected itself to present an article by K. Fyedorov, on the unrest of Western youth. It was a general survey without penetrating insights. Fyedorov mentioned the French uprising in a few words that contained no hints of its significance. Toward the end he cited the Central Committee of the French Communist Party, which had declared in its usual tone that the radical leftist groups were "led by sinister and irresponsible elements." In addition, wrote Fyedorov, the French bourgeoisie had demonstrated its flexibility by criticizing Communism from the "left" (in quotation marks); it had even, he suggested, disseminated the writings of Trotsky and Mao toward this end. Fyedorov admitted that in the West even "progressive students . . . do not always or immediately accept the ideology of Marxist-Leninism." Naturally he meant the Moscow version of that ideology.

The Agitator, an organ of the Central Committee of the Soviet Communist Party, did not discuss the ticklish subject until October, in answer to an (alleged) letter to the editor. In a very brief survey, "Why are the Students in the USA Rebelling," T. Shmeleva emphasized the economic causes of the academic unrest. Her conclusion: The unrest represented no "short-lived eruption of discontent, but a profound mass movement."

Kommunist Vooruzhennykh Sil (Communist of the Armed Forces) published an article by Yanayev, the Chairman of the Committee of Soviet Youth Organizations. In six meager pages the article disposed of the entire world, briefly even Japan, and therefore superficially. Yet, since it appeared in the fall, it should have discussed the May occurrences in France. For an unimportant event in West Germany, in Essen on the Ruhr, which also occurred in May, the periodical found enough room. To be sure, a hint of Paris emerged in the author's dejected conclusion that leftist elements among student youth sought to divide the students from the workers.

In December, finally, Bykov spoke up in *Molodoy Kommunist.* An associate at the Institute of the International Workers' Movement in Moscow, Bykov would, in the course of the years, write on the same theme again. He began his survey of the "shattered generation" with a brief description of the "Beat generation," adroitly translating "beat" by "shattered" ("raz*bitiy*"), and tying the Beatniks to the existentialism scorned by Moscow. Then he undertook an explanation of the "New Left," remembering all but once to place the words in the required quotation marks, and arrived at a verdict which was rather positive, despite the experience of Paris: The New Left was an "anticapitalist movement"; it rejected anti-Communism, concerned itself with Marx, sabotaged the Vietnam War. *Odnako,* it also had its negative sides: It tended toward anarchism, denied the necessity of discipline, distrusted any kind of leadership.

A footnote of his (page 115) contains misinformation, whether through ignorance or by intent I leave up in the air. Under "Old Left," writes Bykov, ought to be understood "the socialists who reject cooperation with the Communists; the Trotskyites and so-called 'Marxists' who oriented themselves by Mao Tse-tung." Exactly the reverse is true: When the American New Left refers to the Old Left, it means primarily the American Communist Party with its numerous underground and front organizations. The Trotskyites and Maoists, throughout, belong to the New Left. And the New Left's association with the socialists of the Norman Thomas and Michael Harrington wing, at least when Bykov wrote his footnote, was closer than its association with orthodox Communists of the Moscow school.

The weekly *Novoye Vremya* (henceforth cited by the English edition) was rather busy, and in the course of 1968 published seven articles on Western youth: two on West Germany, one on the attempt on Rudi Dutschke's life; two on youth questions in general; one each on Brazil, England, and the United States. The best and longest, at four pages, was Igor Kon's article "Capitalist Society and the Youth," but even it contained nothing new. The remaining articles, again, were essentially sketches. Not one discussed Paris. Only in the following year did an article on events in France appear; written by Robert Telliez, a Frenchman, it was bitter in its assessment of the New Left (6, 1969, 7–9).

In October 1968 the periodical *Teatr* (*Theater*) published a ten-page article on the Parisian theater. It is worth mentioning because it discussed new plays and performances exclusively, as if there had never been those days in May when not only plays, but revolution was performed in the theaters. Only half a sentence noted the students' temporary occupation of theaters that spring.

Three other 1968 articles should be named, but they will be treated in another context. Their two themes would, from now on, frequently occupy Soviet journalism: the Western intelligentsia (*Novyy Mir*, 1, 1968), and Marcuse (*Voprosy Filosofii*, 9 and 10, 1968).

One more work deserves mention here. Although it did not appear until 1969 it had been set in type in November 1968: a small book by Lisovsky titled *Study for a Portrait*. On the basis of ten polls of young Soviet citizens from 1964 to 1968, and similar material, it tries to sketch the outlines of a picture of Soviet youth. In the last chapter, "Lost Generation?" (152–

206), Lisovsky employs Western publications to look at Western youth in unusually objective and in part accurate fashion. As a sociologist he must have been primarily interested in facts and tendencies. Instead of raging at Marcuse's theses, for example, he briefly sums them up. Certainly his picture of Western youth is not flattering, but it generally corresponds to that painted by Western sociologists.

THE NEW LEFT: AN UNSUITABLE ALLY?

To summarize the yield of 1968: Only three articles really discussed the students of Paris (Zhukov, Molchanov, and Rubinsky); six treated the New Left in general (Parsons, Fyedorov, Yanayev, Shmeleva, Breytburd, and Bykov); one discussed the intelligentsia, two Marcuse, and one, with considerable strain, Marx's attitude toward youth. Twelve articles in all— in 1968. Nevertheless this is considerably more than in the previous years. The shock of Paris had at least begun to produce a concern with the New Left.

The essential lesson of Paris was never clearly enunciated but could be glimpsed through the dense verbiage describing the Paris uprising. The gist was this: The New Left was an unpredictable, uncontrollable element which allowed itself to be exploited for provocation even by its enemies, and which, through its radicalism, fueled the population's calls for law and order, thereby stabilizing the existing regime. If, in a Western state, the majority of the population already feared Communism, it became doubly afraid when this Communism, in its eyes, joined with the New Left's anarchistic radicalism. Therefore the New Left was anything but a suitable ally for a Communist party.

In the summer of the following year, in June of 1969, *Voprosy Filosofii* carried an article titled "The Social Dynamics of the May Movement," a kind of summing up of the events of the previous year. Its author, Xenia Myalo, associate at the Institute of the International Workers' Movement of the Soviet Academy of Sciences, downplayed the role of the students; the revolt had become significant, she wrote, only when the workers began to strike. She quoted from a student handbill of May 14: "The struggle of the students has currently been outflanked [by the workers. . . .] The outcome of the crisis lies in the hands of the workers, insofar as they will succeed in realizing, by occupying the factories, those aims which we have only been able to suggest by occupying the universities."

Myalo recognized that the students and workers did not share the same goals, and explained why: The battle of the students against the "consumer society [had] obviously found no support in the workers' wing of the [May] movement" (p. 50). "The basis for contacts [between students and workers] dwindled." This is doubtless an accurate observation.

Equally correctly, Myalo described the difference in the attitudes of the students and the Communist-organized workers with regard to the methods that ought to be used. The students countered the cumbersome, bureaucratic apparatus of the French Communist Party and the Communist labor unions by their local action committees, which of course appeared "atomized" and chaotic to Myalo. Since these action committees remained without effective coordination, they had increasingly, she wrote, fallen into isolation and negativism. That, in turn, had led to overemphasis on subordinate aspects of the cultural revolution: She found "God and Buddha's navel" the objects of student critique in one handbill of those days; even "revolutionary committees of sexual action" had been founded. Mrs. Myalo summarized the development of the French New Left in May 1968 with the catchword: "carnevalization."

> After the students had brought to life a broad social movement they were unable to understand its essential tendencies—which cannot be described by the concepts of anti-consumer ideology—nor were they able to gain its support by clear slogans and a program. On the contrary, the slogans which furthered the revolutionary consolidation of the students, proved to be ineffective outside their narrow [student] context; they were generally unable to show the movement the way. Negation as such, total negation, became the sole function of the students within the movement, and the movement collapsed (p. 58).

This paragraph in the June 1969 issue of *Voprosy Filosofii* might be called Moscow's epitaph to the May 1968 Paris uprising.

When the year 1968 is mentioned, everyone of course thinks of May in Paris but *also* of "Springtime in Prague." We could debate whether developments in Czechoslovakia, between fall 1967 and the Soviet Army's entry in August 1968, do not also belong to our subject, the New Left. In this investigation I did not take them into account. Moscow's relationship to the spring in Prague is a major theme by itself, only mentioned here. But we cannot overlook that the two shocks—of Paris and of Prague—occurred closely together in time, and that the Soviet leadership saw simultaneously two dangerous cracks in the monolithic Communism it so ardently desired.

Let us recall a third related shock, that of Peking. Although China's Cultural Revolution had begun to ebb in 1968, Moscow presumably did not see this clearly at the time; and this revolution, too, was carried by a kind of New Left. (See my earlier book, *Peking and the New Left*, Berkeley, 1969.) We can therefore understand that from spring until fall 1968, as a result of the three "P-shocks," Moscow was severely agitated. But this does not excuse Moscow's inability to analyze the events in Paris quickly and lucidly.

That remains a failure. The Soviet Union sees itself as the exegete and the very center of Communism, yet its journals remained shrouded in silence when, in an important country like France, a profound fissure appeared within the left, between the New Left and the Old.

IV

A PORTRAIT CHANGES (1969-1972)

"The difficulties on the young American's road to the university are constantly increasing. [. . .] The fees are considerably higher than many young people or their parents can afford. [. . .] Obtaining a higher education remains a [special] privilege" (*MEiMo* 6, 1971, 113).

"The central problem for the various opposition groups within American youth is the human problem. [. . .] Life in a society of abundance is responsible for the major stress in the life of the students" (*SShA* 9, 1971, 56 ff.).

The most active New Leftists "belong to the best part of academic youth" (*SShA* 3, 1971, 27).

The shock of Paris ended Moscow's era of blissful ignorance about the New Left. The Soviet leadership was alarmed. An investigation of the unexpected phenomenon, though unpleasant, could no longer be avoided. Discussion opened—within limits.

At the end of February the Presidium of the Soviet Academy of Sciences, a primary ideological control center of the country, held a meeting on the further work of its periodical *Voprosy Filosofii*. At the session there was also explicit discussion on a future stance toward the New Left. The major address was given by the internationally known physicist, Professor Pyotr L. Kapitsa, a former émigré who, in the mid-thirties, had returned to the USSR on a visit and had then been prevented by Stalin from leaving the country. With exceptional candor he told the Soviet philosophers and ideologues that they had lived, until now, in isolation from worldwide intellectual currents. Like athletes, he said, they must now engage in the combat of free competition, if they wished to influence further intellectual developments. (See the document "Out into the Arena!")

The Presidium charged *Voprosy Filosofii* with the task, among others, of "unmasking the aimless conceptions of the contemporary [. . .] 'leftist'

31

revisionism" (*VF* 5, 1969, 145 ff.). Perhaps this resolution opened the way for freer, gradually more realistic discussion of the New Left by Soviet ideologues.

Every Soviet person knows that the United States is the richest, most powerful country in the Western world; most also suspect that America, despite all the self-praise by Soviet leaders, is in the vanguard of the frequently mentioned "scientific-technological revolution." Some may even suspect that America, as a pioneer of progress, experiences many things that less modern states, including the Soviet Union, will only live through in the future. Perhaps all this contributes to the Soviet people's lively interest in the United States before any other country. It is no wonder that the revolt of youth is also seen and researched as a primarily American phenomenon. In fact, as many articles on American youth have appeared in the Soviet Union as articles on youthful unrest in all other countries combined.

Soviet publications on the New Left peaked numerically in 1970 and 1971; after that their number declined considerably. Two books can be called temporary culminations: Brychkov's *Young America,* which despite its 1971 imprimatur did not circulate until 1972; and Salychev's *The "New Left": For Whom and Against Whom?* (imprimatur November 1972). But we can expect further stages. As the last chapter has shown, concern with the New Left began belatedly in Moscow; perhaps now that interest is in full gear, in that frequent time lag characterizing the Soviet Union, it will end more slowly.

Two aspects of the unrest of American youth presented Soviet authors with no difficulties in interpretation: the Vietnam War and the racial question. In both cases they were satisfied with orthodox formulas.

That there are just and unjust wars has frequently been proclaimed by Moscow, most obviously by Khrushchev. America's war in Vietnam was an unjust war, goes the logic, therefore the war against such a war was a just war, regardless of who waged it. When American youth rose against the Vietnam War its action was praiseworthy. In reports on the fight against the Vietnam War, however, the youth motif was stressed less than the anti-war motif. (See the contributions by Daymond; Herbert Aptheker, "The American"; Bereshkov, "After"; Freeman, "American"; Borovik, "Confusion"; Linnik.) Not surprisingly the 1968 and 1970 mass demonstrations were highlighted.

And not surprisingly Soviet observers noted with satisfaction that through the years more and more groups joined the antiwar movement. Although the movement was at first "associated particularly with the intelligentsia [with academic circles, the students, etc.]," later it became one of the movements "with the greatest influence on the masses, one of the most effective, politically, in American history" (Linnik, 108). The same author, an associate of the Moscow Institute of American Studies, already noted with agitation the "lethal smell of revolution" in America's atmosphere (p. 112).

More than any others Linnik also expressed his open discontent over the New Left's role in the movement against the war. For him its "anarchist, ultrarevolutionary" aspect was "one of the most serious problems" of the American antiwar movement, because the "ultraleftist, extremist groups weakened the movement from within." These groups

> seek to isolate the [antiwar] organization from the remaining [Leftist] movement; calling for the "purification" of their ideological positions, they refuse to work together with "peace candidates" [i.e. candidates sponsored by the American Communist Party] during elections, or to join workers or blacks, claiming that their struggle carried no "revolutionary character" (p. 110 ff.).

Thus, as much as Soviet authors hailed the movement against the Vietnam War, they saw the New Left as an irritating fly in the ointment. Ideally they preferred a continuously spreading antiwar movement, *without* the New Left, under the leadership of the Communist Party. In Borovik's words America needed "a unity of student and worker, of white and black, of young and old, a unity of the people as proposed by the Communists. Only such unity can give the decisive force to demonstrations against the war" (*LG* 20, 1970, 15).

A similar attitude is apparent toward American blacks' struggle for equality: a loud YES and a soft, pained *ODNAKO*. (Compare Geyevsky; Zhil'nikov; Meshcheryakova, "The Party.") In other words, there is complete agreement with black protests against discrimination by white American society and, not least, agreement with the activities of the Black Panthers, the vanguard of this attack against white bastions. From conversations in the Soviet Union I have deduced that such agreement is not simply a question of propagandistic slogans; despite reports of racial discrimination I find that Russians—observe their policies in Siberia and Central Asia —share fewer racial prejudices than some other colonizers, and have stronger empathy for the attempts of oppressed races to better their situation.

ECONOMIC CAUSES AND—ALIENATION

Odnako: "As so often among young, inexperienced people, they [radical blacks] suffer from leftist, sectarian opinions that doubtlessly must be overcome" (Lightfoot, p. 104). It is striking that Moscow authors criticize this black attitude not in their own words but by quoting American Communists. *Kommunist* took over the quotation above, for example, from the American Claude Lightfoot. Geyevsky quoted the assessment of another American Communist, in whose view the Black Panthers lacked "theoretical maturity," "they cannot really orient themselves in the class system of bourgeois American society," they had not fully recognized their mistake in "underestimating the historic role of the working class," and they "have not yet learned to see reality in all its complexity, as demanded by Marxism-Leninism." They had not understood, in particular, "that a guerilla war, in the American situation, would simply lead to their isolation" (*SShA* 1, 1970, 115–118).

In other words, here as with the opponents of the Vietnam War: Everything would be fine if the black movement were subordinate to Communist command and if the inconvenient "leftists" did not exist.

Things are easiest for Soviet authors when they discuss the students as students, when they describe the problems at the universities as causes for the rise of the New Left. Because here material is abundant; a vast flood of studies and critiques of higher education has been appearing in America for years.

As loyal Marxists, of course, they first mentioned economic reasons for the student unrest (Aleksandrova; Brychkov, "From Unrest," "The University"; Pumpyansky, "Must One."). They described in detail the high cost of higher education, the insufficient scholarships and financial aid. The Soviet reader, knowing the low cost of such education in the USSR but not the high incomes in America, was no doubt impressed by such statistics. He was confirmed in the belief that higher education in the West was exclusively for the children of the capitalists. Only gradually did Soviet authors point out the broad social basis of American student bodies. Novinskaya ("Student Revolution," p. 99) even included a statistic overpowering to a Soviet reader: that "families with low incomes," who supplied 16% of the students, earned up to $7500 annually! This equals the salaries, in roubles, of Soviet professors and factory directors.

The weakness of explaining student unrest by economic causes is apparent. Neither the families of the students, nor the students themselves, have experienced the kind of dramatic decline in their economic situation at the beginning of the sixties, or dramatic improvement at the start of the seventies, that would plausibly account for the flow and later ebb of university unrest. The standard of living rose fairly steadily in those years, yet student unrest rose suddenly and as sharply dropped. Soviet observers have yet to explain this phenomenon. Such explanation is difficult in any case, and especially by looking for it in economic conditions.

Soviet authors are quick to point to American critics of unequal opportunity in the United States. ("In 1966 the proportion of working class children among students was less than 16%," Aleksandrova, p. 15.) They also note discrimination against blacks and unemployment among college graduates, and report on student grievances against the higher education system: the formalism of examinations, the many secondary duties which keep the professor from his primary responsibilities to the students. For Soviet authors all this, by basic arithmetic, equals student unrest.

Facts and details on student unrest the Soviet reader rarely finds. For example, in Sharikov's article on the *Scranton Report* on campus unrest, authorized in 1970 by President Nixon, the reader is informed of Nixon's reaction: He disapproved of the report's soft approach and allowed it to slip from view; but the article contains nothing on campus events themselves.

Brychkov penetrated deeper, using the word "alienation," now stylish even in the Soviet Union. Unlike many of his countrymen he did not use the word as magic formula that explained everything. Instead he recognized that student alienation differed substantially from that of workers— he called it "existential"—because unlike the workers' it was not tied in with the process of production. (See the document, "The Students Are More Complicated.")

Naturally the authors writing on higher education also regretted that the academic youth was split up into sects, that it was unwilling to subordinate itself to the Communist Party. Needing a scapegoat, they found it in the "reactionaries" which, through their capitalist-imperialist propaganda, exerted corresponding pressure on youth, and in the conservatives, among whom they listed the former ambassador George F. Kennan and New York's Sydney Hook, who supposedly waged a "war against youth" (Lisenkov; Pumpyansky, "Must One."). Brychkov listed several arguments of these conservatives:

The bourgeois ideologues declare that the Communist parties are dishonest in their attitude toward youth, and that they lack sympathy for the wishes and interests of the young generation. They are aped by leftist opportunists, who want to convince youth that the Communist parties have lost their revolutionary spirit and have become "integrated in the system" that exists in the capitalist countries. They explain that the Communist parties have retreated toward "conciliatory, opportunistic" positions, that they fear the revolutionary spirit of youth, that they are afraid of being overtaken from the "left" by the "revolutionary students. [. . .]"

By slander and fabrications the bourgeois ideologues, the "leftist" and rightist opportunists, attempt to refute what the entire history of the Communist movement has proved: that the Communists are in fact the truest friends of youth, that they understand and share youth's wishes and goals, and that they are capable of channeling youthful energy and zest for battle toward the road of struggle for the true interests of the workers.

However, the "bourgeois ideologues," as we are told, also employ far subtler means of dissuading the New Left from the only right way, the way of subordination to the Communist Party: "They seek to represent matters as if the radical student movement consists primarily of the groups and groupings whose positions are ultra-leftist and anarchist, or whose protest expresses itself in repulsive, antimoral fashion; they want to force all under the heading of the so-called 'new left' trend" (Brychkov, "From Unrest," pp. 44 and 47).

For a long time, as we saw, Soviet observers thus cited these causes for the rise of the New Left: distaste for the Vietnam War, the Negro question, the difficult economic circumstances of the students, the antiquated universities, and the seductive powers of reactionary ideologues. In other words, they did not explain the New Left.

Interest in the New Left had begun to ebb in Soviet periodicals, not to mention Western publications; *Novoye Vremya,* in a special issue on the crisis of American society (*NT* 29, 1971), did not carry any article on youth, although on blacks; finally, however, three significant articles appeared in *SShA,* a monthly designed for the observation of American affairs. One was by Kon, one of the most active writers in this area, titled "Student Unrest and the Theory of the 'Conflict of Generations' "; another by N. Yulina, "Rebellious Youth in Search of an Ideology"; and the third, L. Salycheva's "The Student Movement: 1960–1970." Not obvious from the titles, but clear from the periodical's name: All three articles were concerned exclusively with the United States.

AT LONG LAST

Kon's achievement consists not in presenting his own views, but in a comprehensive report on American studies of the New Left; more precisely, his essay might have been called "Student Unrest in the Mirror of American Sociological Literature." The conflict of generations which he emphasizes in his title is mentioned, but not stressed by his American sources. They are not so naive as to explain the New Left by the label "conflict of generations"; they mention the conflict, yes, but are less interested in it than in its causes.

Aside from this minor distortion, there is the obligatory reference, in the last paragraphs, to the class struggle—to which nothing points in the article itself. But Kon's essay is also of interest for a Western reader who wants to know the American theories on the New Left, theories that have developed in the last few years. Kon lists some fifty American sociologists; in the process he destroys the Soviet myth of the primarily economic origins of student unrest, a myth repeated even three months later by his colleague Aleksandrova in *MEiMO* (6, 1971).

Kon writes:

> The student unrest in the United States cannot be explained by group interest, by economic difficulties, etc. [. . .] [In contrast perhaps to France and Italy] these economic problems are far less important for American students. The demand for professional people is sufficiently high in the USA, and among the rebels there are not a few from affluent families, pupils of the largest and best universities. [. . .] The overwhelming majority of the leftist student activists belong to the affluent, socially privileged strata of society (pp. 28 and 37).

Both Kon and his colleague Yulina, who discusses the same theme six months later in *SShA,* use almost identical words in their first paragraphs to emphasize that the youthful campus unrest of the mid-sixties had taken American sociology "completely by surprise" (Kon) and had at first "not been taken seriously" (Yulina). But this is not so. And since both authors know the American literature and know it is not so, we suspect that the editors of *SShA* wanted an alibi for the publication's negligence in covering the New Left. When Kon and Yulina wrote their articles, there already existed thousands of Western articles on the world-wide student unrest, and hundreds of books and pamphlets.

On the basis of the Western literature's almost complete consensus on the subject, Yulina provided the accurate explanation for the behavior of the rebelling young people. "The central problem" for the various New Left groups, she wrote, was "the human problem"; even as far as Marx, his criticism of capitalist values interested them more than his critique of capitalist economy. The "Leftist" critique of the system was moral-emotional, she wrote, not rational-scientific. Further New Left characterizations by Yulina, partly in her words, partly in quotes from Western literature: "the romanticizing of the simple life"; rejection of a life style "overburdened with technology and artificial needs," a rejection formulated by young people "who could not bear the stress [*davleniye*] of industrial civilization" and who believed that this civilization "steadily eroded human individuality, steadily limited the unfolding of man's potential." For the students the worst kind of "stress"—Yulina used the English word—was life in the "abundant society" (*obshchestvo izobiliya*).

BEGINNING INSIGHTS

Yulina correctly observed that "when the 'new leftists' describe the ideal future society, they are more interested in its moral and spiritual than its material foundation." She continued: Their goal was a "community of equals" who had "thrown off the economic and political yoke, overcome alienation, based social and personal relations on love, and found true happiness in nature and in each other"; a "free society" with "a new kind of community, new family structure, new sexual morality, new life style, new esthetic forms," as well as a "participatory democracy" (she used the English expression). According to the New Left, all decisions had to be made "by the ordinary man" himself, and "society decentralized into small cells," into communities "in which the citizens truly share in governmental, political, and other matters." The goal of the New Left, she explained, was justice and the abolition of exploitation, its dream was a "community of equal, spiritually rich individuals."

Naturally Yulina censured the New Left's anarchism, its lack of ideology (Soviet-Communist ideology, of course), its negative attitude toward labor, toward the "organizations on a mass scale," unavoidable in the modern world. Especially she censored the New Left's claim that the proletariat was "conservative, apathetic, and increasingly integrated into the capitalist system." Despite this she quoted the American sociologist Keniston; in his *Young Radicals* he had said that sometimes he felt as if *the New Leftists were "the only sober and reasonable human beings" today*. Yulina even concluded that the anarchism and Utopianism she disliked so much in the American youth movement represented its "reaction to conformity and to the political passivity of an important segment of the American working class" (55–61; emphasis added).

Salycheva's assessment was similar: "The starting point of the current student movement in the United States was the protest against the moral-ethical norms of capitalist society" (*SShA* 4, 1972, 24). This judgment would be entirely correct had she spoken of a protest against the norms of contemporary *American* society, which were the movement's target throughout. When it began in 1960 there was no talk of battling against capitalism, but of fighting for racial equality, of attacking the war in Vietnam, later in Cambodia. Only minor currents within the New Left saw capitalism as the root of all evil.

In the last month of the period researched for this study, in the December issue of *Voprosy Filosofii,* Mrs. Novinskaya wrote a clever, summarizing report which she called "The 'Student Revolution' in the U.S. and the Crisis of Bourgeois Values." The reader, by the way, may have been struck, as I have, that some female Soviet authors have shown a special understanding of the New Left.

In March 1968 Novinskaya had published an article on Western youth in the same periodical; its editors proclaimed it the first in a series on the "theme of youth and progress in society," but, without a reason being given, the series never materialized. Her contribution in December 1972 can be viewed as the conclusion of an unwritten series, simultaneously as a kind of endpoint in the concern with the New Left. Even the first sentence of the essay sounds like a funeral oration: "If one asked the most diverse people what, during the sixties, was the most astonishing phenomenon in the social development of the capitalist Western states, in many cases the answer probably was: the mass protest of the younger generation" (p. 89).

Certainly Mrs. Novinskaya, with the help of impressive statistics from many American sources, informs the reader about the radicalization of campus youth during the sixties. But she also mentions the one-time radical student's new concern for "professional and career matters." "This [concern] leads to individualism and social passivity; in many cases it transforms the rebellious students of yesterday into carriers of social conformity and bourgeois ideology" (p. 99). She notes, I think rightly, a growing interest in Marxism among American youth, but no longer identifies this with pro-Soviet feeling. Perhaps because of its catastrophic defeat in the November 1972 elections there is no more talk of the U.S. Communist Party, and the last lines of her thirteen-page article remark drily that a "firm solidarity" between the student movement and the "working class" does not yet exist. Nor does she predict such solidarity for the future.

The American "working class" in general seems to pain Soviet writers. It is not what Moscow would like. Novinskaya even uses an expression that does not belong in the official vocabulary of Soviet Marxism, a phrase she puts in obligatory quotation marks and precedes with "so-called": the so-called "middle class." The term does not fit into the standard two-class scheme usually applied to the West, of bourgeoisie and proletariat, where all social groups must belong or at least tend toward one or the other.

On the basis of American sources, Novinskaya feels able to conclude that American students, although originating from various social strata, like adult Americans "gravitate [to the] norms and ideals of the so-called 'middle class'" (p. 100). The word appears in other writings about the New Left. The prodigal son, wrote Kagramanov, meaning the New Left and its kind, was "typically a 'child of the middle class'" (p. 247). In fact, the Marxist antithesis of bourgeoisie and proletariat has not been applicable in America for decades, because of the existence of a vast middle class including most of the population.

LIBERAL SYMPATHIES

All three of the last mentioned authors, Yulina, Salycheva, and Novinskaya, saw the motives of the New Left more in moral and ethical than in economic grounds. Novinskaya even ventured that the students, just because they were not yet occupied with making a living, had more time and energy for general or, as one now says even in Moscow, for "global" questions. Narrower problems of wages, working conditions, and profession demanded less of the students' attention than that of the employed (p. 101). Even the battle against poverty, which the students led, was viewed by the three authors not as a fight against personal poverty, but against that suffered by others. After all, for the most part the students came from homes that were well-off or affluent. In short, the three articles could have appeared in Western periodicals, authored by a Smith or Miller, without seeming particularly alien.

The newest contributions by Soviet authors on American campus unrest usually display sympathy for the New Left, similar to that felt by many Western liberals in the beginning. Since then many of these have turned from the movement, repelled by the outward forms of the battle: acts of violence, vandalism in occupied universities, dirt, obscene language. Soviet liberals meanwhile—and the Soviet intelligentsia is basically liberal—saw these methods from a distance and were less upset.

The warning, "Nothing can come of you, if you don't join your country's Communist Party right away!" has been less heard of in the last years. Perhaps Soviet authors meanwhile know more about the New Left and its peculiarities, and so there is less hope that the road via an anti-Soviet Marcuse is a minor detour on the way to a Soviet Marx. They openly admit that groups critical of the Soviet Union have a special attraction for New Leftists (Salycheva, p. 30), and that it is the Trotskyites and "revisionists" (i.e. Maoists) who expound Marxism most successfully among the radical students (Yulina, p. 55).

Like Yulina (p. 63) they console themselves by saying: "Today's youth is still searching."

THE NON-AMERICAN WEST

In the previous chapter it was pointed out that until the beginning of 1968 Moscow had overlooked the entire New Left, not only in the USA. This changed after the Parisian May, for America as shown above, and also for the rest of the world. Not suddenly, of course; the articles then commissioned had first to be written.

In summer 1970 *MEiMO* began a series of reports on youth in several non-Communist countries. Reutova wrote on West Germany, including West Berlin; Peschansky on England, Luk'yanova on Spain, Shlikhter on Canada, and Onyshchuk on France. In *Molodoy Kommunist* appeared reports on countries along the western coast of Latin America, by Volkov and Vessensky; on Italy by Yaropolov; Sweden by Konstantinov; Australia by Dobkin; and Indonesia by Sevortyan. Other periodicals proceeded less systematically. *Azia i Afrika* carried an article on Turkey by Danilov. In the *Literaturnaya Gazeta,* Molchanov, Bochkarev, and Volzhsky treated France. Repeated survey articles appeared: in *Kommunist* by Minayev, in *Kommunist Vooruzhennykh Sil* by Major Vyalykh, in *Politicheskoye Samoobrazovaniye* by Shmeleva, in *Molodoy Kommunist* by Bykov (who even discussed Thomas Jefferson and Thoreau) and by Lebedev and Tulayev.

The New Left was mentioned throughout, Marcuse frequently. The general feeling was that in itself the left trends were good. *Odnako*: The New Leftists and Marcuse (and his like) were troublemakers, even in distant Indonesia. Frequently they were mentioned in the same breath with the Maoists. Part of the Canadian New Left, for example, "was under heavy influence by the Maoist wing, and entertained sharp polemics with other leftist forces in Canada" (Shlikhter, p. 121). The founding of the pro-Moscow "Spartakus" in West Germany was praised, since "its members saw as their major task the successful conclusion of the task posed by the Communist Party." But at the same time there was the depressing diagnosis "that neo-Trotskyite and other leftist anti-Marxist currents attempt to increase their influence among the students. This tendency contains within itself a great danger for the oppositional movement, the greater the more its goes hand in hand with [. . .] expressions of hostility toward the socialist states [i.e. toward the USSR]" (Reutova, p. 123).

In England "a hostile attitude predominates among part of the 'left radicals' toward mass organizations of the workers, who are considered 'insufficiently revolutionary'" (Peschansky, p. 112). In Italy " 'leftist' students are attempting to force extremist views on the workers" (Yaropolov, 106 ff.). South American "leftists" disrupted the beginning cooperation of students and workers (Volkov, p. 113). A danger from the "left" threatened the student movement in Turkey. The "fame" of the Maoist Red Guard "has rolled as far as the shores of Turkey. Part of the progressive student body displays a tendency toward 'ultra-revolutionary' acts and phrases" (Danilov, p. 13). In France the "leftists" brought grief; Garaudy's dissent had not been recovered from, and the effectiveness of Sartre and André Gorz obviously pained Soviet observers. For the future, however, part of the students was considered an "ally of the working class" (Onyshchuk, pp. 125–127).

Everywhere there was an eager sighting for hints of cooperation between students and the Communist-led workers; wherever such hints were found, they were noted with satisfaction. But there was little opportunity for that. In Canada's case: "Although incidents of the joint appearance of students and workers are not especially frequent, they give evidence of an increased political consciousness in a sizable part of youth" (Shlikhter, p. 122).

The difficulty, suggested commentators, lay not simply in the "leftist" students' attitude toward the workers, but also in the poorly developed "consciousness" (in the Moscow-Communist sense) of working class youth. Kosenko, writing on American youth, found that although it was often in the first ranks of the proletariat, "as always it strongly lacks activity, organization, and class consciousness" (p. 131).

As we have seen, the Soviet picture of the New Left is not unified. It vacillates between sharp reaction and undeniable sympathy, especially when, as in an article by Ambartsumov (*LG* 30, 1969), the theme is partisanship in the quarrel between the New Left and its conservative critics. The generally uneasy feeling toward the New Left originates, of course, from the accurate insight that the "potential allies," as Soviet observers would like to see the New Left, for the most part reject Communist parties and the Soviet Union, and are even hostile to them. As always the consolation is: Things are still in flux. Hence Borisov's article, " 'Left' Radicalism and the Workers' Movements in the Developed Capitalist Nations," speaks of the "decided hostility [of the left-radical movement] toward the working class and its Marxist-Leninist vanguard," namely the Communist Party. But pages later Borisov continues: The youth movement, "notwithstanding its 'leftist' tendencies and excesses [is] a staunch reserve of the political army of socialist revolution, a potential ally of the working class" (p. 49).

The realities presented in the articles were generally described correctly, though naturally from Moscow's perspective. Occasionally errors occurred: The German student Benno Ohnesorg was killed by police in June, not January 1967 (Reutova, p. 120).

The question remains whether the student revolt is a temporary or long-term phenomenon. Since, despite its irritations for orthodox Communists, they judged it as a symptom of Western decline, Moscow likes to see the revolt as the onset of the deepening decay of Western society. The editor's introduction to an article by Borshchagovsky (*LG* 39, 1971) states: "The youth movement in the West is undergoing far-reaching internal developments. Bourgeois propaganda claims that 'the danger has passed,' that young people have been successfully pacified, have been led 'on the right path.' But in reality the insurrection of youth continues."

That may be; I tend to agree that the New Left was no mere episode which is now of only historical interest. But the fact is that an amazing calm has set in after the climax of the unrest in the later sixties. During my 1972/73 stay at Columbia University, New York, there were only two modest little disruptions: One concerned the issue of a separate clubroom at the university for homosexual students, the second a strip-tease performance on campus, disrupted not by the administration, but by conservative students. Five years earlier there had been bloody riots on the same campus.

DAVYDOV, A HUMOROUS CRITIC

The most amusing article on the New Left that I found in Soviet journals was Davydov's "Critique of the 'New Lefts'." Davydov obviously enjoyed writing it. His reasoning is not always that penetrating. He attempts for example to carry the theses of the New Left's fathers to absurdity by saying: If your teaching of the one-dimensional man is correct, then you must also be one-dimensional; but since you are able to recognize one-dimensionality, you yourself cannot be one-dimensional (otherwise you could not recognize it); therefore your teaching is incorrect (p. 73).

This is sophistry. But Davydov deserves praise for dispensing with deadly earnestness (as in his essay on Marcuse, which will be discussed). He even waives quotation marks, something that may have required courage, and unabashedly writes: the New Left. (Except in the heading; here the chief editor presumably insisted on obeying the rules.) Davydov even allows himself to discuss the conflict of generations without defensive mechanisms (p. 81), something no one else had dared because, as is well known, there can only be a "conflict of classes."

The author also ignores ritual repetition of the basic formula that everything, including the New Left, was to be explained on economic grounds. He expresses things like this: The protest of the New Left philosophers against the latter-day bourgeois world is "neither economic [hunger] nor erotic [frustrated sexuality], but primarily of a moral nature. . . . This moral position lent pathos to their demands . . . and brought them the sympathies of the New Left, *whose protest against latter-day bourgeois society had also, primarily, a moral character*" (p. 74; emphasis added).

But alas, Davydov continues ironically, the young extremists did not want to admit to old-fashioned values like morality or conscience, and therefore reduced everything to "existence."

> If you ask a young man today why he struck a drunk in the mug for molesting a girl, nothing in the world will induce him to say: because my moral sense was offended. And in fact, why a moral sense at all? Maybe the girl was a whore and the drunk who molested her a pimp. What, in fact, does all this have to do with morality? If you are lucky the young man explains his spontaneous action with an esthetic reflection (My esthetic sensibilities were offended [he could say], because the drunk's vulgarity was so irreconcilable with the grace of the girl); but it is one hundred to one that he will invoke his "existence," which "rebelled."

Next Davydov amuses himself with existentialism. Existence, he writes, is

> a redeeming concept. The more vague, the more redeeming. If we sub-
> merge the variety of our moral feelings in the dark ground of "existence,"
> we need not account to ourselves for their true content: it is enough to
> act, "to be beside ourselves," that is—to use the language of existential-
> ism—to exist. Our fist into the dirty mug and we can be at peace, al-
> though the real reason for this "being-beside-ourselves" might not have
> been that ugly face at all. But when we begin to analyze the reasons, we
> can succumb to "endless reflection" or even total inaction, like the cen-
> tipede that stood forever still when it began to ponder which foot should
> initiate its movement (ibid.).

Movement, however, is the New Left's concern.

> Every clash seems so natural, so self-explanatory to them [the New
> Left], and everything that opposes it so boring, so dull and small, that
> there is nothing to discuss: "Conflict, that's the real thing"—and there
> is nothing more to say. . . . In a word, everything points to creating a
> disturbance first. Then one can go on from there (p. 96).

> Still in good spirits, Davydov mocks the New Left's progenitors, takes
> it by way of Sartre and the atom bomb (he calls the New Left the "atom
> bomb generation," p. 79) at last to art, particularly ecstatic, wordless and
> abstract art, since the use of language, in the eyes of the New Left and its
> philosophers, would already mean undesirable limitation, a hardening into
> ideology. "In the end it is difficult to recognize anything, or even to dis-
> tinguish artistic action from the action of some drug addict. [. . .] Every
> ecstasy is esthetic, simply because it is ecstasy and therefore [. . .] a phe-
> nomenon of art" (pp. 94 and 97).

> For the Western reader it is a breath of fresh air to read the few such
> contributions which treat a serious subject with irony instead of sour in-
> dignation, especially when, like Davydov's, such articles occasionally hit
> the bull's-eye.

> Moscow, of course, does not appear happy with the current course of
> debate with the New Left. Three years after the resolution mentioned
> early in this chapter, a leading article of the same periodical, *Voprosy
> Filosofii* (1, 1972, 15 ff.), complained of the "leftists'" ideological activities.
> The editors of the journal promised an ongoing analysis of "all these com-
> plicated ideological situations and displacements which, in the ideological
> battle, continuously result in the area of theory."

> The battle continues.

V

READING THROUGH THE KEYHOLE

"The state has turned into a rigid administrative bureaucracy, which consists of a numerically small elite and a huge disfranchised mass" (*MEiMO* 10, 1971, 114, quoting from Charles Reich's *Greening of America*).

To the most positive developments of the post-Stalin era belongs the appearance of Western authors in Soviet publications, not only of Communists or fellow travelers published even in Stalin's time, but of others as well. I am not thinking of authors in the literary sense, though a writer like Heinrich Böll, with Soviet editions in the hundred thousands, no doubt provides Soviet readers with food for thought with his abhorrence of any repression of the conscience. Rather, I am thinking of non-Communist Western authors who are concerned with current sociological and psychological developments, insofar as they touch directly or indirectly on the problems of youthful unrest. Some of their names are as follows:

Raymond Aron, Daniel Bell, Joachim Bodamer, Zbigniew Brzezinski, Agatha Christie, Régis Debray, William O. Douglas, Peter F. Drucker, H. M. Enzensberger, Frantz Fanon, Jay W. Forrester, Erich Fromm, John K. Galbraith, William Golding, Paul Goodman, Gil Green, Günter Grass, Richard Hofstadter, Kenneth Keniston, George F. Kennan, Alfred C. Kinsey, H. Marshall McLuhan, Herbert Marcuse, Margaret Mead, C. Wright Mills, Vance O. Packard, Charles A. Reich, Jean-François Revel, David Riesman, Theodore Roszak, Jean-Paul Sartre, Arthur M. Schlesinger, B. F. Skinner, Alvin Toffler, Martin Walser, Andy Warhol. (Agathie Christie belongs in this context because her detective fiction is called an opiate for youth, and Günter Grass—see Mlechina—because of his depiction of young people in *Local Anesthetic*.)

Naturally, commentaries on these Western authors, and the decisions on which of their works to translate, are shaped by the specific aims of Soviet media politics. It is as though Soviet citizens observe Western intellectual life through a keyhole which provides a limited view especially selected for them by Moscow's cultural functionaries. But over the decades Russians have learned to read through keyholes. "One must read the white space, not the black," is a motto they learn early, hence even slanted commentaries and excerpts provide them with valuable insights.

Of course not all the authors just listed have received equal attention. Herbert Marcuse drew the most comprehensive reaction, enough to merit the next chapter. Among the rest Charles Reich is leading with *The Greening of America*; followed by Theodore Roszak, *The Making of a Counter Culture*, 1969; Marshall McLuhan, *Understanding Media*, 1964, and *The Medium Is the Message*, 1967; and B. F. Skinner, *Beyond Freedom and Dignity*, 1971. Gil Green is often cited on the subject of the New Left, but because he is an orthodox Communist this is less revealing. Soviet commentaries on Andy Warhol, Hans Magnus Enzensberger, and Frantz Fanon should be mentioned. In all cases what is interesting, of course, is not these writers' actual words or deeds, but Moscow's reaction to them.

Let us begin with Charles Reich. In Germany his American bestseller, although the translation appeared within a year of its American edition (Vienna, 1971), caused no major discussion. For many it remained a book for young people. Not so in the Soviet Union; there, among all pertinent Western books, it has had the strongest effect.

In October 1971 *MEiMO* published a seven-page excerpt from the book, and for ten additional pages a commentary by Arab-Ogly and Zhiritsky. At the same time a shorter version of this material appeared in the *Literaturnaya Gazeta* (p. 41, 1971), filling an entire newspaper page. Just previously Novikov commented on the book in *Inostrannaya Literatura* (9, 1971); barely a year later the same publication treated Reich extensively with an article by Kagramanov. Reich was mentioned in many other articles primarily on the basis of *MEiMO*'s October 1971 contribution.

Reich's essential thesis, of course, is that among restless youth a new consciousness has already developed, which he calls "Consciousness III," and which is characterized by a turning away from traditional values; "Consciousness III" is about to transform America from within, to bring it without violent revolution to a "greening."

Soviet authors' assessment of the book was predominantly positive. It would, they hoped, have a favorable influence on the West's New Left, because unlike much of the Leftist literature its orientation was positive in Soviet eyes, not pessimistic about culture or violently antimodern. In addition, much to Reich's credit, his analysis of contemporary American society relied in many ways on Karl Marx (though on the early Marx whom Moscow handles with kid gloves), despite his being no Marxist and being burdened by "abstract humanism and petty-bourgeois radicalism." Not least, they praised him for his rejection of Marcuse.

VISION OF A GREENING GARDEN—IN THE WEST

Reich's weaknesses are, of course, contrasted with all this: He overestimated, the Soviet authors maintain, the role of consciousness as a factor in transforming society. A changed consciousness was no doubt very nice, went the feeling, and it was a necessary part of society's transformation, but the transformation itself required "class struggle and revolutionary force." In addition Reich erroneously believed that a new consciousness would evolve spontaneously. "He thereby diminishes the role of theoretical thought and of political organization [meaning: of the American Communist Party!] in preparing and carrying out fundamental social change. At this point Reich the realist withdraws permanently behind Reich the Utopian" (Arab-Ogly, pp. 125 and 128). And of course Reich was reproached for his permissiveness with regard to marijuana (Kagramanov, p. 250). The document "Green Grow the Reichs" brings an excerpt from one of the reviews.

Interesting, however, are not only Soviet comments on Reich, but rather what Soviet readers discover about his ideas. The quotations presented to them create for them the following picture:

Existing circumstances are ripe for change. Corporate society, as Reich calls this condition in his somber description, cannot be totally unknown to the Soviet reader. *MEiMO* quotes from Reich's book*:

> The state has turned into a rigid administrative bureaucracy, which consists of a numerically small elite and a huge disfranchised mass. [. . .] Much of the power of the state does not rest in the hands of the legislature, but with the administrative authorities. [. . .] The bureaucracy displaces step by step the power of the law. [. . .] The police, the army, and state security forces swell in number. . . . Like work, life becomes more and more mechanical and senseless. Many major tasks need to be fulfilled, tasks which demand quick decisions, but working hours are

---

* This and the following quotation have been translated from the author's German because *MEiMO*'s text does not give a precise source and is, for the most part, Moscow's summary of Reich's ideas from the *New Yorker* and the later book. *Trans.*

wasted on all sorts of things useful to no one: the manufacture of unusable or harmful products or the servicing of bureaucratic structures (*MEiMO* 10, 1971, 114 ff.).

This Leviathan corporate society, says Reich, is so powerful that any frontal attack is futile. Fortunately its end is in sight: A new kind of man emerges! What Soviet readers learn of this new man must affect them positively: He wants to love, not hate; wants to lead a meaningful, not a senseless life; wants to experience work as joy, not drudgery. Such a man, according to Reich, already exists: the young American. And not only that. This new man is already in the process of changing today's odious society into a beautiful and pleasant one by transforming it from within. Universities, law firms, industrial concerns are already caught up in this transformation, since the younger generation grows into them everywhere. There is hope, in fact, that members of the ruling stratum will convert to Consciousness III. Again a quotation from Reich:

> Even the millionaire will be happier when he prefers personal freedom to the artificial world of material affluence. [. . .] Although in varying degrees, all of us today are employees, even exploited employees of the corporate state. In this sense there is no class struggle because there exists only one class. In Marx's terms one can say that we are all proletarians now, and that there is no ruling class aside from the technological-organizational apparatus (ibid., p. 119).

The nine-page-long quotation ends with Reich's happy news that the new consciousness was growing like a flower from the asphalt of the streets, transforming America into a "greening garden."

From the Reichian texts presented to him, the Soviet reader could deduce three points: that in the evil capitalist society there existed men who confidently envisioned a better, more humane future; that the new man could arrive by a different route than the Marxist-Leninist way preached to him ad infinitum; and not least, that according to reasonable people in the West it was possible to transform an all-powerful state from within, through a new generation growing into that state.

As in America, Theodore Roszak's book on the counter culture received less attention in the Soviet Union than Reich's. Roszak's essential thoughts first appeared in *The Nation* in spring 1968, just before the events in Paris, and as a book in 1969. The April 1971 issue of *Voprosy Filosofii* contained the most detailed Soviet review. There, together with Reich's, the book was treated in 16 pages by the husband-and-wife team of Zamoshkin-Motroshilova. They judged Reich's *The Greening of America* the better, but also reviewed *The Making of a Counter Culture* positively. Of course, they treated Roszak's critique of the technocratic society as if it had in mind only the West. The Soviet reader was not told that Roszak also excluded, in the same breath with the conservatives, the Communists from the new youth culture because they were defenders of a "technocratic totalitarianism." Nor did he hear Roszak characterize the Communists as people "who tend the ashes of the proletarian revolution, in the hope that a spark might leap from them" (Roszak, p. xii).

The two Soviet authors emphasize several times that Roszak's critique applied only to the West (pp. 54 ff.). Whether Russian intellectuals agree with this interpretation I leave in the air. Much of what the two reviewers, on the basis of Roszak's book, say about Western bureaucracies may remind the Soviet reader of his own country's bureaucrats. Zamoshkin and Motroshilova explain that in the bureaucratic system there exists

> conflict between personalities, an irrational play of feelings, sympathies, antipathies, and above all the possibility of drawing advantages from the mere fact of one's *holding* a post in the bureaucratic system [emphasis by the two authors]. Hence the almost pathological fear of the professional bureaucrat, the specialist, of losing his position, and thus his willingness to sacrifice his own dignity and the fate of others, his feverish efforts toward higher status (p. 49).

Some readers of *Voprosy Filosofii* must have been impressed—as the two Soviet reviewers were—by the fact that followers of the New Left "more and more demonstrate their willingness to renounce all pleasures and comforts of the consumer society, rather than pay the highest price: dignity, personal autonomy, and convictions" (p. 50).

The reflections of the two Soviet philosophers prove that Roszak is right in excluding the Soviet Union from the new youth culture. Roszak believes in the counter culture as an alternative to the current technocratic-bureaucratic system, but the position of the two Soviet authors is that no road exists outside that of the scientific-technological revolution's further development. They write:

> Without a functional, rational organization of industry and management, without people exclusively and professionally concerned with efficiency and with the perfecting of technology and managerial meth-

ods, it is today impossible to increase mankind's affluence and power over nature, to improve the conditions for work and permeate them with creative possibilities (p. 48).

The vast majority of people in the West, including Western Communists, including Western establishments—but with the exception of the New Left—would express the idea of the industrial society in approximately these words of Zamoshkin and Motroshilova.

Soviet commentators regret the "influence which McLuhan has especially on student youth." Kravchenko compares McLuhan to Goebbels, describes him as a nihilist, a distorter of reality, a creator of confused conceptions, illogical and without ideas, as a man who presents "the goals of the youthful protest movement in a false light" and "barbarically assaults the facts," as a useful tool of the ruling class: "McLuhan's circus philosophy pleases the bourgeoisie which, with its help, and despite the growing ideological vacuum, hopes to channel the energies of the radically inclined strata of society away from the social struggle" (*MEiMO* 4, 1971, 147). Previously the *Literaturnaya Gazeta* had published the entire translation, from the English, of a bitter attack on McLuhan by Sydney Finkelstein (3, 1969, 13).

The most recent critique of McLuhan is by the Doctor of Philosophy Mozhnyagun (*LG* 50, 1972, 15). Without naming his sources, but evidently on the basis of passages from McLuhan's books and French essays (in *Le Monde, Figaro, L'Express*), Mozhnyagun sees in McLuhan above all a corruptor of youth. With surprise he notes McLuhan's thesis that Western youth walked about in rags, half naked, with tangled hair, "unwashed, with amulets around their necks," because it had turned from the establishment, from the "big machine." Quickly he adds that the "big machine" meant capitalism, although McLuhan also sees it in the USSR.

Mozhnyagun especially resents McLuhan's calling Soviet Communism passé, a piece of the nineteenth century, and that like Reich he envisions the coming of a new man, turning from technology and logic back to sentiment. Hence he labels him, simply, the public relations man of the American electronics industry.

In the fall of 1971, when B. F. Skinner's *Beyond Freedom and Dignity* appeared in New York and quickly became a bestseller especially among students, it was clear that the book would arouse the strong interest of Soviet ideologues. Little more than a year later, the same Arab-Ogly whom we just saw reviewing Reich's book, tore into Skinner's in the *Literatur-*

naya Gazeta (49, 1972, 15). He had so much to say that his allotted newspaper page was insufficient, and long paragraphs were set in fine print.

Arab-Ogly annihilates the American psychologist, calling him a "philosophical primitivist" who degraded men to the level of "super mice" and who saw in the anthill the ideal society. He even compares Skinner with the devil, cheating men of freedom and dignity. In fact the spectacle is ironic. On the one hand: the famous inventor of the teaching machine, with which he revolutionized education; a professor at Harvard, one of the major universities of the West; who now assures us that mankind can no longer permit itself freedom, dignity, and individualism if civilization is to survive, and who warns us (in Arab-Ogly's pointed epigram): "The more mankind clings to the mirage of personal freedom and dignity, the surer and more quickly will it create hell on earth."

And on the other hand: the Soviet ideologue and journalist (a Russian despite his Azerbaijan name) as defender of freedom, dignity, and individualism, of moral values and democracy; a representative of the materialist world view who accuses Skinner of degrading man by applying, to him, experimental data drawn from doves and mice.

Is it an inside-out world, with upside-down fronts? Or simply Skinner's view of a postdemocratic world, as Daniel Bell's is postindustrial—while Arab-Ogly, along with his friends among the Soviet intelligentsia, lives among people who still view democratization and industrialization as desirable goals, with the same certitude as Skinner's American fathers and grandfathers not long ago?

The Americans, with their ability to coin brief and pointed phrases, speak of "time lags" if the same event happens, and must happen, at place B as has happened at A, except some time later. Much of what is good or bad in America today will come, with varying time lags, to Europe, and then to the Communist countries.

When an American like Skinner feels that in America, because of time-consuming democratic cautions about the violation of individual rights, only a fraction of all criminals can be convicted while others are free on minimum bail committing further crimes, then he is seeing democracy with very different eyes than the Soviet intellectual Arab-Ogly, who witnesses the deportation of Soviet intellectuals to Siberian prison camps because they participated in modest, by Western standards meek demonstrations. One seeks peace and order because of the excess of democracy surrounding him, and hopes to find them through experiments with doves and mice; the second, surrounded by an excess of quiet and order, yearns for democracy and is horrified at Skinner's postdemocratic pessimism.

STRUGGLE OF GENERATIONS OR BETWEEN CLASSES?

Since the Soviet intelligentsia is primarily concerned with those keyholes that yield glimpses of *America,* it is noteworthy when it turns to *European* authors. Of these the German psychiatrist Joachim Bodamer has aroused its special interest, particularly his article "Cult of Youth and Horror of Age," printed with minor editing in the *Literaturnaya Gazeta* (24, 1972, 15).

Bodamer's essay deals with the conflict of generations. His conclusive, perhaps consciously emphatic thesis is: "On the contrary, the social class struggle has become the struggle of generations; the different age groups have stepped into battle against each other, and from the dictatorship of the proletariat has risen the demand for a dictatorship of youth."

Alexander Borshchagovsky attacked this thesis in an essay published simultaneously with Bodamer's. He called Bodamer an enemy of progress and democracy who "declared war on youth." Borshchagovsky's counter-thesis is of course: The struggle of generations is a "myth"; there is only the class struggle. It followed, for him, that two completely different groups existed among youth, a good, "a progressive youth," and an evil one consisting of "fanatic little bands of extremists, using the most out-rageous, most criminal methods": "Maoists, anarchists, Trotskyites, neo-Trotskyites and other pseudo-revolutionaries playing into the hands of reaction and baited by the reactionaries." The often used Western term "struggle of generations" is being rejected by other authors, too. In a long article Onyshchuk devoted an entire chapter to the theme; the West took the easy way out, he said, when explaining youthful unrest by a conflict of generations (*MEiMO* 3, 1970, 111). True. But Soviet ideologues also take the easy way out in explaining it by a class struggle.

But to return to Bodamer. Without his emphasis on the struggle of generations, Moscow's reaction to him might have been less negative. Many of the Soviet older generation agree wholeheartedly with Bodamer's critique of the New Left: its anti-historicism, its fanaticism about equality, its struggle "against orderly human relations," its excessive surge "toward the power and control centers of the apparatus." And of course a conflict of generations exists in the USSR as well (see the poetry of the young dissidents), except that the conflict is less obvious in a very controlled society than in the open West.

With the critics of the New Left, its idols are also rejected by the Moscow authors. Andy Warhol, Hans Magnus Enzensberger, and Frantz Fanon, for example, find no mercy.

Pop artist and film-maker Andy Warhol merits this comment: "This son of a humble Czech emigrant" is not an artist, but a typical art merchant of the consumer society, a cynic and destroyer; he directed the "most boring" films and made a career of picture montages, consisting of poster clippings for soups and tomato sauce. His work is without content, without ideas, inhuman. In rare support the conservative *Daily Telegraph's* view is invoked: "deadly boredom" (*LG* 24, 1972, 14). The possibility of covert social protest in Warhol's work is not even considered; here *The Daily Telegraph* and *Literaturnaya Gazeta* agree.

There is agreement again, this time from Moscow's *Literaturnaya Gazeta* to Hamburg's *Welt,* on Hans Magnus Enzensberger. Enzensberger is attacked with several colleagues, among them Wolfgang Neuss and Max Bense; their contemptuous attitude toward the cultural heritage of the Germans arouses the indignity of Soviet observers (*LG* 40, 1970, 15). They hardly know whether to laugh or cry, and are totally unwilling to believe that this attitude had revolutionary intent. (See the document, "Against Enzensberger and Other 'Gravediggers of Literature'.") The attack on Enzensberger and those like him characterizes the conservative attitudes of Soviet ideologues toward the New Left and toward art.

Frantz Fanon, the black ideologue who even speaks for American blacks, is also an undesirable. Any rival on the left, the "left" in Moscow's view, is rejected. The document "The Moor . . ." provides the example of his case.

Several years later in a different context, in *Voprosy Filosofii,* the judgment on Fanon was more muted. Mrs. Myalo, known to the reader from her concluding report on the Parisian May, contributed a sensible essay on "The Problem of the 'Third World' in the Left-Extremist Consciousness." Quoting the *New York Times Magazine* (May 5, 1968; 80), she called Fanon one of the seven heroes of the New Left. The seven were: "Three moralists (Albert Camus, Paul Goodman, Noam Chomsky), three immoralists (Ché Guevara, Régis Debray, Frantz Fanon), and a professor (Herbert Marcuse)." She also named Jean-Paul Sartre, whose preface to Fanon's *Wretched of the Earth* influenced youth no less than the book itself. But even she, of course, could not induct Fanon into the pantheon of revolutionaries.

Angela Davis' chances of reaching it are much greater. Her membership in the American Communist Party even erased the sin of having been Marcuse's pupil. But in contrast to Fanon, and especially to Marcuse, she elicited no discussion among Soviet ideologues. True, the papers reported extensively on her political fate, her trial, her triumphal visit to the Soviet Union (for example *New Times* 28, 1971; 3, 1972; 24, 1972; 37, 1972). But she caused no intellectual waves. And how could she? Having joined the American Communist Party, even being elected to its Central Committee, she had qualified for the pantheon, but despite her obvious intelligence had failed to qualify as a subject for intellectual debate.

There was also praise for Supreme Court Justice William O. Douglas. The periodical *SShA* reported comprehensively (1, 1970) on his life, which involved the transformation from a pillar of American society to its bitter critic, who called youth's revolt against the American establishment justified.

MAO, TROTSKY, BAKUNIN: THE CORRUPTORS OF YOUTH

In contrast to the Western interpreters and prophets of the New Left (Marcuse, the most important, will soon be discussed extensively), Soviet readers hear amazingly little on the influence of the man who had an enormous reputation among youth during the years of unrest: Mao Tsetung. The entire literature combed for this book contained not one essay on Mao's influence on Western youth. Of course countless articles and dozens of pamphlets and books on Mao and Maoism, wholly negative, have appeared in the Soviet Union, but not on Mao as idol of the students. Mao's influence is not kept secret. But in page-long treatments of the New Left he is mentioned in but a few lines. Two examples: In Volzhsky's retrospect on the four years in France since May 1968, we read in the last paragraph: "The Maoists and Trotskyites [in France] continue to pin their hopes on the politically most unstable, anarchistically-oriented, declassed youth." And in a nine-page, fine print analysis of Western students by Diligensky and Novinskaya we read:

> Maoist demagogy, which preaches an "absolute [. . .] revolutionary élan [*revolyutsionnost'*] acknowledging no objective considerations whatever, and which opposes the movement of the workers supposedly

in the direction of *embourgeoisement,* with the "revolutionary spirit of the poor nations of the Third World," is able, despite its primitiveness, to lead astray a few extremists of the student youth.

This negligible treatment of Mao's influence, of a man never treated in friendly fashion otherwise, is difficult to explain. The intent, it almost seems, is to keep from Soviet youth any knowledge of Mao's influence on the world's youth in general. But nothing points to any special receptiveness of Soviet youth to Maoism, so this explanation is not convincing. In the last chapter I will attempt another explanation.

More understandable is the discreet treatment of Trotsky's considerable influence on rebellious youth; there is a Trotskyite tradition in the USSR, which of course cannot be nurtured. At any rate, however, the periodical *Agitator* published an article by Ognev, who discussed Trotsky's influence on Western youth, not least during the May disturbances in Paris. Basmanov has even written a longer essay whose subject is what the title indicates: "Contemporary Trotskyism and Its Intrigues in the Youth Movement." (Also see his 1969 article and his 1971 book on Trotskyism.)

A third "ism" is often mentioned in one breath with Maoism and Trotskyism as a corruptor of youth: anarchism. The attack on anarchism is much easier for the Soviet author. Certainly anarchism is bothersome, but its impracticality is easily laughed at; it is also safe ground, since Marx and Engels struggled with it for decades. To find all arguments, in fact, one simply flips to "A" in the index of the "classics."

Mamut's contribution is typical of this method. Although attacking today's anarchism, he moves on rutted roads: Bakunin, Proudhon, and Stirner are mentioned nineteen times, Cohn-Bendit, Dutschke, and Marcuse just once each, and today's leading anarchists not at all.

Mamut admits openly that contemporary Western anarchists attack the state as such, in other words also the Soviet state. (The document "Does That Hold Only for the West?" supplies the corresponding example.) But Mamut's defense of the Soviet state is not strenuous. A quotation from Engels is convenient; in addition Mamut points to the enormous differences between the capitalist and socialist states, which, he thinks, make criticism against the first inapplicable to the second (pp. 45 and 47). For the rest, he is satisfied to dispose of the anarchists as "reactionary romantics," as "dyed-in-the-wool dogmatics," as thoughtless adventurers (pp. 26, 49, 51). Yemelyanov's procedure is no different; for him anarchism is an "ideological potpourri" (*meshanina*), which "leads into the ideological swamp of the bourgeoisie."

My observations of the Soviet Union suggest that broad sectors of Soviet youth have as little sympathy for anarchism as for Maoism or Trotskyism. Many Soviet citizens, not least young people, are vexed by the omnipotence of their outrageously bureaucratic state; they would gladly loosen it up, "democratize" it, make it more "humane." And some may wink at each other when reading Mamut's report on the Western anarchists' reproaches against the system. But the idea that the state must be destroyed would sooner meet with their abhorrence than with acceptance.

But what are the Soviet reader's thoughts when—instead of Mao, Trotsky, and Bakunin—he sees marching past, if only glimpsed through the keyhole, the Western critics of Western society that we discussed in this chapter? In view of a lack of public opinion polls we can only guess. Presumably he thinks two things. First, that the West must actually be in crisis, a crisis which allows meaningful inferences on the future of modern civilization. Secondly, that Western intellectuals have an unbelievable, at once frightening and exciting opportunity to analyze and criticize their own system.

VI

THE THIRD M

"Marx—the god,
Mao—his sword,
Marcuse—his prophet"
(*Pravda,* May 30, 1968, and *Molodoy
Kommunist,* 4, 1968, 18).

No Western political writer in recent times has occupied Soviet critics as
much as Herbert Marcuse. Not including newspaper articles, 16 major
essays (up to 34 pages) appeared from 1968 to 1972, and a book of 137
pages (Batalov, et al.) in fall 1970. Of the publications, there appeared:

1968: 2 (Ulle; Zamoshkin and Motroshilova)
1969: 5 (Kosolapov and Pechenev; Cheprakov; Bykhovsky; Khristov;
    Mozhnyagun)
1970: 7 (Cheprakov, Valyuzhenich, Steigerwald, Novikov, Davydov,
    Ivashkevich, as well as the book by Batalov, Nikitich, and
    Vogeler)
1971: 2 (Besonov, Lakshin)
1972: 1 (Nikitina)

Literaturnaya Gazeta carried three articles on Marcuse; *Inostrannaya
Literatura, MEiMO,* and *Voprosy Filosofii* each published two; and *Vestnik Moskovskogo Universiteta, Voprosy Literatury, Kommunist, Molodoy
Kommunist, New Times, Politicheskoye Samoobrazovaniye,* and *SShA*
each had one. Marcuse was mentioned in many other articles not specifically devoted to him, beginning with Zhukov's *Pravda* article on May 30,
1968.

Zhukov's article (see the document "The Three M's") set the tone; also
significant were contributions in *Voprosy Filosofii* in October 1968 and,
in January and April 1969, in *Molodoy Kommunist* and *MEiMO* respec-

tively. The theoretical party monthly *Kommunist* (8, 1969) did not comment until May 1969. Publications on Marcuse, and in fact the New Left, attained their peak in 1970.

Whoever knew Marcuse's thoughts must have told himself that his Soviet critics would reject four of his theses in particular: that the USSR was no longer true to Marxism; that the proletariat had become integrated into bourgeois society and was therefore no longer capable of revolution; that Western Communist parties also played by establishment rules now, thus transforming themselves into "doctors at the bedside of diseased capitalism" (Kosolapov, p. 18); that despite this a revolutionary situation existed in the world, though not among the workers, but among other revolutionaries: the students, the alienated and asocial, the blacks.

But what do Soviet critics really say?

Voprosy Filosofii's first major Russian article on Marcuse appeared in October 1968 (prior to that, in September, one by Dieter Ulle, translated from the German). The article's title promised much: "Is Herbert Marcuse's 'Critical Theory of Society' Really Critical?" but the content disappointed. Zamoshkin and Motroshilova, the husband-and-wife team we know, took the easy way out. They rebuked the author of *One-Dimensional Man* for a teaching that was itself "one-dimensional." He criticized not real people, they commented, but man as portrayed by Western sociology.

Living as they do in the classical land of authoritarianism, where the Party tells the intellectuals what to do, the authors' outrage about American sociologists following orders from the powers-that-be sounds rather hollow. To support their charge the two authors mention W. W. Rostow. Moscow has never forgiven Rostow his non-Marxist teaching, widely read especially in the Third World, on the five stages of economic growth (*The Stages of Economic Growth: A Non-Marxist Manifesto,* Cambridge, [Engl.], 1960).

Certainly Rostow for years had close ties to the White House, from 1966 to 1969 as Special Assistant to the President, and in his official capacities also published defenses of official policy, especially of the Vietnam War. But his book on economic stages, so sharply rejected by Moscow, was written by him as an independent scholar, not on orders from the government.

Other Soviet critics attacked Marcuse himself as a puppet of, and commissioned by, monopoly capital to confuse youth and push it in a wrong direction. In an article on hippies Rozental' creates the impression that the lords of Wall Street had cunningly built up Marcuse and loosed a "popularization campaign" for him in order to turn youth from the true revolution led by Moscow-oriented Communists. Or, there is Novikov's judgment: Marcuse's philosophy "disorganizes ideologically the radical groups of the intelligentsia and of youth [in the West], making them receptive to the ideology of 'leftist' opportunism, above all Maoism and Trotskyism. The writings of Marcuse are therefore a weapon of ideological diversion by the imperialist bourgeoisie" (*Politicheskoye Samoobrazovaniye* 9, 1971, 79).

In his press the Soviet intellectual reads daily about his American colleagues' attacks on American society and government. Therefore he knows the remarkably wide range of American journalism and its critique of the system, and perhaps thinks of his own country rather than of the United States when the article on Marcuse mentions authors who are "stamped by ideological guidelines [. . .] conditioned by apologetic forms of the uses of the social sciences, by the social mandate decreed by the bureaucracy, by the functional induction of these sciences into the ideological atmosphere of the society in question" (p. 72). It might be, in other words, that deep inside the Soviet reader is skeptical when reading in the same article: that American sociologists had developed, in the employ of monopoly capitalists, the very picture of American man and society which suited their employers; and that Marcuse aimed his pseudoattack against this picture, and thus—since the picture was inaccurate—was tilting in a void.

In the opinion of the two Soviet critics, Zamoshkin and Motroshilova, Rostow and Marcuse thus used the same false picture as their starting point, except that Rostow affirmed it and Marcuse rejected it. In fact, they claimed, Marcuse really supported the false portrayal by treating it as though it were accurate. Rostow's apologia and Marcuse's "critique" (in quotation marks) were therefore to similar effect. The Soviet conclusion: Marcuse's "rejection of capitalism is based on today's fetishist bourgeois consciousness."

AGAINST MARCUSE: THE WORKER WANTS REVOLUTION!

Zamoshkin and Motroshilova mention Marcuse's real sin only in passing: For him modern society, they wrote, was identical with developed industrial society, which he saw in America as well as in the Soviet Union;

hence there were, for him, no "effective differences between today's capitalism and socialism" (p. 73).

In fact, as early as 1958 in his *Soviet Marxism,* especially in the chapter "The New Rationality," Marcuse wrote that "both systems [in the West and in the Soviet Union] show the common features of late industrial civilization." Among other things he meant by that the "joint rule of economic and political bureaucracies" and the lock-step standardization of man through "the mass media, [. . .] entertainment industry, education." In a preface to the 1961 edition he added that "the common technical base [. . .] could assert itself even through such fundamentally different economies as nationalized or private enterprise" (Vintage edition, pp. 66 and xi).

Zamoshkin and Motroshilova cautiously do not mention Marcuse's book on Soviet Marxism. Clearly a man like Marcuse, who sees in the Soviet Union simply another industrial society instead of something fundamentally new and—compared to everything that has gone before—something fundamentally good, almost by definition would be judged an enemy.

Hence the question posed in their article's title is answered: Marcuse's critique is not criticism, but serves to support the capitalist system.

The second major article on Marcuse also has two authors, perhaps for mutual protection. Kosolapov and Pechenev's title again asks a question, "Where Does Marcuse's Philosophy Lead Young People?" and again the article skirts the real issue. This time both authors concentrate on the extent to which Marcuse is accurate in claiming that Western industrial society had succeeded, basically, in solving the problem of poverty. They are willing to agree with Marcuse that the workers' standard of living had improved in some capitalist states, even that, "judging by key statistics, it is higher than in the socialist states" (p. 20). But this conclusion, they remark, is valid only for the workers' material well-being, which the crafty bourgeoisie had elevated to the standard of general welfare; it is invalid for the workers' other needs. Their sentence, in bold type, is as follows:

> Capitalism need no longer pocket its profits at the expense of the masses' obvious [physical] hunger [*nedoyedaniye*], but does use every opportunity to enrich itself at the expense of their chronic intellectual-spiritual [*dukhovniy*] hunger. Only the form of exploitation has changed, its essence has remained the same (p. 21).

Here a comment is necessary. For millennia the poor have demanded the overthrow of existing powers, to overcome hunger by revolution. All socialists—Utopians as well as the many shades of Marxists, also the social democrats—always assumed that freedom from material want would make mankind happier and more free. By this reasoning, wherever material hunger has been satisfied, contentment must reign. Instead Western youth is rebellious, precisely the youth of those social strata that have not experienced physical hunger for some time. Many young people turn in outrage from society precisely when society realizes the age-old dream of mankind: the satisfaction of material needs. Hence there must be another kind of hunger—the intellectual and spiritual hunger. So far so good. The West has long ago reached this conclusion, to which the New Left has contributed. Now Moscow picks it up. Just when the West has satisfied, without revolution, the material needs of hundreds of millions of people to an extent inconceivable to Marx, the Soviet ideologists prophesy a new revolution for the fulfillment of the intellectual and spiritual wants of the Western citizen.

This is not the place to discuss in detail the problem of these two kinds of hunger. It is true, much has been done in the West to satisfy intellectual and spiritual hunger; educational facilities have been established throughout the West in steeply rising numbers. However, despite this, spiritual dissatisfaction is more acute today than several decades ago, most likely because the satisfaction of material wants has pushed non-material needs into the foreground.

However that may be, it is unjustified to accuse Marcuse of neglecting man's intellectual and spiritual needs. His concern for them is precisely one reason for the fascination he holds for youth. For us it is interesting that Moscow is concerned with the theory of the two hungers; thereby Moscow basically incorporates Marcuse's thesis, though in different words, that the Western worker is economically integrated into his society, exactly the theory Moscow does not wish to accept as true.

In passing, the two authors, Kosolapov and Pechenev, regret Marcuse's influence on the Parisian events of May 1968, although more mildly than Zhukov. Without naming the French Communist Party they defend its actions; under its leadership, they comment, French workers had refused "to gamble [by revolutionary means, we must add] with rights and freedoms already won, even though these are circumscribed by the bourgeoisie, or to give in to Marcusian despair and plunge headlong into the whirlpool of so-called 'deliverance' [by an] uprising of outcasts" (p. 25). Their article ends by reproaching Marcuse for trying to split the New Left from the Communists, and with a summons to the New Left to join the "decisive revolutionary force," the proletarian movement led of course by the Communists.

Only the third major article, Cheprakov's "On the Social-Economic Concepts of Herbert Marcuse," dealt with one of the decisive controversies between Marcuse and Moscow. Cheprakov, Professor of Political Economy at the University of Moscow, and associate at the MEiMO-Institute, discusses Marcuse's thesis that the carriers of revolution today were not the workers, who were integrated into the bourgeoisie, but the outsiders of society, namely the students, asocial "ghetto" dwellers, and the Third World (*MEiMO* 4, 1969). The paragraphs on the ghetto and the Third World are contained in the document, "Proletarians or 'Outsiders'—Or Neither?" Cheprakov's thoughts on ghettos are basically sound, but this thinking on the Third World is vague and unconvincing. His brief comments on the students are not worth mentioning.

Xenia Myalo's commentary in *Voprosy Filosofii* is more intelligent, though not aimed specifically at Marcuse. She remarks rather correctly: Fanon's and Sartre's (but of course also Marcuse's) picture of the Western world, "with the emphasis on the totalitarian and repressive character of its civilization, is the effective center around which—trying to explain itself—contemporary 'left' consciousness arises" (1, 1972, 83).

Marcuse is not the only Western author who has commented on the worker's integration into Western industrial society, although in the Soviet Union this view has come to be connected primarily with his name. This thesis has even reached the Urals, which may not be the best place to pass judgment on it. The "leftists," writes Zhemanov from Sverdlovsk, in *Voprosy Filosofii,* claimed that the workers were conservative and no longer felt the urge for revolutionary battle. Actually, he admits, in England 30 percent of the workers had voted for the Conservative Party. Nor does the counter-argument, the increase in strikes, wholly convince Zhemanov either. Thus his conclusion follows: "Everything said here proves the necessity of further discussion of the bourgeois-sociological conception" (12, 1970, 13). Marcuse's thesis (and not only Marcuse's) of the integration of the working class thus causes waves in the Soviet Union as well.

Perhaps Marcuse is the one who was honored, though negatively, in an important Communist analysis: According to the so-called main document of the International Meeting of Communist and Workers' Parties (Moscow, June 17, 1969), imperialism uses ever newer methods "to split the workers' movement from within, to integrate it with the capitalist sys-system" (*Kommunist* 9, 1969, 6).

MARCUSE'S GREAT SIN: CRITICISM OF THE SOVIET UNION

The most delicate subject, Marcuse's criticism of the USSR, was not treated in a Soviet periodical until May 1969, in the party organ *Kommunist* (8, 1969). Marcuse's *Soviet Marxism,* then eleven years old, had for ten years interested only specialists in the East and West. Only when the antitotalitarian New Left also turned against Soviet totalitarianism; when the rebelling students in Paris and Berlin went their own way, sharply separate from party Communists; when Daniel Cohn-Bendit and his brother, in the second half of their book on the May events in Paris, marched under the banner of Marcuse against "Stalinist bureaucracy" in France, and against "the strategy and essence of [Russian] Bolshevism"— only then did Moscow recognize that further silence was untenable.

Bykhovsky's essay consisted of two parts. The first requires no elaboration; it discussed Marcuse's books on Hegel (1932 and 1941) and aimed at discrediting Marcuse as an expert on Hegel. With this basis established, Bykhovsky could attack *Soviet Marxism.* He had begun the first part with the question, Who is this Marcuse of whom no reference work speaks? With equal irony he began his second part by asking, "What is 'Soviet Marxism'?" and answered: "Marxism is Marxism. There is Marxism and anti-Marxism. 'Anti-Soviet Marxism' [of which Marcuse had not even spoken] is just as irrational as 'Soviet anti-Marxism' " (p. 118), which Marcuse again had not even discussed.

After these and similar pranks (Marcuse, he wrote, was trying to prove that "two times two was no stearin candle," p. 119), Bykhovsky attacked Marcuse on Marxist dialectics. The following is a sample, with quotations of Marcuse's actual words in the first half, Chapter VII, *Soviet Marxism:*

MARCUSE	BYKHOVSKY
There is no Marxian theory which may be meaningfully called a "world outlook" for post-capitalist societies—whether they be socialist or not.	In a word, the socialist revolution and the creation of a socialist society are represented [by Marcuse] as a negation of the Marxist world-view (p. 120).
There is no Marxian theory of socialism because the antagonistic-dialectical laws which govern pre-socialist history are not applicable to the history of free mankind.	Where socialism begins, Marxism [for Marcuse] ends. . . . [Marcuse] is kindly prepared to "preserve" Marxism, but without its philosophical basis and without social-political conclusions (p. 120).

More is contained in the first half of chapter VII, "Dialectics and its Vicissitudes," in Marcuse's *Soviet Marxism,* and on pages 120 and 121 of Bykhovsky's article.

Only now does Bykhovsky turn to the issues, to Marcuse's three accusations against the Soviet Union. The document "Marcuse—'Pseudo-Revolutionary Phrasemonger' " contains Bykhovsky's counter-arguments.

Only one Soviet author, Davydov, judged Marcuse without grim outrage; he found a more elegant and, I think, more effective means of attack. Davydov compares Marcuse with Faust, more precisely, with Thomas Mann's Faust-like Adrian Leverkühn. Through the portrayal of Leverkühn, in Davydov's view, Mann had made one of the "most important discoveries of our century," the discovery of the type of man who recognized the real world as a hopeless blind alley, despaired of it, and in his despair was tempted by the devil, for the price of his soul, to seek salvation in *one* major breakthrough. The breakthrough formula (*formula proryva*) can be applied, thinks Davydov, to the contemporary "people of Western culture."

But Satan's real art lay in persuading the seduced, that is Marcuse, that he was also the savior who would show humanity the way out of that blind alley. Today's Adrian Leverkühn, Herbert Marcuse, according to Davydov despairs of "one-dimensional humanity" because he believes that the working class, the class that could find the way out of the blind alley (of capitalist society), was so integrated into the consumer society that it no longer aspired beyond it. Until suddenly Marcuse discovers the chance of a breakthrough and passes on this glad tidings to humanity, especially to the students.

Davydov allows the inference that Marcuse is both devil and seduced. First Marcuse points out the unmitigated horror of the blind alley in which mankind finds itself, until it shrieks in panic for a way out. "That is exactly the condition in which [Marcuse] [. . .] wants to put his reader, in order to present him with the happy formula of the breakthrough" (p. 76).

Marcuse's breakthrough is, of course, the revolt of the unintegrated in the universities, the ghetto, and the Third World. Marcuse himself, remarks Davydov, did not believe in the success of such a revolt; Davydov points to the words "without hope" in the next-to-last sentence of Marcuse's book on one-dimensional man. Therefore Marcuse had to seek other possibilities of breakthrough, among them the revolt of art (*An Essay on Liberation,* 1969). But this road was also impassable, since art, however radical, would soon be absorbed and neutralized by the established society (ibid., p. 74). With great satisfaction Davydov concludes that Marcuse's attempt to break through the blind alley would lead him into a further blind alley, the attempted breakthrough there into a third, and so on, without his being able to escape the maze of blind alleys.

Among the critics Batalov wrote the only serious challenge to a basic conviction of Marcuse, one that was especially difficult to understand for the nonleft readers of Marcuse and for most observers of the New Left: Marcuse's astonishing confidence in imagination. We might think, for example, of the posters that were inspired by him and carried along the Seine in May 1968: "Put Imagination into Power!" and "Be Realistic— Demand the Impossible!" It goes without saying that Moscow also had a negative reaction to this side of Marcuse's teaching.

Marcuse's reasoning, enthusiastically taken over by the New Left, is simple; it is contained in these key sentences from his *Essay on Liberation*:

> This situation gives all efforts to evaluate and even discuss the prospects for radical change in the domain of corporate capitalism their abstract, academic, unreal character. The search for specific historical agents of revolutionary change in the advanced capitalist countries is indeed meaningless. Revolutionary forces emerge in the process of change itself; the translation of the potential into the actual is the work of political practice. [. . .] (p. 79).

> We are still confronted with the demand to state the "concrete alternative." The demand is meaningless if it asks for a blueprint of the specific institutions and relationships which would be those of the new society: they cannot be determined a priori; they will develop, in trial and error, as the new society develops. [. . .] The possibilities of the new society are sufficiently "abstract," i.e., removed from and incongruous with the established universe to defy any attempt to identify them in terms of this universe (p. 86).

Batalov deals with the issue of imagination in a collective work, directed against Marcuse and to be discussed later, but especially in his article "Imagination and Revolution" in *Voprosy Filosofii* (1, 1972). Naturally he understands that an inner relationship exists between Marcuse's refusal to be tied to a concrete vision of the future, and his refusal to participate in industrial society (East or West), in other words his Grand Refusal. And so Batalov formulates something we can accept: "Imagination is the midwife . . . of Marcuse's grand refusal" (p. 69).

Batalov also understands that he cannot get away this easily. He admits that Marcuse's conception of the imagination's role, even if rejected, "demands the most serious attention." It is informative to watch Batalov, occupied with Marcuse's conceptions, begin to make concessions to these ideas. Let us recall the naive optimism of 1961 with which the Central Committee of the Soviet Communist Party, in its third party program, described the transition to Communism, and Communism itself, as just around the corner. But in view of this the following quotation from Batalov shows that the posters appearing on the Seine had their effect on the Moskva River. The New Left's vehement opposition against a rigid picture of the future, and simultaneously against totalitarian Soviet-Communist reality and its vision of the future, makes it difficult for the Moscow ideologists to continue to insist, blithely and uncritically, on their own picture of the future. Batalov writes:

> A *concrete* socialist alternative, as a project of the new society, cannot in fact be found outside living political practice. The structure and organization of the new society cannot simply be "discovered" a priori, to manifest themselves like something finished, suddenly and completely revealed to the gaze of the conceptual faculty [*soobrazhayushcheye soznaniye*]. In the real and historical creative process, whose end products can only be guessed with a certain measure of probability, their necessity does not "manifest" itself; rather this necessity is born, within the objectively possible, in the process of the practical "acting" of men. Seen from this aspect, revolution is the transition from one necessity to another, a transition which does not possess the character of unequivocality [*odnoznachnost'*], but which is formed in the struggle of forces generated by the process of historical "acting." Thus, although the project of restructuring society is based on historical necessity, the latter, in turn, is formed in the context of the existence and the goal-oriented realization of the project; this project aims, on the one hand, at a clear ideal, and on the other hand originates because of the analysis of the relationships—in the society under question. One must never forget: During the whole process of the work of the conceptual faculty and of historical "acting"—"acting" aimed at realizing the social project, which is oriented toward a historically determined ideal—in the course of this process the real and what is conceptualized by the imagination interact, correcting and determining each other. The imagination cannot and may not break either with reality or with the strategic and social class ideals. Of course it does not discover a "finished" alternative "hidden" in reality, but it works to reveal a widening circle of possibilities, of which some are realized, while others disappear in the course of historical evolution (p. 74).

This translation reproduces, I hope, the precise sense of the Russian original, and on close reading says what Batalov tried to express in his tortuous style: that Marcuse was not entirely wrong in concluding that today one could not expect concrete alternatives for a future, since this future was still inconceivable and, for the time being, could only be sensed by the imagination. To legitimize his recognition of imagination, Batalov also cites a figure from Russian revolutionary history, G. Plekhanov, whom Lenin once addressed in contempt as "Mr. Ex-Socialist." In a polemical exchange with the German social democrat E. Bernstein, Plekhanov had written: "The authors of the manifesto [i.e. Marx and Engels] did not play the prophets, but simply pointed to various possibilities. [. . .] When someone engaged in practical action does not wish to be overwhelmed by events, he must [. . .] weigh every direction they might take" (ibid.).

Batalov's more pointed debate with Marcuse, written jointly with Nikitich and Janjürgen Vogeler, provides another example of the "feedback effect" which Marcuse elicited in Moscow; the book's title anticipates the final judgment: *Marcuse's Campaign Against Marxism* (Moscow, 1970).

In the last third of this collective work, written by Batalov, he defends the Communist parties against Marcuse's accusation that they had lost their revolutionary fervor, that they had been "parliamentarized," that they had "become components of the bourgeois-political process and concentrated their attention on economic demands" (like higher wages), that their attempts at slowing down the revolution had been overcome only by outside pressure, especially from the intelligentsia, and that the party apparatus had always opened itself to revolutionary developments only after such developments had spread widely, and even then only to regain control over such developments (p. 117).

INFLUENCE ON MOSCOW'S THOUGHT

Marcuse's accusations are bitter medicine for a Moscow ideologist. Batalov answered them with the arguments used by Western liberals to criticize their countries' New Left: Radical action on the left would only "play into the hands" of the right and allow it to move from passive to open suppression of forces intent on change. For example, writes Batalov, citing a French Communist, if the French Communist Party had acted differently in May 1968, there would have been civil war, a military dictatorship would have been established, and the building of French socialism would have been delayed "by two to three generations." Batalov continues:

A legal Communist Party is, under the conditions of a capitalist state, as much "integrated" into the contradictory political organization of society and the social superstructure, as the working class is "integrated" into the capitalist basis (one is tied to the other). And as the party of the social opposition it cannot avoid participating in the "game" with the political forces of the bourgeoisie (just as the proletariat cannot keep from being embroiled in the "game" with capital). In this "game" it [the Communist Party] uses the most various levers, among others the "parliamentary" lever and the entire technical and social-psychological arsenal and the totality of mass communications media employed by the "Party of Order" [i.e. the right] (p. 118 ff.).

These arguments of Batalov and the French Communist Party may be entirely logical. But then, we must ask, why is Marcuse wrong when he diagnoses the parliamentarization and derevolutionization of the Communist Party?

Naturally Batalov, as other authors, fights Marcuse's conceptions of the Third World as the reservoir of world revolution. Batalov notes with regret: "Marcusianism and Afro-Asiatic left-radicalism further each other and obviously affect each other, if not on the plane of direct theoretical influence, then at least on the plane of preparing public opinion for the absorption of left-radical theoretization" (p. 121). Marcuse's major sin is that he contrasts the Third World, that outsider of international society, with the developed industrial states, *including the Soviet Union*. Since, according to Moscow's version, the USSR is the truest, most reliable friend of the Third World, such thinking "disorients" the Third World (p. 130).

Batalov, Nikitich, and Vogeler's collective conclusion on the subject of Marcuse is important enough for Marcuse, and the entire New Left, to be included entirely as a document in the appendix: "The Fertile Soil for the New Left Remains."

It is interesting, finally, that in his essay Batalov speaks of Marcuse without elaborately introducing him. His readers already know the Californian professor's name. Batalov also forgoes ironic references to Marcuse as "philosopher" (in quotation marks) or, like Yuri Zhukov in the appended document, as "former CIA agent." The easy argument used, for example, by Lebedev and Tulayev (p. 36), that Marcuse's success was due to "bourgeois propaganda," has also ceased. His key phrase "one-dimensional" has become, as *"odnomerniy,"* so much a part of Soviet jargon that it is no longer connected exclusively with Marcuse, as in Novinskaya's essay on "The Student Revolution" (p. 89).

Though Marcuse claims the title of Marxist, his Soviet critics naturally deny him this honor. In Batalov's words: "Marcuse remains within the confines of a left-radical Utopian socialism, which is politically and ideologically alien to Marxism and hence its enemy" (p. 140).

Since the crest of 1970, as explained, the interest of Soviet writers in Marcuse has receded. Moscow has also noticed that Marcuse's fiery theories have been less than fiery in practice. Marcuse has not been successful in breaking through the blind alley, to return to Davydov's words. Moscow has noted with pleasure that Marcuse's prophetic verve, his attractions for youth, have lessened; and Nikitina remarks that in his latest book, *Counterrevolution and Revolt* (1972), Marcuse views revolution as a matter of generations and gives capitalism another hundred years.

But his sins are not forgotten, especially not his worst: With his "theories" (again the obligatory quotation marks) he so affected the student movement that, to quote Valyuzhenich, "in a series of acute political situations they did not join the workers."

VII

THE INTELLIGENTSIA:
WHERE DOES IT STAND?
WHERE IS IT GOING?

"The activity of the intellectual approaches that of the worker."

The intelligentsia becomes "more and more bourgeois" (Molchanov, *Literaturnaya Gazeta,* 1, 1970, 13).

Make up your mind!

If we plug the words "student unrest" into a Soviet writer's brain there follows automatically, after a little delay, the catchword "intelligentsia." In no other nation has the elite been so intensely concerned with the intelligentsia's essence and role. Hence it is not surprising that Soviet ideologists would connect the intelligentsia with the unusual phenomenon of occupied lecture halls and bloody clashes at the universities. And this led them on familiar roads, where they found the usual reassuring signposts and quotations from Lenin.

After the 1917 Revolution it would, of course, have been clear even without Lenin that the existing, in other words the old intelligentsia, had to be put to use first (Kurylev, p. 109), after which, as soon as possible, a new intelligentsia loyal to the Bolshevik state had to be created. This pragmatic aspect of the question of the intelligentsia requires no further words and no quotations from Lenin.

The ideological-sociological aspect is a different matter, in other words the question of the nature and position of the intelligentsia. For Lenin this meant, and perforce for today's Soviet writers this means, the question of its "class character." (See especially Kurylev.) A quotation from Lenin has become dogma on the subject: The intelligentsia "is no *independent* economic class and therefore is no *independent* political force" (December 20, 1906, in *Proletary,* no. 10).

Soviet writers have not dared to upset this dogma when, in recent years, discussing the issue in relation to the new climate among students and intellectuals in general. But their manner of describing the Western intelligentsia provided nuances and accents that are of interest here. (See for example Ivanova; Kon, "Reflections"; Kurylev; Mel'nikov and Sonov; Mikul'sky; Molchanov, "The Western"; Nadel'; Semenov; Velikovsky.)

We need not detail the history of the intelligentsia, which for Kon begins with the ancient Egyptian priests; our concern is to assess the Western "intelligentsia" of the sixties and seventies. I will use the word "intelligentsia" throughout, since Soviet authors use this key word to designate that segment of humanity; to avoid ambiguities, I will refer to the *Western* intelligentsia when speaking expressly of it.

Something that needs little emphasis is the great difference between the classical Russian intelligentsia—it still exists in the USSR in principle and also in reality alongside the new Soviet intelligentsia—and, on the other hand, intellectuals in America or Western Europe. From Radishchev, Turgenyev, and Gorky to Solzhenitsyn, the classical Russian intelligentsia has always viewed itself as the voice of the people against the autocratic government, as a kind of unofficial parliament. The Western intellectuals, on the other hand, especially Anglo-Saxon, have for a long time belonged to the established elite, or have, after youthful storm and stress, grown into that elite; they were never outsiders; numerous platforms have been at their disposal: besides the parliaments, also the press, publishing houses, theaters, university chairs, and lately the mass media's inconceivable import.

Another difficulty in understanding arises from Soviet use of the word "intelligentsia," which refers not only to the Western intelligentsia but very loosely to today's Soviet intelligentsia. Part of the latter, however, feels a continuing responsibility to the tradition of the classical Russian intelligentsia, and little allegiance to the party's desire for a "toiling" intelligentsia largely synonymous with the proletariat.

Soviet authors agree on two points: first, numbers and significance of the intelligentsia are steadily increasing (throughout the world); second, this is a result of the "scientific-technological revolution." This revolution holds a lively interest for Soviet ideology. Neither Marx nor Lenin foresaw it to its current extent and acceleration, hence no reassuring "classical" quotations on the subject exist.

Naturally this scientific-technological revolution is affirmed by the Soviet Union, because it must join it or fall hopelessly behind. But with great misgivings Soviet authors also see what this Pandora's Box has already wrought throughout the world, and the anxious question is whether the same will happen with some delay in the USSR. *Kommunist* systematically investigated the effects of the scientific-technological revolution on industrial workers (Masol and Matsegora), the effects on the party (Degtyarev), and on the competition between the two major economic systems (Mikul'sky). *Voprosy Filosofii* also carried a series on the topic, which from July 1968 extended for years. Books on all aspects of the scientific-technological revolution appeared, up to Afanas'yev's investigation of its administrative effects.

Moscow's favorite dialectical thesis, however, always worked as a tranquilizer: What was bad in the capitalist system was good in the socialist; in its wake the scientific-technological revolution brought severe dangers for the West, but only advantages to the East. Let us simply note the thesis here; the next to the last chapter will comment further on the Soviet Union's claim of immunity to the dangers of modern civilization.

THE DIFFICULT INTELLECTUALS

Soviet authors agree, at least outwardly, on yet a third point: Under no circumstances can the intelligentsia be the leading force in transforming society. First of all, according to Lenin the intelligentsia is not a class, but a stratum, and only a class can be a leading force; besides, according to Marx and Lenin, that leading class is doubtless the proletariat. (That this is so, is never proven, it is simply a given.) But where does that leave the intellectuals and the students, their most active members, who since the early sixties have put their stamp on developments throughout the Western industrial states? This is the real issue for Soviet ideologues, and here their views no longer coincide.

Starting with the assumption that the proletariat is the leader on the road to socialist Communism, the authors in Moscow differ when assessing that other potential leader, the intelligentsia. Velikovsky calls the students instigators and leaders (*zastrel'shchiki*) of the workers; another, Kon, views the intellectuals primarily as "critics of society"; a third, Molchanov, sees them as "new mandarins"; and Semenov is prepared to recognize in them something entirely new. Obviously the differences are considerable.

In part, of course, this depends on the different Western sources used by individual Soviet authors. In general the lack of originality among them is notable; they not only take their facts from Western, primarily American studies—that goes without saying—but also derive their categories and judgments from the West, from L. Baritz among others, and Y. Bensman, L. Coser, J. Galbraith, A. W. Gouldner, R. Hofstadter, P. F. Lazarsfeld, C. Lasch, S. Miller, C. W. Mills, B. Rosenberg, E. Shils, G. Sykes, W. Thielens, W. H. Whyte, H. Zetterberg, to name a few.

Above all there are two phenomena which Soviet authors are able to reconcile with official ideology only by great effort. In the West, first of all, it is the intelligentsia, not the proletariat, which clearly sets the pace toward socialism, and secondly, the Western intelligentsia's dreams of socialism and democracy are very different from Soviet reality.

Soviet ideologists try hard to shut their own and their readers' eyes to the second fact. Whenever the Western intelligentsia speaks of socialism, they pretend that Soviet socialism is meant; every Western call for socialism is simply taken as acknowledgment of the USSR although, except by party members in the West, something very different is meant: a democratic, unbureaucratic kind of socialism. This basic attitude of the New Left and of the liberal intelligentsia in the West must be known to the Soviet authors studying so many Western sources, yet they try to overlook it.

The Western intelligentsia's call for more democracy is interpreted by Moscow's ideologists as if it were an option for the Soviet system. Only one author, Velikovsky, dares to tackle the slippery concept of democracy, by discussing the intelligentsia's desire for participation in all decisions by all people concerned. But the Soviet Union, with its emphasis on a centrally planned economy, has no intention to give its workers, employees, and intellectuals more than the formal right of participation in decisions; Moscow's rage at the workers' councils of the "Prague spring" reminds us vividly of this. Velikovsky, in his "The Intelligentsia in the Contemporary Class Struggle," therefore saves himself by arguing that all talk of participation—talk by intellectuals, or by entrepreneurs in a Western, perhaps Gaullist state—that such talk was humbug, that by definition such participation was impossible in a capitalist state (p. 115). He does not investigate why no such participation exists in the Soviet Union, which he praises for its socialism.

Citing many examples, he does reprimand the French intelligentsia for demanding, in May 1968, the general right of a voice in decisions. French intellectuals, he writes, had "advanced rashly" and most had afterwards "reprimanded leftist politicians [without quotation marks, hence mainly the French Communist Party!] for their caution" in not trying to obtain the maximum of participation from the Gaullist state ("The Striking Intelligentsia," p. 245).

But Moscow's writers cannot avoid explaining the other function of the Western intelligentsia, its function of pacemaker in the general development. They have therefore developed several theses. The most favored is that of the progressive proletarianization of the intelligentsia. In his essay "The Western Intelligentsia" Molchanov formulates the theory in this way:

> In view of their social position more and more intellectuals find themselves in the same role as the workers, that is, the role of the exploited. This is the most important aspect of the current problem of the Western intelligentsia. [. . .] The activity of the intellectual approaches that of the worker (p. 13).

To be sure, the same author, in the same article, also says the opposite. He accepts the conclusion of Paris' *L'Express* that, although the Western intelligentsia "curses the bourgeoisie, it becomes at the same time more and more bourgeois." Molchanov also points to the intelligentsia's self-confidence, to its claim of "being the decisive developmental force of humanity, [. . . and] of ruling in the second half of the 20th Century." Reminding us of Einstein, he continues: "The time when science was only the servant of the production process is over; today science precedes that process and begins decisively to guide it" (p. 13).

Kon calls the intelligentsia the "most important component within the basic social classes and alongside them." ("Reflections," p. 179.) These basic social classes are the bourgeoisie and the proletariat. Since, as we know, the intelligentsia may not be a separate class, it is at any rate "the most important component" of the two basic classes, and also "alongside them." My cautious "alongside" translates Kon's Russian *naryadu,* which can mean not only "alongside" but "equal."

THE UNDERESTIMATED INTELLIGENTSIA

There are contradictions between the actual influence and self-confidence of the Western intelligentsia on the one hand, and the Soviet claim of its dissolution in the proletariat on the other. To resolve these contradictions Soviet authors developed the thesis that the intelligentsia's power and confidence were only apparent, that in reality the Western intelligentsia existed only as an instrument of the rulers, as "mandarins" deployed by those rulers, without authority except what they required to fulfill their tasks. The significant role of intellectuals in Washington under Kennedy, Johnson, and Nixon is explained away by saying that the final decisions were still the president's. But that, after all, is precisely his task.

Soviet authors further explain the avant-garde stance of the Western intelligentsia by pointing to its innate tendency to hurry out front, to be ultraradical, to be "leftist" (*levachestvo*). While the proletariat, from long experience, knew how far it could go, the intellectuals liked "enterprises [that were] not too well thought out." Their "all too radical leftist course" (*poleveniye*) showed itself in the "increasingly frequent eruptions of the long dormant [*zastarelyye*] childhood diseases of left-ism." In this circumstance Velikovsky also sees "the source of that shocking and irresponsible intellectual anti-technologism, which in May [1968] and afterwards crazed not only the young people—without mustaches, but with beards—but also many an older, stronger, and wiser head." The author describes the "terrifying r-r-revolutioneering" of the intelligentsia, which unfortunately had "not [been simply] a bad joke"; it was clear by now that, left to its own devices, the intelligentsia vacillated between a "technocratic and a 'left'-Utopian ideology" ("The Striking Intelligentsia," p. 247).

All this leads Soviet authors to conclude that intellectuals must subordinate themselves to the proletariat. We know what this means, and one author expresses it clearly: "The intelligentsia is subordinate to the leadership of the working class, and that leadership is guaranteed by the Communist Party" (Kurylev, p. 116). In other words the American intelligentsia, which numbers ten to twenty million people (depending on the criterion), is to subordinate itself to a party which, in the 1972 U.S. election, received a tiny fraction of one percent of the vote!

An accurate synopsis of current Soviet attitudes toward the Western intelligentsia appears in the second part of an article by Mel'nikov and Sonov, "The Working Class and its Allies." Naturally they parrot Lenin's word that the intelligentsia is not a separate class; to argue with them here would be a waste of time. Politically decisive is not the definition of the intelligentsia, but the role it will play. Four such roles are theoretically possible: (1) The intelligentsia can be an autonomous, perhaps even the dominant historical force, (2) it can subordinate itself to the bourgeoisie's interests, (3) it can join the proletariat and bow to its leadership, or (4) it can split in two, one part joining the bourgeoisie, the other the proletariat. For the two Soviet authors no doubts dare exist: The Western intelligentsia will split in two, with the majority joining the proletariat, the minority the bourgeoisie. (See the document, "Who Leads—the Proletariat or the Intelligentsia?")

For ideologically rigid Soviet authors, and much less for the pragmatic West, therefore, much depends on whether the workers' leadership in future developments can be demonstrated so convincingly that any claims of the intelligentsia to such a role are conclusively stopped.

Since the days of Marx an extensive literature exists to demonstrate just that. Our two authors specifically discuss the question of whether the intelligentsia or the proletariat is the leading force, and they provide the quintessence of the Soviet-Marxist argument in favor of the proletariat. But the argument is weak. Mel'nikov and Sonov remind the reader of the long historical and practical experience of the proletariat, by which it was "elevated to the level of the one class which is in a position to lead the socialist revolution to victory." As evidence for this leadership role the two authors point out that the proletariat, since it fought for progress in all areas, "defends not only its own interests, but expresses at the same time the interests of all working strata of the population" (p. 77).

If it was *only* the proletariat which fought for progress, this argument would be convincing. But this is not so. Most ideas and catalysts for progress come not from the proletariat, but precisely from the intelligentsia; this would explain Lenin's life-long battle against the pragmatic "economism" of the workers. If the right to leadership is to be based on progressive ideas, that right belongs to the intelligentsia, not to the proletariat.

MORE SOPHISTICATION

A few authors in Moscow have managed to see the question of the Western intelligentsia in a more sophisticated light, especially Semenov. In 1966 appeared a two-volume collective work on sociology in the Soviet Union, Moscow's first such attempt; it contained a contribution by Semenov on the intelligentsia of the Eastern Bloc (I, 414–428). In 1969 he published his own book, *Capitalism and Classes,* which was remarkable for its information about his sources (a rare thing in Soviet social science literature), as well as for a bibliography (including 107 Western titles), and a 15-page index.

Semenov's starting point is the scientific-technological revolution since the middle of our century, which, for Semenov, compares in significance with the first industrial revolution of the nineteenth Century. But just as the natures of the two revolutions differed, so did the new social groups they brought forth. From the first industrial revolution emerged the proletariat, writes Semenov, while the scientific-technological revolution produced the intelligentsia.

Both, according to Semenov, are anticapitalist by nature: The proletariat is completely dependent on wages, the intelligentsia is increasingly so. But from this Semenov does not draw Marcuse's conclusion, that today's intelligentsia has become the leading force for social change. On the contrary: "The facts show that today's toiling intelligentsia [in the West] as well as the employees do not hold positions which, either objectively or subjectively, can be compared in significance with those of the working class" (p. 356). For Semenov such reasoning is necessary to show that the proletariat, in accord with official dogma, is the only leading force in the struggle with capital, the struggle for social change, while the intelligentsia's function is merely auxiliary.

In contrast to most of his colleagues, however, Semenov is not satisfied with claiming that "the proletariat leads, the intelligentsia has no autonomous role." He tries to prove this belief by pointing out three differences between the intelligentsia and the proletariat, because of which the intelligentsia is not suited to leading the revolutionary battle:

First of all, the intelligentsia (even when "toiling" and dependent on wages) was interested in maintaining private capital and property, since its income is based on them. Secondly, in contrast to the proletariat, the intelligentsia was already in a privileged position since it made its living by mental, not physical labor. Thirdly, since in part it was occupied with leadership tasks which allowed it to work closely with the owners of capital, it was paid correspondingly more. Semenov's final conclusion, emphasized by him through italics, is that "the working class and the working intelligentsia . . . are *qualitatively different components* in one system of paid labor" (p. 358). Semenov thus acknowledges the *qualitative* difference between the proletariat and the intelligentsia; unlike many of his colleagues, he does not let the intelligentsia dissolve anonymously in the proletariat.

This differentiated portrayal by Semenov is closer to the dominant Western conception, namely that the intelligentsia, even the wage-dependent intelligentsia, is qualitatively different from the workers. Semenov does not take the next logical step, the conclusion that in the first industrial revolution it was the proletariat which led and pushed toward social change, while in the scientific-technological revolution it is the intelligentsia. To take this view would bring him dangerously close to Western sociology and to Marcuse.

We can accept Semenov's conclusions up to a point. We can agree that the intelligentsia and the proletariat are "qualitatively different," and we accept his three reasons (among others that might be added) for that. All else must be rejected as assertion without proof: that at the end of a long-term process, which he too deems necessary, the Western intelligentsia would convert to socialism and subordinate itself to the leadership of the proletariat.

Semenov's sleight of hand in suggesting this conclusion to his readers depends on his use of the word "socialism." He rightly points to the socialist tendencies within the Western intelligentsia. But nothing in the intelligentsia's use of the word indicates that it will bow to the proletariat and, secondly, that with the proletariat it will subordinate itself to its country's Communist Party. Under the auspices of the vague slogan "socialism" the Western intelligentsia seeks a thousand things, but Soviet socialism is not among them. Few Western intellectuals can say exactly what this desired socialism should be; but this they know: It should not be like that of the Soviet Union.

This suggests the basic error of the Soviet ideologues: their equating of socialism and Soviet Union. In Germany in the twenties, for example, much was heard about the German people's "socialist yearnings." We know where that led. The socialist yearnings of today's Western, and especially today's American intelligentsia, will certainly not lead to a Hitler, but just as certainly not to a Brezhnev.

THE AMERICAN COMMUNIST PARTY: A DWARF

On November 7, 1972, 124 years after the Communist Manifesto and about twenty years after the full advent of the scientific-technological revolution, these election results occurred in the country that has gone farthest in this revolution, the United States:

Richard M. Nixon (Republican)	47,042,923
George McGovern (Democrat)	29,071,629
Gus Hall (Communist)	25,222

Even if all Communist voters had been nothing but old intellectuals, this number is grotesquely small. The two other parties of the left (both anti-Communist and closer to the New Left), the Socialist Labor Party and the Socialist Worker's Party (Trotskyite), both received more votes than the Communist Party: 53,614 and 65,290 respectively. The extreme right American Party obtained forty times as many votes as the Communist Party: 1,080,541.

The Communist Party's pitiful share of the vote has not remained entirely unknown to Soviet citizens. Leo Gruliow, Moscow correspondent of the *Christian Science Monitor,* reported in the January 11, 1973 edition on a public discussion of the Lecture Society *Znaniye* in Moscow:

> "What was the Communist vote [during the U.S. elections]?" someone asked.
> Mr. Smirnov [the speaker] thought it was 17,000, or, no, about 25,000. . . . "But you must remember," he hastened to add, "that the U.S. Communist Party functioned in very difficult circumstances and conducted its campaign primarily to publicize its program, not to garner votes." The audience was silent, weighing the fact it had elicited.

Contrary to Soviet claims, it is clear that in America the vanguard in the battle for social legislation, for slum clearance, for modern health services, and so on, does not consist of the workers, not of the major labor unions, but of the intelligentsia: the students, the liberals, and the leftist liberals. They are represented, for example, by *The New York Times,* whose editors include not one proletarian, or by countless citizen initiatives which are concerned with everything—from the pros and cons of abortion to the pros and cons of prison reform—to an extent unheard of in Europe.

The leftist tendency of many Western intellectuals disappoints Moscow because generally, and especially in America, these intellectuals do not lean toward Moscow but shy away from it. With few exceptions they are not a pro-Moscow Left but an anti-Moscow "Left." Few among them regard Moscow as a desirable model; in fact Moscow knows, from its conflict with Mao at the latest, that the "Left" can be very irritating, even dangerous for Soviet politics.

Semenov makes his most interesting comment in the last lines of his last chapter: "At the present time," he writes, "the working class is the leader and ruler of all the employed, including employed intellectuals." The phrase "at the present time" suggests for the first time that it may not always be so. And these questions, continues Semenov, "demand further careful analysis." They have not been conclusively explained; Soviet intellectuals have not finished their say on Western intellectuals. Thus the two questions posed in the title and after the epigraphs to this chapter are still open for Soviet intellectuals. And what about us?

On the basis of personal observation in many countries, decades of acquaintance with American universities, and a recently finished two-semester stay at Columbia University, New York, I conclude that American intellectuals are mainly liberal, in second place conservative. Only a small minority is left-radical in orientation, and of these, despite the special Soviet interest in American intellectuals, hardly anyone leans toward Soviet Communism. Many Western intellectuals are deeply concerned with questions of social, cultural, and political change. But the proletariat (or workers) seldom figure in their strategic deliberations, and the Communist Party never.

VIII

IS THE WEST DECAYING?

"The protest of [Western] youth [. . .] leads to empty and hysterical frenzy [. . .], it detracts from true political struggle" (*Literaturnaya Gazeta,* 26, 1970, 13).

The hippies are "nothing but pathetic victims of bourgeois civilization and for the most part incapable of political activism" (*Teatr,* 8, 1970, 156).

"[. . .] weird lights of Walpurgis Night, community created by song, bacchanal and drugs" (*Inostrannaya Literatura,* 8, 1972, 248).

Two things fascinate the Soviet observer about Western, especially American youth: its bias toward the left, which we have discussed, and its spiritual and moral condition. But before we ask what common explanation he has for these two phenomena, we need to look at the picture he paints for his readers of this spiritual and moral condition.

All articles relevant to this chapter, except those by Spitsyn, Petrov, Bykov ("Paths"), Kon ("Sex"), Konstantinov, Sharikov, and L'vov, come from the *Literaturnaya Gazeta.* This periodical seems less concerned than some about the effect, on young Soviet readers, of portraying the lax morality of Western youth.

The most accurate report on the spiritual and moral situation of America's Leftist youth occurred in *Teatr,* a periodical where I least expected it (7, 1970). The article was "Around the Woodstock Festival" by V. Vul'f; as I began to read, I expected, judging by the titles of the periodical as well as of the article, a description of the summer 1969 rock festival near Woodstock in upstate New York. But though it fills nine long pages, the article contains only a few paragraphs on the festival itself; the rest describes the life style of a part of American youth, especially of the hippies, who at that time experienced their last grand happening. Of this movement, which for the Soviet reader is not easy to understand, the article paints a generally undistorted picture. The author comments on the most important themes: sex, drugs, religion, crime, alienation, protest.

The concluding judgment is negative, of course. The hippies are seen as "pathetic victims of bourgeois civilization and for the most part incapable of political activism." Many Westerners would agree with this verdict. The question remains, however, whether we are dealing with victims of bourgeois civilization or with victims of civilization in general. (See the document, "Love, Drugs, and Hysteria in Sodom and Gomorrah.")

It is not surprising that the hippies in particular fascinate Soviet authors. First of all they are, or were, a colorful and eccentric folk, as if specially designed for journalistic treatment; secondly, they can be used to exemplify the dissolution of Western society.

Their predecessors, the Beatniks, were also suitable in this way. Bykov, research fellow of the Institute of the International Workers' Movement, discussed them earlier (*MK* 12, 1968, 113). In the word "Beatnik," by the way, he detected a Soviet influence; he says it is coined from *beat* (beaten generation) and sput*nik*. I have never heard this explanation. The suffix *nik* comes from the Russian, true, but has occurred in non-Russian usage for some time, as in "kibbutznik."

At any rate Bykov has little sympathy for the Beatniks. Their life, according to him, revolved around "love, parties, jazz, and drug abuse," and their name was associated with "riotous scandals which, not infrequently, ended with police intervention and arrests." They had explained their origin with disappointment in the bourgeois world, in which it was senseless to seek a major goal. One of their leaders, Allen Ginsberg, had according to Bykov confessed that he was a rioter, not a revolutionary.

Bykov considers the Beatnik influence on the younger generation considerable; "in many ways they mirrored its moods, tastes, and morality." What would become of American youth he found difficult to say. However, Bykov ended with an optimistic note as far as Moscow is concerned: Youthful distaste toward Soviet Communism was lessening, he thought; therefore one could hope that the young American successors of the "beat generation" would no longer be a "beat" generation but one "beating" the bourgeois system.

Literaturnaya Gazeta devoted an entire newspaper page to the "Confession" (the title) of a hippie (42, 1972). Borovik, who often writes on America, reported that a hippie named Mark Hallert, from Seattle, Washington, had accidentally crossed his path in Ecuador. The Soviet

journalist's tale of the young man is not unconvincing: a break with the
bourgeois father, acquaintance with drugs, the life of a tramp, first run-
ins with the police, the morally corrupting influence of military service
in Vietnam, escape to South America. This confession and Hallert's picture create an impression that is not unsympathetic, and which, for the
Soviet reader, is probably more revealing than sweeping judgments on
Beatniks and hippies. (In the meantime I have heard from Mark Hallert; he seemed to be on the way to a middle-class life.)

Rozental' reports on a young Californian in similar fashion, in an article in *Novyy Mir* (1971), doubtless the country's best literary monthly
when Alexsandr Tvardovsky edited it. Since his January 1970 departure,
not entirely voluntary, the periodical has suffered in quality, but Rozental's story is worth reading.

As Soviet correspondent in Geneva, Rozental' had an opportunity to
observe the Western young. His description of a talk with a hippie
named Barry, a hitchhiker whom he picked up in Switzerland and accompanied to his forest camp, provided many Soviet readers with their
most vivid look, until then, at the thoughts of these young people. Like
Hallert, Barry (family name not given) is not maliciously caricatured.
There are such hippies, I have heard them talk in similar fashion, even
in Katmandu, which is mentioned by Barry. The document "The Hippies in Their Forest Camp" contains part of Rozental's conversation with
Barry. His polemic with Herbert Marcuse, by the way, is the weakest I
have read in the major journals.

THE VICES OF WESTERN YOUTH . . .

On the theme of sex, the sociologist Kon is especially comprehensive.
He takes us on a tour of history, from the rituals of prehistory through
antiquity and the Middle Ages, the Renaissance and Victorian Age up to
the present. Besides a few verses from Pushkin and mention of Tolstoy
and Makarenko, remarkably little is said about Russia; one might almost
think the sexual drive existed only outside Soviet borders.

Professor Kon's comments on Western sex are reasonable throughout.
His attitudes, of course, derive primarily from Western books, among
them Vance Packard's *Sexual Wilderness,* David Riesman's *The Lonely
Crowd,* John Updike's *The Centaur,* D. H. Lawrence's *Lady Chatterley's
Lover,* and of course *The Kinsey Report.* And he has seen Western films,
Antonioni's *Blow-Up* and Bergman's *Silence.* Hence he also knows what,

according to Western authors, influences the present form of sexual behavior: the collapse of traditional values, rapid urbanization, lonely modern man's quest for self-confirmation, the acceleration of sexual maturity, increased leisure, female emancipation. He even uses the Western word *"seksapilnyy."*

What is the gist of Kon's article? He mentions two, in his view equally wrong interpretations of the problem of sexuality, a rightist and a "left" one. The first, which suppresses sexuality, includes, he says, Freud's teaching on sublimation. In contrast to Freud, Kon does not believe that some degree of asceticism is necessary to the development of culture, because "not austere and chaste Sparta, but tolerant Athens became the center of the highest flowering of Greek culture." Here the ambivalence of the traditional, classical intellectual is apparent. Like every good intellectual, East or West, Kon must be convinced of the rightness of this particular sentence, but he overlooks—or does he not?—that the extremely intolerant Soviet Union is not exactly Athens.

More important for us is Kon's criticism of "left" conceptions of sexuality (naturally he uses quotation marks). Other authors take over his thesis; we can therefore regard it as the general attitude of the Soviet intelligentsia, particularly the older intellectuals. It appears in the document, " 'Left' Sex is Wrong."

Of course we, and the Soviet reader, would like to know what Kon thinks is the significance of all this for Soviet youth. But Kon cautiously avoids this treacherous issue. For the umpteenth time he cites Lenin's famous "glass of water" statement, reported by Klara Zetkin in her *Recollections of Lenin*; it is wrong, in Lenin's view, to treat the sexual act as something as "simple and inconsequential" as drinking a glass of water. Nor does Kon neglect to mention the view of the 85-year-old Engels, who in many ways remained a true son of his hard-working, rather puritanical hometown Wuppertal. Only the last seventeen lines of Kon's long article deal with the Soviet Union. As expected, he sees the Soviet Union as moving between the "irrational taboo" of the right and the "irresponsible sexual anarchism" of the "left." On the pace of Soviet development on this road, his words are rather cautious: "That is a long and difficult process which needs more time than the life of one generation."

What Kon does not say but surely knows is this: Precisely between those extremes of repression and anarchy the West is also seeking its way. Certainly the extent of the "sexual wilderness" is very different in East

and West; it is relatively small in the Soviet Union. But the problem—
sex in the modern industrial and consumer society—is the same. And the
direction of the desired path, as Kon has just told us, is also the same.

The fronts have reversed themselves. In the twenties and thirties the
West thought Bolshevism the destroyer of marriage. Today it is the
Soviet Union that defends marriage, and it is Soviet authors who hold
up as a warning to Soviet youth the immoral behavior of Western
spouses. Gerasimov's "Marriage, American Style" tells Soviet youth of
America's rapidly rising divorce rate, of nine million fatherless children,
of the spread of wife-swapping, of efforts to contract "marriages for limited periods" (with the possibility of extensions), and of a growing aversion to having children. In short, Gerasimov reports on the "decay of the
family, the germ cell of society" (*LG* 41, 1972). Indeed, times have
changed.

Morality in nearby Sweden is also observed closely. Konstantinov, special correspondent for *Molodoy Kommunist,* visited Swedish sex-shops,
conversed with their profit-hungry owners, and with a "young woman
lecturer at the University of Lund." The last conversation went as follows:

> "What do you, a teacher by profession, think of the wide-spread
> erotic decadence of youth?"
> "We have freedom in every way. We are a free, democratic land."
> "In other words freedom to corrupt morally? Let's call things by
> their right name."
> "That's your explanation, others see it otherwise. One thing is certain:
> prohibitions are harmful."
> "Then nothing is forbidden?"
> "Nothing."
> "But if you develop that basic idea, can't you carry it so far as to
> legalize robbing and killing? The possibility of killing without punish-
> ment—couldn't one also call that freedom?"
> "Well, and what if? We'll reach that point some day."

Konstantinov reports that the young woman's last words were said without irony. He finds them abhorrent (as do we).

. . . ARE DELIBERATELY PROMOTED BY THE CAPITALISTS

Decay everywhere, in other words, including art. Borovik, who inter-
viewed the hippie named Hallert, filled more than a page with the cyni-

cal disclosures of pop musician Charlotte Moorman: Since mere cello-playing would get her nowhere, she had to think up one sensation after another, with whose help she received publicity and attracted the public. Her partner, for example, stretched strings across his back, on which she would play; the same thing could be done with a mock-up of an atom bomb; from time to time she played in the nude. Her complaint was that it was increasingly difficult to think of something original. "At first all my appearances involved scandal, protests, even being jailed. But today everything's allowed. People have already seen enough of everything. They sit around, are bored, applaud" (*LG* 7, 1970, 13).

To Soviet readers rooted in Western and Russian classicism, accounts of such happenings must seem rather strange (though the word "happening" has meanwhile become part of the language). Archipov reports on a coed's strip-tease during a lecture of the aged Professor Adorno in Frankfurt, on the affront inflicted by "leftist" students to "ancient academic tradition" during a ceremony (corresponding to an American commencement) at the University of Munich (the students "somersault, walk on their hands, kick their legs, make faces, giggle, snort, and meow"), and on students' "exhibitionism, sadism, bloody orgies, vandalism, obscene behavior, destruction of food, of sandwiches [spoiled] with beetle larvae."

The author's sympathies are unequivocally with the "ancient academic tradition"; he is honestly indignant at the students. Nor does he accept that their tactics are meant to achieve constructive political aims. His concluding judgment: "The protest of youth which uses primarily the mode of the happening ends in empty and hysterical frenzy, in blind anarchistic revolt."

Not unexpectedly Soviet observers note the laborious Western experiments with communes (for example Bol'shov, "Without," pp. 198 ff., 211 ff.) or with the living theater (pp. 213 ff.); others are concerned about other Western phenomena—the Jesus freaks, the spread of Satanic and witches' cults, of occultism and Asian mysticism; they comment on a "pursuit of miracles," on a "superstition industry," which manufactures "spiritual surrogates" and releases grand spectacles like *Jesus Christ Superstar,* and huge editions of related books, periodicals, and records (*LG* 46, 1972 and 33, 1971, p. 15 each).

For Soviet observers Western moral decay, the soil which nurtures Beatniks, hippies, and the New Left, is closely tied to drug abuse, sexual anarchy, and superstition. But what causes such abuse, anarchy, and superstition? The answer of Soviet authors is so uniform that we have to infer central directives. Reduced to essentials this answer, in my words and with my emphases, is as follows:

When the "leftists" speak of liberating man by unchaining the sex drive, they are speaking nonsense. The contrary is true: *The capitalist system itself unchains and promotes an over-emphasis on sex among youth, in order to steer youth from actions dangerous to the system, and to realize fat profits from pornography.* Whether ultra-right or ultra-left, the aim is the same (Kon).

Through the sexualization of life the bourgeoisie attempts to "*keep* young people *from the real problems*" and to make profits (Konstantinov).

"Happenings are useful to the ruling class because *they distract from the political struggle*" (Archipov).

Religious charlatans and other "manufacturers of miracles *want to keep the masses of the people from the class struggle*" (L'vov).

According to the establishment, it is better for youth to play at being Jesus freaks, instead of *demonstrating against youthful unemployment, the Vietnam War, racial discrimination.* The "Jesus market" with its musicals, records, and decals is also *good business,* even if, in the process, "the Bible is kicked into the dirt" (Gribachev).

An article reprinted from *Le Monde* also serves as emphatic evidence from the West: "Confused and lacking a moral orientation, people, especially young people, are adroitly *exploited* by all sorts of crooks and adventurers who call themselves creators of new 'philosophies' and 'religions'" (*LG* 30, 1971).

Rozental', already mentioned for his description of the hippie forest camp, takes the prize for simplistic absurdity. In a section of his article, called "*Eskalatsiya Seksa*" ("The Escalation of Sex"), he asks why the sexual explosion in the West happened to occur between 1968 and 1970, and promptly answers: The capitalists, especially the likes of John D. Rockefeller III, had loosed the sexual explosion at the crest of youthful revolt, in order to channel the energies of rebelling youth "*from the barricades toward free love.*" At last we know it, thanks to Rozental.

Rozental' believes to have found evidence for his thesis in a Rockefeller quotation from the December 1969 *Saturday Review*. Referring to the revolt of youth, which concerned him then and later, Rockefeller had said: "A unique opportunity appears before us—the joining of our generation with its experience, its money, and its organization, with the energy, the idealism, and the social consciousness of youth." How this supports Rozental's theory is not clear. Nor does he explain why, as he points out, the Rockefellers should have promoted the sexual explosion above all in Denmark.

Thus the slogan "opiate of the people" is still in evidence. Do Soviet observers really believe that the bourgeoisie drives its youth, its own flesh and blood, toward drug abuse, sex, and superstition just in order to neutralize it politically?

WHY NOT EXPOSE WESTERN DECADENCE MORE?

A brief aside is appropriate here. As indicated, we have to read beyond the black print in the totalitarian press. Soviet authors rarely elaborate on serious aspects of Western decadence—drug abuse, unrestrained sexuality, violence, juvenile delinquency. All this is mentioned, but only fleetingly; it is painted in pale, and not in strong colors. Lately, it is true, Yevtushenko's "Under the Skin of the Statue of Liberty" and a film on America, *Washington Correspondent*, have used a livelier palette, but again the emphasis is more political than moral. Generally the evildoers pulling the strings are the insatiable capitalists. Even the specialized law journal *Sovetskaya Yustitsiya*, in an article by Pisareva on Western juvenile crime, concludes that such crime was intentionally fomented by "unchained mass media propaganda for immorality and crime" (pp. 28–30).

It attracts attention that Soviet journalism exploits the theme of Western decadence far less than we would expect, as it is so potentially useful ideologically. Critiques of Western decay are much more extensive and more bitter in Western than they are in Soviet periodicals. Over breakfast in New York, on any given day, we can read more in *The New York Times* about sex and crime in the city than we can read on Western degenerative symptoms in the Soviet press in a month. The Soviet press ignores a subject which would have more anticapitalist propaganda potential than any other. Why?

The morass of sin into which Western society is sinking can be used to illustrate the decay of capitalist society, but what if Eastern readers were corrupted by Western vices?

Or: If it was not monopoly capital which, with evil intent, created the New Left, in all its peculiar and in part disquieting aspects, how then did it originate? The New Left cannot arise from contemporary industrial and consumer society (where the New Left itself and many Western analysts see its origin), because the Soviet Union is also moving, as quickly as possible, into this direction. Whoever would dare to call the New Left a child of modern society, would simultaneously predict its future rise in the Soviet Union.

The question posed at the beginning of this chapter, how Soviet ideologists can reconcile Western youth's bias toward the left, on the one hand, with its decadence on the other hand, can now be answered. First of all, according to Soviet observers, there was no trend toward the left, only a trend toward the "left"; secondly youth's decadence did not arise from within youth, nor automatically from the modern industrial and consumer society, but was in large part implanted in youth by the establishment, by monopoly capital, by the bourgeoisie, and by the profit sharks.

We must ask ourselves: Why this great effort at interpretation when the Soviet Union, as we have been told, is so radically different from the Western world that Western laws of development do not apply in the USSR, that the USSR, in other words, can enter without fear the industrial and consumer society without also picking up that society's illnesses?

IX

IS THE SOVIET UNION REALLY IMMUNE?

"There is no such thing as drunk nations and sober nations. Each nation has a large sober segment and a smaller part of drunks" (Levin, *Literaturnaya Gazeta*, 11, 1970).

The question posed in the title of this chapter occupies not only Western observers. We might ask, in fact, if the distaste of Soviet leaders for the Western New Left is not due to concern that the same causes which produced a Western New Left are effective, or will be effective in the Soviet Union too.

Most Western and some Soviet authors, as we saw, regard the New Left in the West as a plant which grew in the soil and the climate of the contemporary industrial and consumer society. If that is so, two questions arise: Have Western winds carried seeds of this plant to the East? And are the Soviet soil and climate hospitable to such seeds, can they take root and flourish?

Moscow's answers to these questions vary. Most commentators, as I have pointed out, say they will not. According to them, the seeds only arrive in very small quantities and furthermore cannot develop because the socialist state is able to absorb what is positive in Western developments, and to reject what is negative.

But there are other voices. Vsevolod Kochetov's novel *Just What Do You Want?*, which appeared in the fall of 1969 in the literary journal *Oktyabr'*, gave the most pessimistic answer. Kochetov sees enormous dangers: The West, so goes his thesis, intends to destroy the Soviet Union. But because of Soviet military might, this cannot be achieved by force; therefore the West concentrates on the spiritual undermining of the Soviet people. One of Kochetov's fictional characters, an American woman who symbolizes the alleged Western policy, explains how this will be accomplished:

"A very clear program for the dismantling of Communism, of Soviet society exists: penetration of its spiritual life. We'll attack from three directions. First—the old, the older generation. On them we'll work with the help of religion. When life approaches the end, men involuntarily begin thinking of what awaits them up there, there!"

She points toward the ceiling. The number of Soviet believers in Christianity was increasing, she points out; in the province Moscow, for example, every sixth newborn was baptized within the church, though before the war only one in fifty.

Secondly, she continues, concerning the middle-aged: Their desire for consumer goods had to be awakened, whereupon they would concentrate on their private lives and turn from the collective. Their demands would escalate, and since their income was insufficient they would steal or embezzle.

"Even today that's how it is. The Soviet press is full of complaints about embezzlement. Embezzlement, embezzlement, nothing but embezzlement! And how many cases of embezzlement never reach the press!"

And third, Soviet youth.

"Youth! That's the most fruitful soil for our seeds. It's the nature of young people to protest against all restrictions to their stormy nature. If you entice them with the possibility of complete liberation from restrictions, from all responsibilities, let's say toward society, adults, toward parents, toward any morality—then you've got them. That's what Hitler did when he threw out of youth's way the Biblical 'Thou Shalt Not Kill,' because it inconvenienced him. And Mao Tse-tung did the same, when he mobilized masses of boys to smash the party of the Chinese Communists."

To fell the mighty Russian tree by putting vermin underneath the bark and thus destroying it from within is, according to the author, the West's ambition.

Kochetov's primary concern is the third danger, the corruption of Soviet youth by the West. The West brought "sexbombs" to the Soviet Union, for example a black American singer, whose performance was so erotic, Kochetov wrote, it would get sterile women with child; then there were "long-haired youths with the boring mugs of homosexuals and guitars hanging from their necks," and pornography and strip-tease, even slits in men's jackets, two of them now, so that "the massive hind parts, through this invention of foreign fashion designers, were thrust into the open."

The successes, according to Kochetov, could not be denied. There were, in the Soviet Union,

> intellectual unrest at the universities, underground journals [in the USSR these, by the way, are literary and not pornographic] and leaflets, the complete destruction of earlier idols and authorities, the glorification of brashness. [. . .] the sexualization of the environment. [. . .] Komsomol is in atrophy, its congresses, its political schooling are becoming mere formalities, mere façade, behind which the private and sexual life is played, free of all commitments. Among such people, indifferent to the common good. [. . .] one can shift people step by step into leadership of the various decisive organizations that prefer the Western system to the Soviet, to the Communist system.

Kochetov exemplifies the thrust toward a comfortable life, toward the consumer society, in a conversation between two young Muscovites, one good and one bad. The evil one talks of manifold ways of making money by embezzlement. The honest youth then asks:

> "Then you've studied the methods of left [black] market gains. [. . .]?"
>
> "Not at all! Not even Bender knew them all! [Bender was a corrupt confidence man in Ilf and Petrov's novels of the 1920s.] Besides, if you want to know the truth, Bender was a child compared to those making money today!"
>
> "But what the devil do you want with the money[. . .]?"
>
> "What? I'd find something. Now, do you need a car? Of course you need a car. I'd get myself a little Mercedes from some foreigner. You've got to have a dacha [country house]? Yes, must have a dacha. I'd build a little toy like that. *Amerika* [American magazine in Russian] prints such pictures—they would knock you over!"
>
> "Oh? And what else?"
>
> "You can have an apartment in a housing cooperative, custom-made and furnished. Special places will do that for you. You can have them with halls [the English word is used], with black toilet fixtures, with a mezzanine—in short, everything just proper and right."
>
> "What else?'
>
> "All kinds of gadgets. Tape recorder, movie camera, color TV, this and that."
>
> "And . . . ?"
>
> "Whatever's left you save, the savings account brings a percentage.

Three percent per year. You put 100,000 roubles down and three little thousands float down toward you all by themselves. 250 per month, down from heaven. You don't need to exert yourself anymore at all."

"That's quite a little program you've got!"

"Well, what of it? Don't you want one, too? All your life you jump early in the morning, at the sound of a buzzer, to march somewhere. Where does that leave freedom, the harmonious development of the personality? And the realization of man's golden dream?"

Imploring Soviet youth, Kochetov cries out: "When Western 'democracy' arrives, with which Western propagandists tempt you young Russians, it will not bring you stores crammed with consumer goods, but first of all your people's ruin, the destruction of your state, the ruin of Russia."

In his novel Kochetov warns in detail of the effects of the West's "undermining propaganda": A young man, instead of working, lives from the sale of icons to foreigners, with whom he runs around. A director makes a film that seems anti-Hitler but is really anti-Stalin—and receives a prize! A young man commands high fees for his portraits of foreign diplomats; Kochetov calls him a whore because he lets himself be praised, without protest, by an "émigré swine" on Western radio. A parasitic young poet also has his Western admirers, among broadcasters in London and Munich.

At a party in Moscow, to continue, young Russians are pleasantly indignant when looking over Western pornographic magazines; their fathers, among others, are a vice-minister, a general, a man "who does something abroad and hardly ever lives in the Soviet Union," and the boss of a fashion design studio. One of the young Russians boasts that his grandfather spent time in Stalin's prisons; he has even written a poem called "Verses On My Grandfather." Another young man makes his career with an organization "that has to do with foreign countries." The young people know each other from the resort where their high-ranking parents, in other words the new class, spend their weekends and vacations. The parents, by the way, are also under the influence of the West. One family has succeeded, by somewhat shady methods, in obtaining a large apartment on Moscow's prestigious Gorky Street, and refers to the individual rooms by English words: sitting room, dining room, bedroom, study.

Again and again Kochetov describes the bridge-building over the East-West abyss, initiated by the West, as a deadly danger for the Soviet

Union. The West, he believes, has only one goal, to create a pro-Western, anti-Soviet mood in the USSR, and to bring on eventual civil war between followers and opponents of the regime.

Kochetov's novel is an exaggerated, probably intentionally exaggerated cry of alarm; the average Soviet youth is hardly as susceptible as Kochetov's main characters. Contrary to Soviet claims, the monopoly capitalists of the West have no intention of destroying their own youth or that of the USSR through sex and crime. Kochetov's pessimism has been criticized, we might add, in his own country, for example by Yevtushenko in his address before the Fifth Congress of Writers; without mentioning the name, Yevtushenko clearly attacked Kochetov's work by speaking of a novel that had "aroused regrettable interest," though it falsely portrayed Soviet youth as susceptible to Western decadence (*LG* 28, 1971, 11).

Another author, though he belongs to the optimists and has appeared in *Molodoy Kommunist,* Komsomol's basically optimistic periodical, is not wholly convinced of Soviet youth's ability to resist Western currents. Novopashin does attack the Western view that the Western crises which result from the scientific-technological revolution would finally appear everywhere, including the socialist states. But he agrees that even in a socialist society there existed "certain contradictions," namely "between the objective necessity for a stable administrative mechanism [. . .] and the necessity of continually adapting this mechanism to developments of the productive forces and to the demands of the scientific-technological revolution" (p. 102). He thinks, however, that such contradictions within socialism can easily be resolved.

Here one has to disagree. There is plenty of evidence that the socialist bureaucracies, which are particularly cumbersome and vast—and they basically are what Novopashin calls the "stable administrative mechanism" —make adaptation to the demands of modernization not easier, but more difficult.

The "certain contradictions," Novopashin also admits, call forth in the USSR youthful resentment and demands for the "exposing and removal of deficiencies" (p. 104). Pointing to experiences in Czechoslovakia, though not limiting himself to them, Novopashin finally concludes that youth sometimes did lack "immunity against bourgeois ideological maneuvers [*diversity*] which [. . .] are directed especially toward young people." His comment at this point is worth quoting, since it coincides with thinking heard in the West: Today's young people do not know the older generation's strenuous exertions and therefore do not appreciate their achievement. The lack of understanding for the achievements of the parents' generation

> is easy to explain. The generation entering life still lacks its own experience of historically creative work. The older generations see the social relations under socialism as the result of their efforts; in the process they compare them with the social relations they inherited from their predecessors, they see how far they have progressed, and measure what has been attained by the difficulties of the socialist development. But young people most seldom judge reality, when entering life, from the viewpoint of the ideal to be attained, a speculative ideal which they know from writings and textbooks. Such judgments are influenced by their meager experience with life, by youth's naturally high expectations, and by overreaching social orientations during their education (p. 105).

Since Novopashin is an editor of *Problems of Peace and of Socialism,* the world-wide Communist periodical, his comment is particularly interesting.

Thus Kochetov and Novopashin do not deny that the young generation has some susceptibility to ideas related to Western phenomena. Ever more Western ideas are being disseminated in the Soviet Union, since Moscow, for various reasons—for example to import Western know-how, or to collect hard currencies through tourism—has opened the country's doors much wider than in Stalin's time.

The answer to the second question posed early in this chapter is even more important: Do seeds of Western influence die on the Soviet soil, or do they find favorable conditions for their growth?

For years the West has been thoroughly and self-critically concerned with the causes of the phenomena discussed in the last chapter; it believes there are many such causes. Some can be expressed by these key words: earlier maturing (= acceleration), more leisure, urbanization, consumer mentality, alienation, loneliness, breakup of families, feminization of education, increasing interest in sex, escape into drugs, "hot music," crime.

The question is, are these aspects of civilization and their effects found only in the West, or does evidence of them also exist in the Soviet Union? Once again, we will check the periodicals investigated for this book. We shall not study the solemn declarations by party leaders, but the day-to-day life, the *byt,* as the Russians call it, the *byt* which can be found in short stories, satires, feuilletons, occasionally in films and on the stage. Let us look at the most important trends and ask: Can they be found in the Soviet Union, too?

AKTSELERATSIYA AND OTHER PHENOMENA OF CIVILIZATION

Earlier Maturity? Yes.

The Soviet reader knows that his country's youth is subject to an ever faster *aktseleratsiya;* among others, articles by Nikolayev and Vlastovsky point out that, instead of growing in size until the age of 22 or 23, today's youth reach full growth much earlier, the girls by age 16 or 17, the boys by 18 or 19. Young people are also from 6 to 8 inches taller than their age group a hundred years ago, and "their sexual maturity is attained three years sooner," more so in the city than in the country, which means that rapid urbanization speeds *aktseleratsiya* even more.

In fall 1972 *Literaturnaya Gazeta* published a letter by an engineer from Leningrad (38, 1972, 12). The engineer, Kondakov, worried about his adolescent son. What he disliked about him, millions of Western fathers also dislike about their sons: He drank and smoked, adopted extreme fashions (hippie fashions, we can assume), had no interests, lived as if "in a vacuum," and scorned his elders with the usual symptoms of the generation gap.

It hardly matters whether this letter is real or fictitious; it is interesting because it elicited a detailed reply by Vlastovsky in the same issue of the weekly. The young man's behavior, according to Vlastovsky, was caused by a double dose of *aktseleratsiya,* a physiological as well as psychological-intellectual one. This acceleration, coupled with the son's slow process of social mauration, he explained, produced "various deviations in the development of the young man's personality." The schools, for example, limped three and four years behind the student's accelerated development. In other ways, too, the "whole complex of conditions essential to life" was changing. The author notes: "Human communities are breaking up, communities which have been self-contained ways of life for centuries."

More Leisure? Again Yes.

In the Soviet Union working hours have decreased; according to the 1971 statistical handbook of the Soviet Union (p. 121), they have decreased, in industry, from 47.8 hours in 1955 to 40.7 hours per week in 1970, a decrease of seven hours. Many Soviet citizens now have two days off per week. Of course part of this free time is spent in illegal employment, in shopping and errands, still incredibly cumbersome and time-consuming in the Soviet Union, but certainly not more than before and less among the young than among adults. Overcrowded theaters, cinemas and bookstores, and crowded libraries and museums indicate that many young people know how to use their free time. Others have no idea and get bored, and, in the Soviet Union as everywhere, this leads to mischief. Drinking, which can lead to alcoholism, often begins with boredom (Levin, *LG* 2, 1971, 13).

No statistics on boredom exist, but feature page articles give descriptions, for example L. Zhukhovitsky's "Around the Dance Floor": Twenty percent of the young people are dancing, the rest are bored, or even, out of boredom, involved in mischief. "A strange folk," comments the author. "Locks down to their shoulders, fringes on their jackets, fringes on their pants, fringes at their knees," he describes a sixteen-year-old. "Where does he get all that stuff? Unbelievable. Maybe he's clipped his neighbors' drapes?"

Drinking, rowdyism, long hair, barefoot dancing—why, asks Zhukhovitsky, do they do all this? To attract attention, he answers, "to solve their private problems" in this way. But apparently they do not succeed. "There is nothing that one can discuss with them," the girls complain to Zhukhovitsky. The "joys of human companionship" do not materialize. The young men and women standing around the dance floor, says the author, have not felt them: "Many will have the same experience tomorrow, and again next month and next year. There will be drama. [. . .] Some will have their run-ins with the militia [police]. For some it's a relief to chase the blues with vodka—for an evening, maybe for two or even more, but over a period of years, this too becomes a burden. Others won't be happy either, although nothing very upsetting happens in their lives; it isn't upsetting, this monotonous and quiet life in which only one thing is missing: joy." More concern was needed, says Zhukhovitsky, for the problems of leisure time. This does sound familiar to us.

Lately the popular thrillers and detective novels have been called a lamentable way to pass free time; this form of relaxation, so popular in the West and so unproductive materially, has gained in influence in the USSR. Soviet thrillers now even have their own 014, a hot competitor of agent 007, handling revolvers and women like his model James Bond. The 014 book was issued by the Komsomol publishing house *Molodaya Gvardiya* —Western decay has penetrated the innermost bastion of Communist youth! (*The New York Times,* February 18, 1973)

Urbanization? Yes.

As in the Western industrial states, a rapid population displacement from country to city is occurring in the Soviet Union too. In the three decades from 1940 to 1970 the village population (in 1940 still twice as large as the city population) decreased from 131 to 105 millions, while the urban population more than doubled from 63 to 139 millions. The significance of this for the social structure and psychology of a nation is clear.

CONSUMER MENTALITY AND "VASES WITHOUT FLOWERS"

Consumer Society? Yes.

The Soviet population wants more today than it had yesterday—an urge for which it cannot be blamed in view of its previous low standard of living; part of its leisure is therefore spent in the pursuit of additional consumer goods. The people are increasingly demanding. During the Stalin years and even for years after, when, for example, shoes appeared in a store, anyone who had the money ran to buy a pair, regardless of the color, style, quality, sometimes even of the size. But this period of scarcity is over, everyone wants to choose, and therefore to be able to judge the goods' quality. Since 1968—May 22, 1968, to be exact—consumer clubs exist in the Soviet Union. It is openly admitted that these are modeled on corresponding American organizations, and their function is to advise the consumer (*LG* 41, 1969, 11).

Consumer advisement, of course, does not mean consumer mentality, but there are hints of that too. Just because it takes such time and energy to obtain them, consumer goods have great significance when finally obtained. Soviet youth's overemphasis on material things is attacked in a satire: Instead of devoting the wedding night to the delights of love, a young couple spends it calculating the value of their wedding presents. (See the document "Unromantic Wedding Night.")

It is not only through satires that we learn about consumer mentality. From time to time the results of surveys are published in the Soviet Union, results intended to prove that Soviet youth, in contrast to Western youth, aims for lofty, not selfish material goals. A book by V. Makarov tells us that when asked "What kind of work do you find satisfying?" 70 percent of the young people questioned checked the answer: "The most useful [probably: publicly useful] work." Praiseworthy, but is it that unique? An eighteen-year-old German girl, just finishing high school, tells me in a letter about her aim in life: "I want to serve society and do something really useful for it." Millions of young people, in America too, would subscribe to this view.

Even in Makarov's book an associate summarizes, after questioning young people: "The young [Soviet] worker wants his own flat, a motor coaster or a motorcycle" (p. 99). Makarov also includes in his book, without any negative comment, the "Self-Portrait of a Soviet Citizen Growing Up." The portrait shows a likable, but clearly consumption-oriented young man, whose goals in life differ little from those of a German or Californian of the same age. (See the document, "Self-Portrait . . .")

Another phenomenon might be listed under the consumer mentality, one which can be supported by statistics: the well-known spectacular decline in the Russian birthrate, especially in the cities. Many Soviet couples believe that *one* child is enough; the Soviet press campaign against this attitude invokes arguments also heard in the West. Professor Urlanis, for example, calls children the "flowers of life," and a marriage deficient in children a "vase without flowers."

The attitude of "one child is enough" is strongly, though not exclusively tied to consumer mentality. Excerpts from readers' letters, published last year in Moscow and included in the document "His Personal Life is Everyone's Own Business," show how strong this connection is, especially when the attitudes in the letters are compared with comments in the West. In both East and West the reasons given arise from the same consumer mentality. These statistics seriously worry the Kremlin: On the eve of the First World War 7.2 million children were born in tsarist Russia; just before World War II there were 6.1 million births in the Soviet Union; and in 1970 (in a greater territory) only 4.2 million births.

Alienation? Yes.

Alienation in Marx's sense is, according to the Soviet view, only possible in a capitalist society. The most frequent argument is that under capitalism a blue- or white-collar worker experienced alienation because he toiled only for the capitalist, while the products manufactured by workers under socialism belonged to all the people, which—allegedly—made alienation there impossible. This reasoning need not be analyzed in detail. Clearly, an auto worker in Detroit is more likely to own the car he helped build than his colleague in Gorky.

Of course there is alienation in the Soviet Union. Gradually this is recognized, though with hesitation and reservations. Klyamkin's essay "Man at Work" is an example, as is the reaction by Tochilovsky, both in *Komsomol'skaya Pravda*. Here we learn that socialism has not removed the technological causes of alienation; in fact, the division of labor made necessary by progress prevents labor from being enjoyable. The authors point out that often "a man must do what he does not want to do" because thus

he makes his living. As in the mounting Western literature, they ask by what methods the joy of labor, lost through alienation, might be regained. But their very question proves that alienation exists in the USSR. And we know its significance as a cause of discontent among youth.

True, the USSR has developed a whole series of methods for mass persuasion, methods for counteracting the alienation of laborers in their place of work, and some of these methods may be useful. On the other hand there is the excessive bureaucratization of the Soviet economy, of Soviet life in general, which is a bottomless source of new alienation. Numerous plays cautiously satirize this phenomenon, and in turn are castigated by the critics. (See Hedrick Smith's two articles from Moscow in *The New York Times*.)

As in the West, and with similar reasoning, there are demands for leadership training for managers, in order to close the gap between them and their personnel. One description of a boss reads like this: "His attitude toward the workers was bad, he was nervous, inharmonious, suspicious, often rude, unjust, arrogant." In the future, goes the argument, managers needed to be trained not only in party history, but in sociology, psychology, pedagogy, ethics, and esthetics (*LG* 43, 1972, 11, and 2, 1970, 10).

COMPUTER MARRIAGES

Loneliness? Yes.

And a special kind of loneliness, not the normal human aloneness that has always existed, but the loneliness of the modern industrial society, perhaps in the sense of the Beatle's line, "All the lonely people—where do they all come from?" The Russians were not always a nation of lonely people; on the contrary, Russian literature and literature about Russians proves them gregarious. Modern developments have thoroughly changed this. Huge apartment houses for dozens of millions are anti-social in East and West, as are huge industrial complexes. In the Soviet Union there are factories, especially in the textile industry, in which thousands of women work and almost no men, and others with thousands of men and almost no women. A reader's letter says: "We have 'cities of brides' and 'cities of bridegrooms'" (*LG* 9, 1973, 11).

In a society where the stigma against not being married, of having remained on the shelf, is still strong, especially the women suffer. Male aversion to marriage is increasing in the Soviet Union as well. According to Perevedentsev, these statistics applied between 1959 and 1970: in only twelve years, the proportion of unmarried males aged 25 to 30 rose from 200 to 228 per thousand, in the age group 30 to 35 from 78 to 113 per thousand. After the age of 25 women's chances for marriage fade rapidly, he writes, "after 30 they are insignificant, after thirty-five miniscule." Some time ago *Literaturnaya Gazeta* carried a photograph of a dance floor with the caption, "Girls Standing About" (41, 1972, 12). The photograph itself is less interesting (there have always been wallflowers) than its publication in a periodical that tries to deal with topical issues.

Not long ago my Russian friends expressed surprise and amusement at hearing about the Western practice of finding a marriage partner by newspaper or even by computer. Today the pros and cons of such methods are seriously debated.

Late in the fall of 1969 appeared an essay, "Counselor in Matters of Love?" Its author Pekelis introduced his readers to the "electronic marriage brokers" that had appeared in the West and in Japan. Anyone looking for a partner, he reported, filled out a questionnaire about himself, about the personality of the desired partner, and the computer did the rest. At Harvard, Pekelis wrote, such a system had received 90,000 requests for partners in the first few months alone. Naturally no one was obligated to accept the partner introduced by computer, but if he did, he did so on the basis of more precise knowledge of the other person than was usually available by conventional means.

In the Soviet Union, Pekelis went on, there were 65 million unmarried people between the ages of 18 and 60; many of these would have liked to marry but could not find the right partner. He gave statistics on the circumstances under which couples had become acquainted: 27.2 percent during leisure time, 21 percent at work, 9 percent during childhood, 5.7 percent at parties (*vecherinki*), 5.4 percent on vacation, and the rest through relatives, in street cars, on the street. The results did not please Pekelis. He regretted the frequent divorces, resulting in many cases from incompatibility, in other words, insufficient acquaintance before marriage. Why not adopt the Western computer method? After all, diagnostic machines were used by Soviet medicine. He wrote: "In this question one must act without hypocrisy, without excessive conservatism." (His use of the word "conservatism," to describe what he thinks a wide-spread Soviet attitude, is interesting.)

His article had an effect. The editors announced that "letters from the readers keep coming and coming" (*LG* 8, 1970, 13). Several men wrote a joint letter: "We are a group of bachelors. We have read the article and regret that our country does not have such a sensible arrangement. We believe in science. And science, says a famous writer, should improve life." The letters from women were less intent on science, but emphasized the motif of loneliness. (See the document, "You Too Are Somewhere Alone.")

Of course there is opposition, too, like that of the linguist Shreyder and the sociologist Kharchev. But a summary of the readers' letters indicates that three-fourths favor creating a neutral institution of the computer type for matchmaking. Shlapentokh, who worked on the incoming mail, concluded: "The leitmotif of the letters is: It is currently very difficult to meet people." The larger the city, he writes, the more difficult it is (*LG* 24, 1971, 12).

Family Breakup? Yes.

The Russian family has withstood the victory of Bolshevism, but is less prepared to withstand modern social developments. The proud Soviet summons to "catch up with and overtake" the West has been almost realized in the case of the divorce rate: In 1970 America had 715,000 divorces, the Soviet Union 625,000. Divorces annually are double the figure for second marriages contracted during the same year (*LG* 2, 1970, 12). The theaters are increasingly occupied with marital problems, and there are plays that leave the conflict unresolved. In *Don't Abandon Your Loved One* (Komsomol Theater) the wife ends in an insane asylum (Hedrick Smith, *The New York Times,* December 31, 1972).

Feminization of Education? Yes.

In the West, especially in America, there is much debate about the great preponderance, almost a monopoly, of women teachers; now the Soviet Union also expresses concern about the effect of the *feminizatsiya* on male children. The statistics are unequivocal: In Ukrainian grammar schools, for example, according to a report by Grigor'yev and Khandros, 106,000 teachers are women and only 7000 are men, the latter mostly directors or physical education instructors. "Yet we wring our hands," is the comment, "and wonder why the young boys grow up to be lazy and without initiative."

Like some Western authors, Professor Kon envisions an equalization of the sexes. In his article "Masculine Women? Feminine Men?" he paints the dangers of a "spontaneous revolt of male youth against the dominance of women." He warns that "the male spirit will either be dulled or find negative expression." He returns to this theme in "Why Are Fathers Necessary?" emphasizing the role of the father, a role he and others see endangered by working mothers. In this article Kon admits, though he denies it elsewhere, that in the USSR a generation problem exists, as a result of the modernization process: "The faster social and cultural changes occur, the more striking are the differences between 'fathers' and 'children' with regard to their education, their cultural niveau, their life style, their esthetic appreciation."

Increased Interest in Sex? Yes.

In the Soviet Union, sexuality was a taboo subject longer than in many European countries, partly because of Russian tradition, partly because the ruling elite tends toward prudery. Their view has been that the people, especially youth, should devote their energies to building socialism, not to needless thoughts about sexuality. Sex education of youth by parents or teachers was unusual and is not usual today.

The earliest Soviet article on sex education that I saw was published in 1968 in the *Literaturnaya Gazeta*. Its author, Mrs. Baskina, reported that in 1967 appeared a Moscow translation of a book on marital problems. It was apparently by an East German doctor; there had not been a similar Soviet publication for three decades. When, a year later, Baskina checked at a library, the librarian said, "You're joking, aren't you? Our librarians are standing in line; I haven't read it yet myself." Baskina called her article "Neither Beast nor Angel" because a man once told her, after his divorce, that because of his sex urge his former wife thought him "a beast," while his ex-wife complained: "It's all so brutal." Another wife, continued Baskina, said indignantly after a five-year marriage: "Kissing? We're not lovers, after all. We have children in the family!" A Professor Posvyansky told Mrs. Baskina: "Lack of compatibility in intimate relations is responsible for half, if not more, of all divorces." In Leningrad, Baskina reported, there was a "Laboratory of Sexology and Sexual Pathology" under the authority of the Minister of Health (RSFSR). Although applicants for treatment needed the approval of the ministry, and there was a staff of four doctors and two research associates, the waiting list extended for months.

Again there were letters to the editors (*LG* 24, 1969, 11). Most letters supported sex education, as did the person who handled the mail. The latter also spoke out against restrictions: Important books on the subject, books ready for printing, were not published in the Soviet Union; and no new editions were printed of older works.

ALCOHOLISM

Escape by Drinking? Yes.

The early Communists thought it obvious that, together with capitalism, both drinking and crime would disappear. This hope has not been fulfilled, as indicated, among others, by two long articles by Levin. The first article informs us that use of alcohol, the traditional Russian drug, has increased under socialism, not decreased. From 1940 to 1970 vodka production rose 300 percent, beer 300 percent, and wine 1000 percent; all these are largely consumed domestically. Levin concludes that every nation has its drinkers and nondrinkers. This conclusion is unorthodox; actually he should have preached: There are (capitalist) drunk nations, and (socialist) sober nations.

Alcoholism in the Soviet Union is not disappearing with the older folk. On the contrary, according to Levin 63 percent of alcoholics become addicted before the age of 21. In his second article he details a Soviet phenomenon which he calls "schoolboy alcoholism."

Nor has the connection between drinking and crime lessened. At the turn of the century "half" of all crimes were committed in a drunken state, today "more than half," according to Levin's first essay. In Gorky province 100 percent of premeditated murders occurred under the influence of alcohol; in a part of the city of Perm, 91 percent of willful murders and 100 percent of the rapes. Another interesting fact from the same study: Of drunks committed more than once to a municipal "drying-out" facility (in other words habitual drinkers), "the largest number proportionately" consisted of people who lived in their own *houses;* then came, in order, those with their own *flats,* persons who *shared accommodations,* and finally, subtenants with *one room.* In other words, the higher the standard of living, the higher the chance of waking up in a drunk tank.

Apparently there exists a traditional need for drugs, and a newer need created by the modern industrial society and its characteristic stresses. While the first is decreasing, the second increases. In the West the newer need may be the greater. In the Soviet Union, I assume, the improved standard of living and better education have lessened traditional drinking; therefore, since according to Levin alcohol sales have risen by 350 percent in thirty years, it is the drinking because of modern stress that must have been increasing.

The current drug abuse raging in open Western society does not exist to a similar extent in the controlled, totalitarian Soviet Union. In any case, there is a new law against the illegal cultivation of hemp, the raw material for hashish and marijuana, and against the "unlawful manufacture and distribution of narcotics" (see *Sovetskaya Yustitsiya,* 9, 1966, 29 ff.). It may be that increasing use of alcohol in the USSR is due to similar causes, finally, as increased alcohol *and* drug use in the West.

Comparable statistics do not exist. But as a visitor to the Soviet Union and the United States, it was my impression that alcohol consumption in the USSR is a lesser problem than alcohol and drug abuse in America. John Lindsay, the mayor of New York, when visiting Moscow early in 1973, could easily have told his Russian counterpart: "I'd like to have *your* problems." Yet the 50 percent increase in alcohol sales indicates that even a socialist society is not immune to the traumatic effects of the modern industrial society. In mid-June 1972 Moscow issued pointed decrees against drunkenness, and shortly afterwards decided on the building of a Pepsi Cola plant in the USSR. These decisions are almost desperate attempts to contain alcohol consumption, by penalty and by supplying Soviet youth with an American drink they would consider chic.

"Pill popping," still increasing, is among the phenomena of Western civilization. It was predictable that the USSR, too, would be affected by this current. Recently Professor Tareyev, a member of the Academy of Medical Sciences, openly admitted that this was the case (*LG* 12, 1973, 13). In an interview under the heading "Pills in the Pocket—Good or Bad?" Tareyev attacks the West because of the advertisement "Health is contained in a pill." (I do not remember ever seeing such an advertisement.) The thalidomide scandal is also mentioned. But more than anything else, Tareyev addresses a serious warning to Soviet readers:

Widespread self-treatment with drugs calls forth deep concern and alarm. In this phenomenon we see the other side of scientific-technological progress. [. . .] We are now dealing with a widespread new affliction, the "drug-affliction." [. . .] Today's man is in a hurry, he takes no time to watch his health, he wants to get rid of his inconvenient ailment now, right this minute and without effort, with the help of a comfortable service" [Tareyev uses the English word] he wants to "procure health" just as, these days, he is used to procuring everything.

As an example Tareyev mentions a Russian woman who wanted to buy penicillin without a prescription—because her child had the sniffles. Such unrestrained self-medication, he says, is the more dangerous in the long run because we live in a time of "mass sensitization," a result of the extensive use of "chemical preparations, cosmetics, chemotherapeutic drugs, serums." All this, he said, created allergenic tendencies; if then a medicine was added, "you have the disease."

About nicotine, Moscow reports that in 1970, despite intensive antismoking propaganda, Soviet cigarette consumption had reached 365 billion cigarettes. Money spent on smoking had doubled in the last ten years, to 3.6 billion dollars annually (*The New York Times,* November 21, 1972, p. 17).

Hot Music? (*My inclusive term for all dance music since jazz.*) *Yes.*

Millions of young Soviet citizens enjoy such music, tape it from Western broadcasts, dance to it. If modern industrial society has produced an art form of its own, it is, I believe, such music. I for one hear in it less of the jungle drum than the rumble of machines, the pulse of street traffic, the wail of ambulances. Whatever its origin, the newly mobile youth from Berkeley via Berlin and Moscow to Katmandu calls the new music its true communal language. And no doubt that much of Soviet youth, beyond the relatively narrow circle of the dissidents, is employing this new medium of international communication.

For a long time Soviet leaders, beginning with Khrushchev, were able to keep modern painting out of exhibits in the Soviet Union; "This picture," Khrushchev once commented, "was painted by a donkey, with its tail dipped in paint." But those who know the Soviet Union also know that many Soviet artists paint abstractly not to irritate their country's Brezhnevs, but because abstract painting, like hot music, is the style of the times. In fact it was Russians like Yavlensky and Kandinsky who, with their colleagues of the "Blaue Reiter" school, developed the abstract style.

SOVIET CRIME

Crime? Again, Yes.

Soviet jurisprudence believes that crime is a characteristic of presocialist societies; by solving the problems that result in crime, socialism should also have abolished crime. Insofar as there was crime left in the Soviet

Union, Soviet criminologists taught, it was but a last and dying remnant of capitalism.

Moscow has not published statistics on Soviet crime for forty-six years, strong evidence of its continued existence. Something obviously needs to be covered up, something even more painful than the rising divorce rate and the declining birth rate.

The "remnant-of-capitalism" theory finds less than complete support today. Professor Connor, the author of a book on asocial behavior in the Soviet Union, brought to my attention a revealing essay titled "A Study of the Factors Causing Crime in the USSR." There Professor Struchkov, Acting Director of the College of the Soviet Ministry of Internal Affairs (MVD), explains why half a century after the victory of the socialist revolution there is still crime in the USSR. He lists the reasons we already know—first, crime as a remnant of the past; secondly, corrupting influences from abroad—then goes on to say:

> In our opinion there is a third cause of crime: the existence of incorrect attitudes among Soviet citizens, of attitudes resulting from a distorted understanding of the humane principles of socialism.[. . .] These [false] attitudes arise from wrongly assessing these facts: that the socialist state is concerned about its citizens, provides them with education and free medical treatment, pays for their vacations, also grants them pensions for old age and for inability to work, and much more; these [false] attitudes also arise because some forget that man himself must create society's wealth and secure his own prosperity. The opinion arises that everyone has a claim [on the state] to being taken care of [*ishdivenche-skiye nastroyeniya*], and selfishness arises with it. [At this point Struchkov debates the objections of an opponent, then he continues:]
>
> These [false] attitudes which give rise to the third cause of crime (the belief that everyone has a claim to being taken care of, selfishness, distaste for work, barbaric acts against the products of work), can of course coincide, in content, with attitudes arising from remnants of the past in the people's consciousness. But because of the particularities of their origin, they cannot be counted among the remnants of the past. These attitudes [those that have produced the third cause of Soviet crime] were *born from Soviet soil,* as the result of a false reaction to socialist property relations [p. 100; emphasis added].

If we look at Struchkov's list of elements underlying the "third cause of crime" *born from Soviet soil,* we discover among them some of the best known aspects of the consumer society, which in the West also help cause crime: "the opinion that everyone has a claim to being taken care of, selfishness, distaste for work, barbaric acts against the products of work" (vandalism?); elsewhere Struchkov adds contradictions between the consumers' steadily growing needs and the economy's ability to satisfy them" (p. 103).

The Soviet Union still publishes no statistics on crime, so we do not have absolute figures. But Professor Walter Connor, on the basis of relative figures sometimes published for smaller areas, concluded at a spring 1973 lecture in New York that the proportion of Soviet crime— according to categories like crimes against property, crimes against persons, and so on—did not differ much from crime in the United States.

Muggings, for example, are relatively frequent in the United States; in New York, experience with muggers—on the streets, in hallways, elevators, in homes, for small cash sums or wristwatches—is a frequent subject of conversation. In the Soviet Union, too, there is mugging, although, I would assume, to a much lesser extent. *Literaturnaya Gazeta* reported (38, 1972, 16) in a satirical vein of a young man mugging an intellectual, presumably in Moscow. This account appeared on almost the same day that a colleague of mine, Professor Friedman, was killed by a young mugger a few hundred yards from Columbia University, without one pedestrian rushing to his aid.

Again about this time, on September 9, 1972, the following occurred near Moscow; the journalist Kapler reported in detail: One evening, as a woman named Novikova walked home from a suburb station, she was attacked by a young mugger; because she resisted she was beaten so badly that she required two months in the surgical ward of a hospital. (Nothing might have been made of the case had she not been a recipient of a decoration for merit during the Second World War.) The behavior of pedestrians is the most noteworthy. According to Novikova, there were at that same time some one hundred people on the way home from the station. In her words: "People everywhere, ten steps away, I hold tight to my purse, but again he hits me over the head, over the head. I think: Finished, the end, I'll fall over in a minute.[. . .] An old man I heard saying: 'Citizen, a woman is being robbed.' But no one stopped, and the old man also disappeared." Kapler explains such behavior in this way: "Everyone for himself. This thing does not concern me. I don't want to be called as a witness." Similar explanations can be heard after such incidents in New York.

For the sake of illustration, let me mention a special variant of this new kind of crime. We can say that in the West the industrial society (because of the excess of goods) led to the consumer society; this in turn led to the department store society; and this, again (because of insufficient personnel due to high wages), to the self-service society; finally and unfortunately, though probably unavoidable due to human nature, we are now facing symptoms of a shoplifting society. In the two decades since Stalin's death, the Soviet Union has clearly gone through the first three stages. It was predictable that self-service stores would spring up; this has in fact happened, though not yet to a great extent. And the fifth stage?

"I FORGOT . . ."

There has been shoplifting from the time of the ancient forums. But the self-service store with its thousands of unguarded goods has created a new situation, it is a source of enormous temptation. True honesty can only be proven by resisting such temptation. It was interesting, therefore, to try to predict whether the developments initiated in industrial society would, as everywhere, end in shoplifting in the Soviet Union too. That question is now answered: "The salespeople [in Soviet shops] have thought of a flattering [*galantniy*] expression—coefficient of forgetfulness. Expressed more simply, [. . .] swiping by customers." Thus begins an article by A. Rubinov, titled "Coefficient of Forgetfulness." He reports: "When a customer had to remove his high boots, I saw 18—eighteen!— tin cans roll from them. In the inside coat pockets of another, two bottles of the most expensive cognac were found." He tells of a woman who, without being noticed, brought an empty container of cheap "Hercules" oat flakes into the store; at home she had already used up the oats, and now she filled the container with the store's butter. When she tried to pay the cashier only 37 kopecks for "Hercules" oats the expensive butter was found hidden in the container. Forgetfulness?

In stores that do not operate on the self-service principle, the customers are separated from the merchandise by a "wall"—as Rubinov expresses it and as every visitor has found out. But even here the "coefficient of forgetfulness" is 0.4 percent of the merchandise. Rubinov does not tell us how much is stolen in self-service stores, but he describes how their customers are treated:

A state of nervous suspicion reigns continuously, as in a bazaar, where someone's swiped one's wallet. Even when someone enters [the store], they [salespeople] do not like him if he carries a briefcase or shopping bag. They think of ways to search everyone, if only with their eyes. They're not even reluctant, there, to conduct bodily searches . . . The salesperson in such a [self-service] store becomes a guard whose task is not to sell goods, but to watch them.

Rubinov suggests that some salespeople enjoy an excuse "for poking around in a strange shopping bag."

A year later Rubinov again discussed the subject (*LG* 44, 1972, 12). He mentions that in 1971 the Soviet Minister of Trade, A. Struyev, had proclaimed "Order 186." It decreed that in the future no one could enter a self-service store without a transparent basket or cart provided by the store; in turn, if the customer carried a briefcase, the case would not be searched when he left. But unfortunately no one knew the order. Rubinov describes his difficulties in getting permission from the minister's secretary, V. Morosov, to see the "heavily guarded order."

In a satiric cartoon customers stand in a store before a television screen which watches the merchandise. On the screen they see a man stealing canned food. The caption: "I'd rather they showed us a soccer match."

Despite everything, I assume less shoplifting goes on in the still few Soviet self-service stores than in the West, where shoplifting has become a serious problem. Yet the sorry story also holds true in the Soviet Union: The consumer society leads to self-service, self-service in turn tempts toward shoplifting.

The satirical magazine *Krokodil* makes clear that the Soviet leadership is aware of the similarity between the developments in West and East. On looking through eight volumes of this officially approved satirical weekly, I found nothing on the Western New Left, but quite a bit on how the Kremlin and its caricaturists see restless youth: as an awful apparition of ill manners, if not insanity. *Krokodil*'s Soviet readers get little opportunity to see more of the Western youth movement than the hippie, the long-hair, the good-for-nothing. The picture of the hippies' Soviet imitators drawn in *Krokodil* is similar: They too are long-haired, stupidly arrogant, lazy, in short—contemptible. (Details are given under *Krokodil* in the chapter "Materials.")

When reading Soviet and American newspapers at the same time, one continuously finds parallel symptoms for the two civilizations: from increasing near-sightedness among the young, as a result of "scientific-technological progress" (Malinovsky); to concern about the excessive number of handguns among the population (Leo Gruliow).

We have seen that many phenomena of the Western industrial and consumer society can be found in the USSR, and second, that some of

Soviet youth are susceptible to these phenomena. In conclusion, a reflection:

We can compare the Soviet people to a tube through which, with the help of the mass media, information on the New Left—either accurate or caricature—flows. The question then is: How does the Soviet citizen react to such data? There are two extreme possibilities, with many shades in between. One possibility is that the conduit remains as it was, before the data flowed through it; the second, that some of the data flowing through it combines with the tube, just as chemicals in water are deposited in plumbing and change that plumbing. Which is accurate?

My assumption is that the Soviet reader who accepts information on the New Left is influenced by that information. To his surprise he sees, in other countries, a youth which—notwithstanding the absurdity of its life style or actions—wants to better society, a society which the Soviet reader finds affluent beyond his dreams. He sees that Western youth is willing to make sacrifices toward this goal, a goal which he hardly dares dream about: more love, equality, justice, freedom, participation in decisions, and beauty. Finally, he learns that this youth wants to better society not by joining Soviet-style Communism, but by following a lodestar that can be called socialist-democratic, a combination of words that sounds suspicious to the Kremlin, but promising to many Soviet citizens.

X

CONCLUDING REFLECTIONS

In this study we have posed some questions about Moscow's reaction to the unrest of Western youth. We can now attempt to answer them and also to look for some conclusions.

1. WHAT IS MOSCOW'S REACTION TO THE NEW LEFT?

Moscow would like to see only one, the Soviet-Communist ideology, in the world, but this wish has not been fulfilled. All other ideologies, religions included, are anathema to the Soviet leadership, even though tactical reasons may compel Moscow temporarily to pretend friendship with some of them, the Mohammedans, the Buddhists, or certain Christian groups.

But there are differences. Some alien "ideologies" are taken seriously, others less seriously. Synthetic Western ideologies, whether conservative or liberal—Gaullism or people's capitalism, among others—and religions fads do not worry the Soviet leaders. They respect Western military power and they look with suspicion upon the attractiveness of Western affluence and personal freedom to Eastern youth, but they envisage no ideological dangers. And more fascist ideologies of any import do not exist.

But it is different when it comes to non-Soviet ideologies on the left, whether these are personified by Communist leaders like Tito, Mao, Dubček, or authors like Herbert Marcuse. The Kremlin regards them as its true rivals, for they use the leftward current for their own ends, to the disadvantage of Moscow-oriented Communist parties.

Until Tito's challenge of Stalin, Moscow lived under the illusion that aside from tiny splinter movements and individual traitors Communism and Soviet Communism were identical, and that the Soviet Union was "the fatherland of all workers." Then the disappointments began. The Social Democrat Kurt Schumacher was able to mobilize German workers against Moscow, the Communist Tito stood up against Stalin, and Mao withstood the Khrushchevs and Brezhnevs. Finally there was the New Left, there were Marcuse and his "werewolves."

The irony of it! At last a revolutionary mood had arisen in the capitalist countries: Western students, the pride and prop of the Western world, stormed universities; marched under red banners against the White House, even against that lion's den, the Pentagon; tore and burned draft cards, going to jail or into exile but not into army camps. At last Lenin's dreams seemed to bloom worldwide.

But what a disappointment! All this did not happen under the leadership and for the glory of Moscow, nor even in the interests of the Western Communist parties. These were either ignored or violently criticized as part of "totalitarian Soviet Communism." When students quoted Marx or Lenin, they often did this in order to attack Stalin and his successors, or they quoted them side by side Marx's anarchist enemy Bakunin, or even worse, in the same breath with Rosa Luxemburg and her critique of Lenin's antidemocratic methods.

All this produced an ambivalent stance. On the one hand Moscow hailed the revolt of Leftist Western youth as a symptom of capitalism's approaching end. On the other hand there was dismay at the anarchist, even anti-Soviet nature of the rebellion, its rejection of cooperation with and particularly of subordination to the local Communist party. Soviet observers were forced to watch helplessly how the young rebels analyzed Western society much like they themselves did, while drawing very different conclusions from these analyses. Thus the New Left's rise contributed to further division among the already divided Communist world.

To be sure, one could say that, with Marcuse's help, the New Left had moved at least part way toward Marxism, that one day it would discover the road to the true, the Soviet Marxism. The reader may recall that many Soviet intellectuals seemed to console themselves with this hope when confronted with the difficult Western intelligentsia. And why shouldn't the road via the second and third M finally lead to the first, to Marx?

Such a development is not impossible; in fact the New Left—like Mao and Marcuse—invokes Marx and Lenin. But the history of the great religious schisms does not point that way. Four centuries, for example, have passed since Luther's theses at Wittenberg, but the Protestants have not returned to the Vatican, nor have the sects which grew out of Protestantism. And Mao is more dangerous to Brezhnev than Luther once was for the Pope. Today's Trotskyites everywhere are more bitter enemies of the Kremlin, and more numerous, than the small band of followers that revered Trotsky until his assassination in Mexico. Among today's many New Left groups, no doubt a few individuals will tire of internal conflicts and will one day enter the secure womb, the Soviet Communist party of their country. Some of these will become loyal *apparatchiki*, others will irritate the party with their habit of intellectual freedom and the resulting lack of discipline. But these few will not change the overall tendency, the decay of the Kremlin's authority in the world. Except as pious wish, Moscow today seldom expresses the hope that in due time the New Left will develop into its reliable ally.

Moscow feels the same distaste as Washington for the New Left's long hair and fringed jackets; its scurrilous grotesqueries, disorderliness, and lack of grooming; its Bohemian and hippie aspects; in brief, its unbourgeois behavior. This reaction proves the deeply ingrained conservative, antimodern nature of today's Soviet Communism. In Moscow's view the New Left not only marches in the wrong direction, but also in very vulgar fashion. This vulgarity repels a Soviet leadership intent on respectability and, judging from my own observations, repels a large part of the Soviet population, presumably the vast majority.

Perhaps a formula can summarize Moscow's reaction: "leftists" who become leftists are good. But "leftists" who remain "leftists" and even convert potential leftists into "leftists" are evil, more evil than if they were rightists. How beautiful everything would be, according to Moscow, if there were once again only good leftists and evil rightists, as in the good old times before Mao and Marcuse.

2. HOW DOES MOSCOW REACT TO THE UNEXPECTED?

The New Left attracted world-wide attention from 1960 on (Japan, Korea), especially since 1964 (Berkeley), but the preceding chapters and the appended documents indicate that before the Paris events of May 1968, Soviet ideologists did not take the movement seriously. From conversations I know that even at the end of the sixties, when a young Moscow researcher with insight into foreign affairs wanted to treat the New Left, his professors rejected the project because they thought the subject uninteresting and unproductive. Most of the articles that finally appeared date from 1970, when the Western flood of similar publications had long since ebbed. It may be indicative that the first independent pamphlet—

it also appeared in 1970—was written by a gifted foreign correspondent and Germany watcher, Vladimir Lomeyko, not by a Moscow sociologist.

The reaction of Soviet writing to the New Left involves three phases. For many years, the movement was not noticed; in 1968 came outraged shock and hostility at this new uncontrollable element; finally serious discussions began, an increasingly differentiated picture of the New Left emerged, with the writers taking a line somewhat different from that of the Party, as shown by the appended excerpts from official party explanations, "From the Kremlin On High." The writers' task is not easy. They hail the youthful élan of the New Left's critique of Western society; just the same, they are concerned about the direction and form of the critique; and they know that the party leaders, overwhelmingly, see the New Left as an irritating rival, a source of contagion even for the Soviet population, and only half-heartedly as a potential ally.

The chapter "Materials" will show that the various periodicals did not react uniformly. Authors with a journalistic bent in the *Literaturnaya Gazeta*, or those with youthful lack of dogmatism in *Molodoy Kommunist*, tended to emphasize the positive, or at least the interesting aspects of the new movement. The dignified and stuffy *Kommunist* stressed the negative side and warned foreign youth: Nothing will come of you, unless you acknowledge the authority of your country's Communist Party! Other publications, like *Yunost'* (*Youth*) and *Molodaya Gvardiya* (*Young Guard*), although their names suggested an interest in portraying and discussing what was current, stayed largely silent.

To examine Moscow's reaction to unexpected ideological developments, I have researched Moscow's reactions to the New Left, and several years earlier to Maoism. In each case Moscow acted slowly and ponderously, even more so in the case of Maoism, the dangerous rise of which required more intensive ideological and practical response on the part of Moscow. Other ideological currents caused equally slow reactions: Titoism from 1948 to 1952, the unrest in Poland and the Hungarian Revolt of 1956, the Prague spring of 1968, which had begun in 1967. In Poland, Hungary, and Czechoslovakia, the Soviet Union achieved military but not intellectual suppression of the heresies; its ideological guns were directed mainly at straw figures like the "NATO danger to Czechoslovakia," instead of taking the new reality into account.

However, it seems to me that the Soviet response to the New Left has included greater interest and involvement, resulting in more sensible conclusions, than that to Maoism. There may be several reasons for this. For

Russian journalists, China is a strange world, not to mention the language difficulties. Comments on Peking also might provoke annihilating answers by the powerful Chinese propaganda apparatus, and hence risk blame for a journalistic setback to one's country. Most of all, as I know from many conversations, Maoism has no intellectual appeal for Moscow's ideologists. Without exception they resent Maoism. The Russians with whom I talk always shake their heads uncomprehendingly at my interest in Maoism.

The attitude toward the New Left is different. Of course, it is also a heresy, and not without danger. But it grew from the soil of a related world, it can be understood, for some it is even fascinating. I suspect that the ideas developed by the New Left—on the special role of today's intelligentsia, or on the repressive role of the technocratic state—seem entirely sensible to some Soviet ideologues, perhaps even agreeable. In contrast to Maoism with its curious sayings in the Little Red Book, the New Left uses a familiar language, employs much of the vocabulary known to Soviet journalists from their own tradition, and to the extent that it coins new words, these are accepted without much hesitation by Soviet ideologists like any new scientific terminology.

Here is an alphabetical selection of such words from New Left jargon, which in turn derive largely from the specialized language of sociology. I present them in the Russian form; translation is not really necessary, but some hints might be helpful. The Russians replace the "h," which their alphabet lacks, with the letter "g" or by a letter equivalent to the guttural German "ch," here given as "kh."

adaptatsiya

akulturatsiya

alienatsiya

angashirovanno (engaged, involved)

bikheviorism

de-etatizatsiya (after French "état," or "state")

de-identifikatsiya

de-ideologizatsiya

dikhotomiya

dropaut

ekolog

eskalatsiya

eskapism

frustratsiya

gomogenizatsiya (g = h)

identifikatsiya

ierarkhizatsiya (initial "h")

imaginatsiya

isteblishment

kampus

kheppening (kh = h)

khippi

kontrkultura (counter culture)

manipulirovaniye (manipulation)

marginalnost'

motivatsiya

outsaider

post-industrialnyy

relevantnost'   subkultura
repressivnyy   tich-in
seks   travá (Russian for "grass," but by
sindrom   adaptation from the English,
status   also "marijuana")
stsientism   vibratsiya

I have saved the funniest Russian borrowing for the end: *seksapilniy*;
indeed: the adjective of "sex appeal."

In the chapter on Marcuse, especially, we saw that not only individual
words and concepts are borrowed. Western sociological theory of the
workers' integration into Western society, a thesis from which the New
Left derived its legitimate claim for revolutionary action, became the
theory of "the two hungers." The Parisian poster, "Power to the Imagination," led to Marxist, or at least Plekhanovist attempts to rehabilitate the
imagination, and to a new debate on Utopianism. And reproaches of the
embourgeoisement of Communist parties caused a fresh analysis of the
dilemma between tactics and strategy.

Nevertheless, here again Soviet reaction was ponderous. Soviet ideologists simply have their difficulties with unexpected intellectual developments. In the West we get the opposite, a frenzied burst of activity greet-
ing new developments. As soon as something happens ideologically in the
East—when Khrushchev topples the demigod Stalin, the Cultural Revolution breaks out in China, Czech writers become restless, or a Soviet
marshall joins the Politburo—droves of Western intellectuals immediately
pounce on the event. Not having to protect themselves either on the right
or left, they toss off analyses and predictions. As the flood of thoughts
rains down, most eventually form a common river. But not all accept the
consensus, and this leads to reevaluations of positions. Due to lack of precise information, much is pure speculation, but months or years later the
gradually evolving consensus of the majority of experts turns out close to
the truth.

This "hit-and-miss" process of lively, uninhibited debate is missing in
the Communist countries. Just as no Soviet manager would dare open a
button factory that has not been planned, no Soviet ideologue will give
his opinion on a touchy question—until the party has ruled on the guidelines of discussion, or has, within limits, permitted the debate. However,
that takes time. Soviet journalism has difficulty in explaining events which
have not been anticipated within the ideological system of the regime. To
analyze events independently is dangerous for a Soviet writer. Despite

this, things sometimes surface better than expected: new ideas rarely, but at least information. At any rate this is true for the New Left, a phenomenon that holds a certain fascination for Soviet authors.

3. WHAT DO SOVIET CITIZENS FIND OUT?

An advantage of this study is its limited subject; the number of Soviet books and articles on this theme is not endless. If there should be a person in the USSR (there probably is not) who has taken the trouble, as I have, to read just about everything that the USSR has published on the New Left, his picture, on the whole, would be rather accurate. As elsewhere, however, people in the Soviet Union read only a few periodicals and derive their ideas about the world primarily from the mass dailies, not from small circulation organs like *Voprosy Filosofii* or *MEiMO*. As mentioned, the *Literaturnaya Gazeta* is a special case. No doubt it helps loosen rigid conceptions, but its staple is topical reportage, not major conclusive studies; it is also difficult to obtain outside the large cities.

Again excluding the *Literaturnaya Gazeta,* which does not mention its circulation, generally the larger a newspaper or periodical's circulation, the more polemical and less factual is its tone toward foreign events, the more unreal the pictures it presents to the reader. Apparently the reader of *Voprosy Filosofii* or *MEiMO* is trusted to have a deeper understanding of the teachings of Soviet Communism, and hence greater resistance to Western influences.

My observations tell me that the Soviet *masses* are in fact shocked and repelled when reading press accounts of disorderly radical students in the West. Like their counterparts in middle America, they are decidedly for law and order; they do not want their standard of living, achieved by long years of hard work, modest but nevertheless secure, endangered by any "long-haired punks." These Soviet readers also accept, by and large, the official formula that Western freedom leads to anarchy. The Soviet intellectual on the other hand reacts like a Western journalist or professor; he is willing to see the positive about youth's stormy push for a more humane, more just, more democratic world, but, also like his Western counterpart, he may be repelled by aspects of youth's behavior.

Some reports of the New Left critique of repressive establishments may cause Soviet readers to stop short and tell themselves (quietly, of course): "Actually not a bad idea; we should push similar demands here, too." Sometimes one almost suspects that a Soviet author quotes some New

Left thesis not to condemn it, but to acquaint his Soviet contemporaries with it in a roundabout, safer way.

Since the Soviet intelligentsia has rapidly increased in size and influence, Western discussion on the intellectuals' role in the society of today and tomorrow must interest the Soviet reader. The constantly repeated dogma of the intelligentsia's subordinate role under the leadership of the proletariat (in actuality, of the party) must seem questionable to him by now, when his own periodicals have told him more and more of the leading role and growing self-confidence of Western intellectuals. Having heard all his life about the proletariat's self-evident claim to leadership, he must now reflect increasingly on a question he might already have harbored in secret. A result of such reflection appears in a 1970 book by I. Sabelin, *Chelovek i Chelovechestvo* (*Man and Humanity*; I did not see the original). Sabelin writes:

> There is no doubt that the intelligentsia has now become[. . .] the leading revolutionary class; it came into being on the eve of the space age, and its manifold influence changes and decides the fates of nations and peoples.[. . .] The working class has prepared its own, and the peasants', step-wise growth into the class of the intelligentsia, and it [the intelligentsia] is destined to be the only class in human society—for ever and ever [*vo veki vekov*]. (Quoted after Yakovlev, *LG* 46, 1972, 4)

Sabelin's view is of course strongly condemned. He is reproached for disregarding the existence of classes, and for regarding "the scientific-technological revolution, the population explosion, the advance of man into space" in the spirit of Western futurologists, namely as problems concerning "all of humanity," the West *and* the Communist states (ibid.). But Sabelin's viewpoint exists, and it does appear in print.

The Soviet intelligentsia has developed a marked interest in the "scientific-technological revolution." I suspect that behind it lies that very question: Has this new revolution not created a situation in *all* developed industrial states, including the Soviet Union, in which the relationship between intelligentsia and proletariat must be analyzed anew, and that means: the relationship between the intelligentsia and the party?

One thing is certain: The New Left (and the intelligentsia generally) was being debated remarkably often and thoroughly in Soviet journals once the topic was released for discussion. This kind of interest is natural for authors who, being intellectuals themselves, are primarily interested in other intellectuals. Whether discussing Soviet or foreign subjects, they feel more competent for the problems of scholars, artists, and doctors than for those of the factory or village. When discussing the West they must also cover subjects like strikes or election campaigns, but they lack personal experience of them. But they have all been involved in intellectual or ideological conflicts—more than they cared for.

The Soviet intelligentsia's almost personal interest in Western intellectuals probably accounts for the relatively complete picture of the New Left drawn in Soviet journals in general. Their Marxist starting point dominates, of course. Either from conviction or tactical caution Soviet authors emphasize the economic causes of Western youth's unrest, especially among students (lack of adequate scholarships, poor housing, not enough facilities to handle students). They do not point out that lower class sons and daughters are most eager to finish their studies, and thus reject disruptions of law and order. And Soviet authors underemphasize or ignore the motives that dominate in the theory and practice of the American youth revolt: ideals like humanism, desire for justice, anti-consumer feeling, or individual and psychological motives. This is understandable. They live in a country that is far from affluence, let alone satiety; the mentality of youth in the affluent Western society must seem incomprehensible to them. Their articles admit only with reservations that hippies and rebels come primarily from the upper classes. The Soviet reader who, in the pictures of his newspapers, sees ragged students march in demonstrations or fight police must take them for young proletarians or slum dwellers; by their patched trousers and torn jackets he cannot guess that often they are the sons of the wealthy, demonstrating not against their "poverty" but against their parents' affluence.

In their newspapers, for decades, the Soviet people have read that in the West the poor struggle against the rich. They may see nothing unusual in the march of "poor" students against capitalism, except for the sometimes disorderly manner of the march. If they knew more of the true background, the picture would look very different. If they are young and belong to the intelligentsia, they might be fascinated or moved to know that white American students from wealthy homes could face police clubs and tear gas not to gain something for themselves, but to join their black compatriots in fighting for the equal rights and opportunities of all underprivileged, the blacks included, against the establishment. Presented without bias, such a picture would support Marcuse's thesis: Students and the black ghettos are the vanguard of the revolution. But such a picture is not permitted. Hence to many Soviet readers the New Leftists seem, primarily, impudent disrupters of law and order, worthy of neither sympathy nor interest.

The chapter "A Portrait Changes" pointed out that a Soviet reader interested in the New Left would learn most about America, something of Europe, little about the rest of the world (which has also been affected by youthful rebellions), hardly anything on unrest in the two major Asian nations, India and Japan. Yet I have seen much more violent student riots in Japan than on American campuses; rivaling factions fought each other in big phalanxes, armed with spears, helmets, and shields. The lack of attention these events received in the Soviet press is therefore surprising. Perhaps what I have been told in Moscow is true: "We don't have enough sociologically trained specialists for Japan and the Third World."

To emphasize one point: The New Left is not one of the perennial topics that Soviet writers *have* to write about, rather it is a marginal phenomenon in Soviet writing. Therefore it is studied only by those especially interested. Seldom have I found anyone in the Soviet Union who even knew the New Left's name.

A few months ago I talked with a Soviet scientist who was temporarily in the West. He asked what I was working on; when I said: "On Moscow and the New Left," he was surprised: There was no literature on that in Moscow! Only when he saw my stacks of xeroxed Soviet pamphlets and articles did he change his mind.

We are thus confronted by a contradiction. On the one hand the sum of Soviet publications on the New Left transmits a remarkably extensive, differentiated picture. Among the people, on the other hand, the New Left is hardly known, because the movement is not a central theme for the Moscow opinion manipulators, and because the relevant literature is very scattered.

4. WHAT HAVE WE DISCOVERED ABOUT THE SOVIET UNION?

Everyone knows, and spectacular trials continually remind us that, unlike the Western democracies, the Soviet Union offers none of the conditions for a viable opposition. Western radicals demonstrate on streets and plazas; most of their publications can appear and be circulated unhindered, even though, to make them sound more exciting, they are called "underground press." But in the Soviet Union all opposition is illegal, public dissent can lead to heavy punishment, literary dissent was pushed into the true underground, and oppositional writings are hardly known.

For every antiparty and antigovernment demonstrator in the USSR, there are hundreds of thousands of protesters in America, in Western Europe, in Japan.

But the literature of dissent, known in the West as *Samizdat,* has existed for years. It indicates that dissidents are indeed active in the Soviet—especially the young—intelligentsia. The criticism of the repressive establishment they have in common with the New Left. But unlike the New Left, these dissidents know what revolution is, know its price, know the misery and bondage to which it leads. Hence the dissidents generally oppose force and advocate legal reforms, respect for the state and its constitution. In a word, they are liberal-socialist, not social revolutionaries, certainly not anarchists or Maoists. For them the industrial, the consumer, and the affluent society remain worthwhile, though distant goals.

In the West the industrial society's uniform development is clear. Its form and symptoms—assembly line and automation, alienation and escape into Utopias and drugs—appear in Germany or Switzerland just as in America, though with various time lags. However, whether the same results will appear in the Soviet Union, the population of which also aims for an industrial society (and moves along the road toward it), remains subject to controversy in the West.

Soviet ideology excludes out of hand the possibility of delayed emergence of Western social problems in the Soviet Union; even the mention of such problems is angrily rejected. According to Moscow, industrial progress will lead, in the West, to revolution and the collapse of capitalism, and to its joining the "socialist camp." Hence, in the Kremlin's eyes, Western research and technology has effects different from those of its Soviet counterpart, Western heart disease differs from Soviet heart disease, Western shoplifting is different from Soviet "forgetfulness."

Some Soviet articles on general Western phenomena, especially on the New Left, read like old tales of missionaries reporting from the darkest jungle: of creatures with human face, yes, but savages until humanized by conversion to Christianity (i.e. Soviet Communism).

However, if the USSR were convinced of the basic differences between the two worlds, she could cultivate Western contacts without anxiety. Potatoes lying in one basket with apples remain potatoes: nor would Soviet society, if basically different, be changed in its nature by Western contacts. But while the supposedly decaying West makes every effort to facilitate free, unconditional movement of men and ideas between East and West, the Soviet Union (and even more so East Germany) insists on their complete control. Moscow even announced its intention to hunt down Western television satellites if they should broadcast to the USSR without express consent (Draft of a UN resolution, printed in *Izvestia*, August 11, 1972).

Not surprisingly, the worried leaders in Moscow have no desire for pushing public debate with the West's New Left. The wider a periodical's circulation, the less information it provides on this risky phenomenon. In comparing all publications investigated for this book (as far as they announce their circulation), we find: 70 percent of all articles on the New Left, among them the best, appeared in three periodicals with low circulations (*Voprosy Filosofii* with 31,000; *MEiMO* with 39,000; and *Novyy Mir* with 175,000) and in a fourth (*Molodoy Kommunist*) with 785,000. The remaining 30 percent appeared among fifteen publications with a combined circulation of eleven millions.

Such preventive policy speaks for itself. After more than a half century of Soviet history, Moscow lacks self-confidence, lacks a belief in the essential difference and superiority of the Soviet system.

5. THE LESSON OF THE SAN ANDREAS FAULT

The Soviet state is ruled by old, inflexible functionaries of the revolution. In foreign affairs, they are ready to experiment, but domestically they are unwilling to risk their predecessors' victory of 1917–1921 through any kind of change, not even programmed change which they control. In contrast, the open society of the West must remain open to change in order to survive, and more open than ever before.

In the West we know only too well that we are surrounded by countless, almost insoluble, and sometimes very ugly problems. With the New Left's help we have lost the naïve belief in progress that we held decades ago, we have become skeptical about modern civilization. Its monuments have lost their old glory. New York, where I wrote this book, has become a warning, while yesterday it was a vision of the future. Therefore we need change. We want not only improved methods of production, but social change in the widest sense. And we want such change before global tensions lead to revolutionary eruptions, the kind predicted, in unison for once, by both the New Left and Moscow.

This makes me think of California. There the great San Francisco earthquake of 1906 has not been forgotten, and now seismologists predict a serious quake for the near future. The San Andreas fault, which extends from Southern California along the coast north for hundreds of miles, through San Francisco and beyond, would cause that quake. The strip of land between the fault and the Pacific Coast moves north, up to several inches per year, while the continent east of the fault remains stationary. Along most of the fault, the tension between the two vast land masses results in continuous minute quakes, which are usually noted only by the seismologists, and which dissipate enormous energy in harmless fashion. But around the lower peninsula, for some fifty miles south from San Francisco, such small quakes do not occur regularly; a dangerous tension is being built up. Hence the predictions of a future catastrophe.

This whole process may be compared to the course of technological and scientific progress. This progress, too, creates continuous social and political tensions, tensions that could discharge catastrophically unless resolved in time by gradual change, that is, by reforms. In May 1968 de Gaulle's France was close to such an upheaval when the General could not bear to give to the young and to the workers, demanding participation and change, a voice in the affairs of the country. And in the Soviet Union, which is so averse to basic reforms—have not much stronger tensions been building up for a much longer time?

Despite its known weaknesses, the democratic system has proven superior to the dictatorships. Will we learn from the San Andreas fault? Let us not be upset by the minor quakes of everyday politics. Let them keep us alert, instead, to the necessity of preparing for change by democratically instituted reforms, not uncontrollable catastrophes, for the change that will allow us to survive in the next millennium.

DOCUMENTS

FOR I: THUS SPAKE LENIN

STUDENT UNREST 1901

Student unrest in Kiev at the beginning of 1901 resulted in the induction of 183 students. Although military service was general and compulsory in the tsarist empire of the time, it was the custom to exempt the sons of the upper classes as well as students, so that the actual induction of these Kiev students was in effect punitive. Lenin used the occurrence for his first major essay on questions concerning restless youth. The event and Lenin's vocabulary compare with occurrences in the late sixties.

V. I. Lenin, "The Drafting of 183 Students into the Army," January 1901, in *Collected Works,* English translation of the 4th Russian edition (Moscow, 1960, and London), IV, 414–419.

The newspapers of January 11 published the official announcement of the Ministry of Education on the drafting into the army of 183 students of Kiev University as a punishment for "riotous assembly." [. . .]

The Kiev students demand the dismissal of a professor who took the place of a colleague that had left. The administration resists, provokes students to "assemblies and demonstrations" and—yields. The students call a meeting to discuss what could make possible so horrendous a case—two "white linings" * (according to reports) raped a young girl. The administration sentences the "ringleaders" to solitary confinement in the students' detention cell. Those refuse to submit. They are expelled. A crowd of students demonstratively accompany the expelled students to the railway station. A new meeting is called; the students remain until evening and refuse to disperse so long as the rector does not show up. The Vice-Governor and Chief of Gendarmerie arrive on the scene at the head of a detachment of troops, who surround the University and

* "White linings" were students from the upper classes. *Trans.*

occupy the main hall. The rector is called. The students demand—a constitution, perhaps? No. They demand that the punishment of solitary
confinement should not be carried out and that the expelled students
should be reinstated. The participants at the meeting have their names
taken and are allowed to go home.

Ponder over this astonishing lack of proportion between the modesty
and innocuousness of the demands put forward by the students and the
panicky dismay of the government, which behaves as if the axe were already being laid to the props of its power. Nothing gives our "omnipo-
tent" government away so much as this display of consternation. By this
it proves more convincingly than does any "criminal manifesto" to all who
have eyes to see and ears to hear that it realises the complete instability of
its position, and that it relies only on the bayonet and the knout to save
it from the indignation of the people. Decades of experience have taught
the government that it is surrounded by inflammable material and that a
mere spark, a mere protest against the students' detention cell, may start a
conflagration. This being the case, it is clear that the punishment had to be
an exemplary one: Draft hundreds of students into the army! [. . .]

The government thinks it will teach the "rebels" discipline in this school.
But is it not mistaken in its calculations? Will not this school of Russian
military service become the military school of the Revolution? Not all the
students, of course, possess the stamina to go through the whole course of
training in this school. Some will break down under the heavy burden,
fall in combat with the military authorities; others—the feeble and flabby
—will be cowed into submission by the barracks. But there will be those
whom it will harden, whose outlook will be broadened, who will be compelled to ponder and profoundly sense their aspirations towards liberty.
They will experience the whole weight of tyranny and oppression on their
own backs when their human dignity will be at the mercy of a drill ser-
geant who very frequently takes deliberate delight in tormenting the
"educated." They will see with their own eyes what the position of the
common people is, their hearts will be rent by the scenes of tyranny and
violence they will be compelled to witness every day, and they will understand that the injustices and petty tyrannies from which the students suffer
are mere drops in the ocean of oppression the people are forced to suffer.
Those who will understand this will, on leaving military service, take a
Hannibal's vow to fight with the vanguard of the people for the emancipation of the entire people from despotism.

The humiliating character of this new punishment is no less outrageous
than its cruelty. In declaring the students who protested against lawless-

ness to be mere rowdies—even as it declared the exiled striking workers to be persons of depraved demeanour—the government has thrown down a challenge to all who still possess a sense of decency. Read the government communication. It bristles with such words as disorder, brawling, outrage, shamelessness, license. On the one hand, it speaks of criminal political aims and the desire for political protest; and on the other, it slanders the students as mere rowdies who must be disciplined. This is a slap in the face of Russian public opinion, whose sympathy for the students is very well known to the government. The only appropriate reply the students can make is to carry out the threat of the Kiev students, to organise a determined general student strike in all higher educational institutions in support of the demand for the repeal of the Provisional Regulations of July 29, 1899.

But it is not the students alone who must reply to the government. Through the government's own conduct the incident has become something much greater than a mere student affair. The government turns to public opinion as though to boast of the severity of the punishment it inflicts, as though to mock at all aspirations towards liberty. All conscious elements among all strata of the people must take up this challenge, if they do not desire to fall to the level of dumb slaves bearing their insults in silence. At the head of these conscious elements stand the advanced workers and the Social-Democratic organisations inseparably linked with them. The working class constantly suffers immeasurably greater injuries and insults from the police lawlessness with which the students have now come into such sharp conflict. The working class has already begun the struggle for its emancipation. It must remember that this great struggle imposes great obligations upon it, that it cannot emancipate itself without emancipating the whole people from despotism, that it is its duty first and foremost to respond to every political protest and render every support to that protest. The best representatives of our educated classes have proved —and sealed the proof with the blood of thousands of revolutionaries tortured to death by the government—their ability and readiness to shake from their feet the dust of bourgeois society and join the ranks of the socialists. The worker who can look on indifferently while the government sends troops against the student youth is unworthy of the name of socialist. The students came to the assistance of the workers—the workers must come to the aid of the students. The government wishes to deceive the people when it declares that an attempt at political protest is mere brawling. The workers must publicly declare and explain to the broad masses that this is a lie; that the real hotbed of violence, outrage, and license is the autocratic Russian Government, the tyranny of the police and the officials.

The manner in which this protest is to be organised must be decided by the local Social-Democratic organisations and workers' groups. The most practical forms of protest are the distribution, scattering, and posting up of leaflets, and the organisation of meetings to which as far as possible all classes of society should be invited. It would be desirable, however, where strong and well-established organisations exist, to attempt a broader and more open protest by means of a public demonstration. The demonstration organised last December 1, outside the premises of the newspaper *Yuzhny Krai* in Kharkov, may serve as a good example of such a protest. The jubilee of that filthy sheet, which baits everything that aspires to light and freedom and glorifies every bestiality of our government, was being cele-brated at the time. The large crowd assembled in front of *Yuzhny Krai,* solemnly tore up copies of the paper, tied them to the tails of horses, wrapped them round dogs, threw stones and stink-bombs containing sul-phuretted hydrogen at the windows, and shouted: "Down with the cor-rupt press!" Such celebrations are well deserved, not only by the corrupt newspapers, but by all our government offices. If they but rarely celebrate anniversaries of official benevolence, they constantly deserve the celebra-tion of the people's retribution. Every manifestation of governmental tyranny and violence is a legitimate motive for such a demonstration. The people must not let the government's announcement of its punishment of the students go unanswered!

YOUTH—"SEETHING" AND "INQUIRING"

From September 1, 1915 on there appeared a German-language paper in Switzer-land, the organ of the Socialist Youth International. Lenin commented on the paper in a review published at the end of 1916. The excerpt below marks one of the few places, perhaps the only place, where Lenin comments on the nature of youth, in-stead of simply seeing youth from the aspect of the class struggle. In the Soviet Union, much to the disadvantage of socialism, nothing of course has come of the "complete independence" of youth which Lenin demanded. Also interesting is Lenin's argument with Bukharin ("Comrade Nota-Bene"), during which he speaks out against the destruction of the state demanded by the anarchists and other radicals.

V. I. Lenin, "The Youth International," a Review, December 1916, in *Collected Works,* English translation of the 4th Russian ed. (Moscow, 1964, and London), XXIII, 164–166.

[. . .] Of course, the youth organ *still* lacks theoretical clarity and consistency. Perhaps it may never acquire them, precisely because it is the organ of seething, turbulent, inquiring youth. However, our attitude towards the lack of theoretical clarity on the part of *such* people must be entirely different from what our attitude is and should be towards the theoretical muddle in the heads, and the lack of revolutionary consistency in the hearts, of our "O.C.-ists," "Socialist-Revolutionaries," Tolstoyans, anarchists, the European Kautskyites ("Centre"), etc. Adults who lay claim to lead and teach the proletariat, but actually mislead it, are one thing: against such people a *ruthless* struggle must be waged. Organisations of *youth,* however, which openly declare that they are still learning, that their main task is to train party workers for the socialist parties, are quite another thing. Such people must be given every assistance. We must be patient with their faults and strive to correct them gradually, mainly by *persuasion,* and not by fighting them. The middle-aged and the aged often *do not know how* to approach the youth, for the youth must of necessity advance to socialism *in a different way, by other paths, in other forms, in other circumstances* than their fathers. Incidentally, that is why we must decidedly *favour organisational independence* of the Youth League, *not only* because the opportunists fear such independence, but because of the very nature of the case. For unless they have complete independence, the youth *will be unable* either to train good socialists from their midst or prepare themselves to lead socialism *forward.*

We stand for the complete independence of the Youth Leagues, but also for complete freedom of comradely criticism of their errors! We must not flatter the youth. [. . .]

On the question of the differences between socialists and anarchists in their attitude towards the state, Comrade Nota-Bene in his article [. . .] falls into a very serious error. [. . .] Socialists are in favour of utilising the present state and its institutions in the struggle for the emancipation of the working class, maintaining also that the state should be used for a specific form of transition from capitalism to socialism. This transitional form is the dictatorship of the proletariat, which is *also* a state.

The anarchists want to "abolish" the state, "blow it up" (*sprengen*) as Comrade Nota-Bene expresses it in one place, erroneously ascribing this view to the socialists. The socialists—unfortunately the author quotes Engels's relevant words rather incompletely—hold that the state will "wither away," will gradually "fall asleep" *after* the bourgeoisie has been expropriated. [. . .]

FREE LOVE—FREE OF WHAT?

Inessa Armand, a French devotee and associate of Lenin, informed him in the winter of 1914-15 of her plan to write a book on problems concerning women. Although at the time Lenin was almost entirely occupied by the question of Leftist parties' attitude to the world war, he devoted two letters to the project; he commented primarily on the question of free love. Inessa Armand never wrote the book. After her death of cholera in 1920 she was interred at the wall of the Kremlin.

V. I. Lenin, Letters "To Inessa Armand," January 1915, in *Collected Works,* English translation of the 4th Russian ed. (Moscow, 1966, and London), XXXV, 180–185.

[Berne, January 17, 1915]

Dear Friend,

I very much advise you to write the plan of the pamphlet in as much detail as possible. Otherwise too much is unclear.

One opinion I must express here and now:

I advise you to throw out altogether §3—the "demand (women's) for freedom of love."

That is not really a proletarian but a bourgeois demand.

After all, what do you understand by that phrase? What *can* be understood by it?

1. Freedom *from* material (financial) calculations in affairs of love?

2. The same, *from* material worries?

3. From religious prejudices?

4. From prohibitions by Papa, etc.?

5. From the prejudices of "society"?

6. From the narrow circumstances of one's environment (peasant or petty-bourgeois or bourgeois intellectual)?

7. From the fetters of the law, the courts and the police?

8. From the serious element in love?

9. From child-birth?

10. Freedom of adultery? Etc.

I have enumerated many shades (not all, of course). You have in mind, of course, not nos. 8–10, but either nos. 1–7 or something *similar* to nos. 1–7.

But then for nos. 1–7 you must choose a different wording, because freedom of love does not express this idea exactly.

And the public, the readers of the pamphlet, will *inevitably* understand by "freedom of love," in general, something like nos. 8–10, even *without your wishing it.*

Just because in modern society the most talkative, noisy and "top-prominent" classes understand by "freedom of love" nos. 8–10, just for that very reason this is not a proletarian but a bourgeois demand.

For the proletariat nos. 1–2 are the most important, and then nos. 1–7, and those, in fact, are not "freedom of love."

The thing is not what you *subjectively* "mean" by this. The thing is the *objective logic* of class relations in affairs of love.

Friendly shake hands!

W. I.

[Berne, January 24, 1915]

Dear Friend,

I apologise for my delay in replying: I wanted to do it yesterday, but was prevented, and I had not time to sit down and write.

As regards your plan for the pamphlet, my opinion was that "the demand for freedom of love" was unclear and—independently of your will and your wish (I emphasised this when I said that what mattered was the objective, class relations, and not your subjective wishes)—would, in present social conditions, turn out to be a bourgeois, not a proletarian demand.

You do not agree.

Very well. Let us look at the thing again.

In order to make the unclear clear, I enumerated approximately ten *possible* (and, in conditions of class discord, inevitable) different interpretations, and in doing so remarked that interpretations 1–7, in my opinion, would be typical or characteristic of proletarian women, and 8–10 of bourgeois women.

If you are to refute this, you have to show (1) that these interpretations are wrong (and then replace them by others, or indicate which are wrong), or (2) incomplete (then you should add those which are missing), or (3) are not divided into proletarian and bourgeois in that way.

You don't do either one, or the other, or the third.

You don't touch on points 1–7 at all. Does this mean that you admit them to be true (on the whole)? (What you write about the prostitution of proletarian women and their dependence: "impossibility of saying no" fully comes under points 1–7. No difference at all can be detected between us here.)

Nor do you deny that this is a *proletarian* interpretation.

There remain points 8–10.

These you "don't quite understand" and "object" to: "I don't understand how it is *possible*" (that is what you have written!) "to *identify*"
(!!??) "freedom of love with" point 10 . . .

So it appears *I* am "identifying", while you have undertaken to refute
and demolish *me?*

How so?

Bourgeois women understand by freedom of love points 8–10—that is
my thesis.

Do you deny this? Will you say what *bourgeois* ladies understand by
freedom of love?

You don't say that. Do not literature and life really *prove* that that is
just how bourgeois women understand it? They prove it completely! You
tacitly admit this.

And if that is so, the point is their class position, and it is hardly possible and almost naive to "refute" *them.*

What you must do is *separate* from them clearly, *contrast* with them,
the proletarian point of view. One must take into account the objective
fact that otherwise *they* will snatch the appropriate passages from your
pamphlet, interpret them in their own way, make your pamphlet into
water pouring on their mill, distort your ideas in the workers' eyes, *"confuse"* the workers (sowing in their minds the fear that *you* may be bringing them *alien* ideas). And in their hands are a host of newspapers, etc.

While you, completely forgetting the objective and class point of view,
go over to the "offensive" against *me,* as though I am "identifying" freedom of love with points 8–10 . . . Marvellous, really marvellous . . .

"Even a fleeting passion and intimacy" are "more poetic and cleaner"
than "kisses without love" of a (vulgar and shallow) married couple. That
is what you write. And that is what you intend to write in your pamphlet.
Very good.

Is the contrast logical? Kisses without love between a vulgar couple are
dirty. I agree. To them one should contrast . . . what? . . . One would
think: kisses *with* love? While you contrast them with "fleeting" (why
fleeting?) "passion" (why not love?)—so, logically, it turns out that kisses
without love (fleeting) are contrasted with kisses without love by married
people . . . Strange. For a popular pamphlet, would it not be better to
contrast philistine-intellectual-peasant (I think they're in my point 6 or
point 5) vulgar and dirty marriage without love to proletarian civil marriage with love (adding, *if you absolutely insist,* that fleeting intimacy and

passion, too, may be dirty and may be clean). What you have arrived at is, not the contrast of class *types,* but something like an "incident," which of course is possible. But is it a question of particular incidents? If you take the theme of an incident, an individual case of dirty kisses in marriage and pure ones in a fleeting intimacy, that is a theme to be worked out in a novel (because there the whole *essence* is in the *individual* circumstances, the analysis of the *characters* and psychology of *particular* types). But in a pamphlet? [. . .]

Have you not some French socialist friend? Translate my points 1–10 to her (as though it were from English), together with your remarks about "fleeting," etc., and watch her, listen to her as attentively as possible: a little experiment as to what *outside* people will say, what their impressions will be, what they will expect of the pamphlet.

I shake you by the hand, and wish you fewer headaches and to get better soon.

V. U.

ONLY THE PROLETARIAT . . .

In January 1917 Lenin gave a lecture before young workers in Zurich, on the lessons of the Russian revolution of 1905. In it he laid down the phases characterizing the Russian revolutionary movement: from the aristocracy over the bourgeoisie to the proletariat. In his eyes the students, meanwhile, had lost their position as the "vanguard of the democratic revolution."

V. I. Lenin, "Lecture on the 1905 Revolution," January 1917, in *Collected Works,* English translation of the 4th Russian ed. (Moscow, 1964, and London), XXIII, 242–245.

Russia witnessed the first revolutionary movement against tsarism in 1825, a movement represented almost exclusively by noblemen. Thereafter and up to 1881, when Alexander was assassinated by the terrorists, the movement was led by middle-class intellectuals. They displayed supreme self-sacrifice and astonished the whole world by the heroism of their terrorist methods of struggle. Their sacrifices were certainly not in vain. They doubtlessly contributed—directly or indirectly—to the subsequent revolutionary education of the Russian people. But they did not, and could not, achieve their immediate aim of generating a people's revolution.

That was achieved only by the revolutionary struggle of the proletariat. Only the waves of mass strikes that swept over the whole country, strikes connected with the severe lessons of the imperialist Russo-Japanese War, roused the broad masses of peasants from their lethargy. The word "striker" acquired an entirely new meaning among the peasants: it signified a rebel, a revolutionary, a term previously expressed by the word "student." But the "student" belonged to the middle class, to the "learned," to the "gentry," and was therefore alien to the people. The "striker," on the other hand, was of the people; he belonged to the exploited class. Deported from St. Petersburg, he often returned to the village. [. . .]

A comparison of these 1905 mutinies with the Decembrist uprising of 1825 is particularly interesting. In 1825 the leaders of the political movement were almost exclusively officers, and officers drawn from the nobility. They had become infected, through contact, with the democratic ideas of Europe during the Napoleonic wars. The mass of the soldiers, who at that time were still serfs, remained passive.

The history of 1905 presents a totally different picture. With few exceptions, the mood of the officers was either bourgeois-liberal, reformist, or frankly counter-revolutionary. The workers and peasants in military uniform were the soul of the mutinies. [. . .]

FOR II: OVERLOOKED (1960–1967)

FIRST HINT

In March 1967 an essay titled "The 'Open' Generation" appeared in Molodoy Kom-munist, the organ of the Communist Youth Organization of the USSR. It was the first essay in which a Soviet author dropped any hint of the New Left, although he did not refer to it by name. In a few paragraphs, reprinted below, the author men-tioned some characteristics of this youth, as well as the attention it had received among Western sociologists. His attitude was not unfriendly. For the rest, Reshetov concerned himself with refuting the Western explanation for youthful unrest, namely youth's "satiety."

P. Reshetov, " 'Otkrytoye' pokoleniye" [The "Open" Generation], *Molo-doy Kommunist*, 3 (1967), 18–22. Here pp. 18 ff.

A generation open to ideas, this is how the majority of sociologists and researchers in various nations characterizes the present generation of youth. Probably, scholars and thinkers one hundred or two hundred years ago, and perhaps throughout all history, spoke in the same way about the youth of their time. The problem of the "new generation" is a problem which has always attracted the attention of progressive thinkers and social and political figures.

This problem has risen again in a more acute form to confront modern society. The actions of young people against the foul aggression of the USA in Vietnam, the ever intensifying actions of young people in the capitalist nations for their political rights and for equal opportunities in factories and plants, student demonstrations against racial discrimination, peace marches throughout Europe, as well as appeals to public opinion in the West coming from all sorts of "beatniks" and "teddies," have pre-sented society with the task of reexamining its previous opinions of the younger generation ar.1 looking at these problems from a new position.

The theme of youth has once again assumed a leading role in the pro-

grams of research and propaganda and in the plans of those who materially and spiritually direct the entire propaganda machine of imperialism.
One is "beginning to write" about the younger generation, "studying" it
and "listening" to it. Radio and television programs are dedicated to it,
and the popular newspapers and journals, as well as the largest publishing
houses in the western world, devote their pages to it. Youth is being
"fawned upon," "questioned," talked to, and "flattered." Finally, attempts
are being made to organize it and make this into a business. In the majority of nations of the West, work with youth has become part of the
state's activities. It is planned within the framework of the state and
carried out by special organs. Ministries for the affairs of youth have been
created in a number of nations.

It is really interesting that a generation which, until quite recently, the
ideologists of imperialism considered "lost" and "indifferent," has aroused
such serious attention among politicians and sociologists, military leaders
and merchants, as well as the widest circles of society!

Expensive programs of sociological research on youth are being carried out in the majority of capitalist nations. 1966 was an especially fruitful year for these projects. Questionnaires were poring onto the heads
of young people in Japan, Australia, the USA, West Germany, and
France. [. . .]

To the surprise and concern of many in the West youth has become an
ever more active force, asking not only for its right to disagree, but demanding a right to active participation in the life of society. The opinion
of many psychologists is now unanimous: "Present-day youth is more sincere, more honest, more energetic, and more ambitious than preceding
generations."

The merchants of politics have not succeeded in keeping the interests
of the mass of young people tied to motor scooters and amusements. [. . .]

The ideologists of the West are also being increasingly disillusioned by
those youth who are not in the ranks of the Communist, democratic youth,
are not in the "armies of the Communists," to use the language of the
bourgeoisie, but who, to the great indignation of the latter, are also voicing
their protest. In America these are bearded youths from Greenwich Village in New York, as well as the so-called "hipsters" and "beatsters." In
Amsterdam they are the "Provos," calling for anarchism. In the West
German cities and in Paris they are the "black shirts" carrying out bandit-
type attacks. On the southern beaches of Europe they are the "modish"
young people who organize bloody battles, and in Italy, the "Sacceroni,"

putting the tourists to flight. In Sweden they are the "Raggare" against whom it is necessary to organize formal defenses, and so on. [. . .]

A BRIEF HISTORY

On the eve of events in Paris, MEiMO published a brief history of the American New Left: "The New Left Movement" by V. Churbanov. Excerpts are reprinted here. Its objective tone—in contrast, for example, with the document "The Three M's"—makes clear Moscow's unconcern at that time—before the eruption in Paris. With a sense of the foregone conclusion, the judgment was that the new movement would eventually merge with Communism of the Soviet variety; its deviating opinions were noted without anxiety. The word "left" was not even placed in quotation marks. For the reader who lacks detailed knowledge of the development of the New Left, the article provides a generally accurate summary. SDS, the radical-leftist American student organization, stands for "Students for a Democratic Society."

V. Churbanov, "Novoye levoye dvizheniye" [The New Left Movement], *Mirovaya Ekonomika i Mezhdunarodnyye Otnosheniya,* 1 (1968), 94 ff.

In recent years the social-political life of the United States of America has been characterized by a considerable activization of democratic forces speaking out against the internal and external policies of the government. One of the most notable features of this process is the entrance of a new, radically oriented generation of Americans into the arena of public life. This has formed the nucleus of a widespread democratic movement which has received the name "New Left Movement." The first of the new generation of American radicals appeared in the spring of 1960 in sit-in strikes, peace marches, and in protests against the House Un-American Activities Committee. In the years following, its activities increased sharply. The first large-scale protest demonstration against the aggression of the USA in Vietnam (more than 20,000 participated in it), which was held in Washington on April 17, 1965, indicated that the "New Left Movement" had been transformed into a significant political force which the government would have to take into consideration.

The "New Left Movement" includes young people and students as well as various representatives of the intelligentsia, trade unions, and religious groups. [. . .]

There are many reasons explaining why American young people are gradually being transformed from an inert mass into an active political force. Among them are the successes of socialism, entering the consciousness of young people as a result of the achievements of the USSR in the exploration of outer space, and the growth of the national liberation movement in the nations of Asia, Africa, and Latin America, which have had a major influence on the struggle of American Negroes.

The ultraconservative wing of the American press characterizes the "New Left Movement" as part of the "Communist conspiracy," while the liberal press considers it an isolated political phenomenon having nothing in common with the struggle of the "Old" Left forces which include, above all, Communists. One of the researchers of the movement, Jack Newfield, in his book *A Prophetic Minority,* considers it a revolution against the depersonalization of people, the growing totalitarianism of life in the USA, and the arch-reactionary essence of the military-industrial complex of the ruling elite.

The new political forces, growing on the basis of the democratic movements, have become left forces because in their domestic policies they advocate a radical social renewal of American society, and in foreign policy the renunciation of the export of counter-revolution and of the suppression of national liberation struggles, as well as the renunciation of the reactionary campaigns against the socialist states. [. . .]

The democratic movements now include diverse social elements and are under the influence of petty bourgeois ideology. Empiricism, anarchism, and sectarian views are widespread in their ranks and there is a definite prejudice against theory.

The ideas of Freudianism, existentialism, and so-called alienation have had a great influence on the "New Left Movement." As Jack Newfield wrote, "The new generation of American radicals was educated in the existential humanism of Albert Camus, the anti-colonialism of Frantz Fanon, the anarchism of Paul Goodman, and the poetic alienation of Bob Dylan." The word "alienation," which has recently become quite fashionable in the West, is not, of course, a synonym for the scientific theory developed by Hegel and given a materialistic explanation by Karl Marx. It is, rather, an emotional expression of the isolation of people and the despair and uncertainty so characteristic of contemporary America.

However, these ideas were not the only sources from which the New Left received views. Their convictions are, to a considerable extent, influenced by such figures and writers as C. Wright Mills, Michael Harrington, and Linus Pauling, who have sharply criticized the "social sores" of capitalism and the foreign policy of the USA, but who basically adhere to bourgeois viewpoints. Students and young people, not having, as a rule, sufficient theoretical training, are inclined to approach the problem of social inequality not from a class but from a moral-ethical position. This results in the attempt to work with the declassé elements of society, the poor people of the Negro ghetto, who are felt to be less exposed to the vices of American society. Thus, for example, at the beginnings of its activity the Student Non-Violent Coordinating Committee [SNCC] advocated an alliance of black and white declassé elements and placed its hopes precisely on them. [. . .]

SNCC, the basic force of the New Left, is an influential youth organization leading the struggle of Negro and white young people for civil rights. Its history began in February 1960, when four Negro students entered a café in Greensboro (North Carolina) and demanded service. Within two weeks students attempted to eliminate the race barrier in cafeterias, restaurants, and lunch counters in fifteen cities in five Southern states. During 1960 such demonstrations, the so called sit-ins, took place in one hundred cities. More than 50,000 whites and Negroes participated in them. [. . .]

SNCC actively opposes the Vietnamese war. At the time of the mass demonstrations in New York on April 16, 1967, in which about 400,000 people participated, the then chairman of SNCC, Stokely Carmichael, sharply condemned the shameful role of the USA in Vietnam. [. . .]

The second most significant participant in the "New Left Movement" is the organization "Students for a Democratic Society" (SDS). Prior to 1962, SDS was part of the right-liberal and strictly anti-Communist oriented "League For Industrial Democracy." At a conference in 1962, forty-three representatives from several dozen universities and colleges decided to set up an independent organization, and approved a manifesto which criticized the social inequality and injustice reigning in American society, as well as the foreign policy of the USA. [. . .]

By the end of October 1965, SDS had become the largest and most respected student group in the New Left. It was SDS that, in 1965, organized the first large march to Washington protesting the war in Vietnam. In the fall of the same year SDS came out against the drafting of students into the army and became an object of persecution by the Justice Department, the FBI, and Senate. [. . .] The social composition of the organization is diverse: students from higher educational institutions and colleges, teachers, "beatniks," and others. [. . .]

SDS has a clear prejudice against centralized organizations in general. This has been embodied in the program by the slogan "participatory democracy." The essence of this slogan is that it is only necessary to arouse the consciousness of the oppressed masses, not "imposing" any definite

ideas upon them, letting them decide what should be done. In the opinion
of the leader of SDS, "the workers should have their voice in the management of the plant, the students in the management of the universities, and
the poor in the development of their welfare programs." In order to avoid
leaderism [*liderstvo*] the constant rotation of leadership has been introduced and the "power" has been divided. As a result of this, the leadership
of the SDS has been divided between the National Council and the Chicago Steering Committee. [. . .]

The DuBois Clubs have a special position in the "New Left Movement."
This is a young peoples' socialist organization founded in San Francisco
in June 1964. Members of the organization state that they adhere to a
Marxist-Leninist philosophy, welcome a wide-ranging coalition of liberal
forces, speak out against violence, and stress the dangers of the ultra
right. [. . .]

The Communist Party of the USA supports the efforts of left leaders
directed at the consolidation of the movement and the development of
common platforms for various progressive organizations. However, as
Gus Hall, the General Secretary of the Communist Party, noted, the effective cooperation of left forces is hindered by the provocative ideas of some
of the ultra-left groups, and the practice of excluding Communists from
the movements, as well as disagreements with regard to the role of the
working class in general and to its revolutionary leadership in particular.

It is still difficult to determine how rapidly the New Left will succeed in
overcoming all difficulties and in uniting representatives of various social
strata and political tendencies. In the camp of the New Left there are still
disagreements on problems of the tactics of the electoral struggle. [. . .]

FOR III: THE SHOCK OF PARIS (1968)

THE THREE M'S

This article by Yuri Zhukov, one of the most respected Soviet journalists, was written during the last days of the Red May in Paris. It is a document of cold rage, a disgusted examination of the unhappy course of developments (in Moscow's view), and at the same time one of the most revealing documents on the subject of Moscow and the New Left.

Marcuse's Parisian lecture, occasioned by the 150th anniversary of the birth of Karl Marx (May 5, 1968), has since been published ("Re-Examination"). That the lecture coincided with the onset of events in Paris is pure chance; in contrast to the unrest it had, as Marcuse has told me, been planned for months.

At the time Zhukov could not know that 1968 would be the year of the "three P's" as well: Paris, Prague, and Peking. By chance, however, a report on the misdeeds of the Chinese Red Guards was printed directly next to his article.

Yuri Zhukov, "Oborotni" [Werewolves], *Pravda*, May 30, 1968, p. 4.

Marcuse, Marcuse, Marcuse. The name of this seventy-year-old German-American philosopher, who has stepped out of the darkness of unrecognition, is repeated endlessly by the Western press. In Bonn he is Markuze, in New York he is Markyuz, and in Paris, Markuz. This resident of California, accustomed to denouncing Marxism, is advertised like a movie star, and his books just like the latest brand of toothpaste or razor blades. Writers have even thought up a clever formula: "The Three M's"—"Marx = god, Marcuse his prophet, and Mao his sword."

"Well," say many readers, "has not Mao Tse-tung been considered worthy of such adulatory commercials in the bourgeois press?" Imagine, in front of me lies a pile of newspapers expressing the formula "Three M's" in various ways. This is no accident. Back in February of last year, a directive sent by the director of the United States Information Service (USIS) to all of its centers stated that workers of this service "should use all possibilities to strengthen the position of the followers of Mao," for the

145

United States desires that "Mao and his group stay in power" as long as
their activities are directed against the Communist Party of the Soviet
Union and other Communist parties. (This secret document was published on May 19 in the *Tribune*, a Ceylonese weekly.) However, let us
return to Marcuse.

The Dream of the "De-Communization" of Marxism

Recently this gentleman visited Paris. There he spoke at a UNESCO col-
loquium dedicated to the 150th anniversary of the birth of Marx. His report was entitled "The Revision of the Marxist Concept of Revolution."
However, it was really not even a revision of Marxism but an attempt to
refute it. Pitiful and inconsistent, but nevertheless an attempt. As the newspapers reported, Marcuse stated that at the present time the "working
class, having integrated itself (?!) into the capitalist system, can no longer
play the revolutionary role which Marx had intended for it. The power
of capital can, consequently, be overthrown only by forces located outside
the system: people of the colonies, Negroes or young people, still not integrated in the system."

As one would expect, the philosophers-Marxists participating in the col-
loquium gave this false prophet the refutation he deserved. Some were
amazed: Why did Marcuse say that the working class "could no longer
play a revolutionary role" at the very moment when in the capitalist
world, and in particular in France where he spoke, the wave of an acute
class struggle was breaking so highly? However, the more far-sighted
people understood: Marcuse was catapulted from far-off San Diego to
Paris just for this reason. It was necessary to put into use all means in
order to attempt to interfere and bring chaos into the ranks of those
struggling against the old order, and—mainly!—to attempt to put young
people, especially students, in opposition to the basic force of the working
class.

There was thus a good reason why, at this time, the *New York Times*
invented a new term, "THE DE-COMMUNIZATION (!) OF MARXISM." There
was also a reason why, with clear sympathy for the Paris students of Marcuse, it wrote that their flag "IS THE BLACK FLAG OF ANARCHY, AND NOT THE
RED FLAG OF COMMUNISM."

The Paris newspapers *Figaro, Le Monde*, the weeklies *L'Express* and
Nouvel Observateur, published during these days extensive interviews
with Marcuse, his biography. (A significant biographical detail: during

the war Marcuse worked for the American Intelligence, and later he spent many years in the well-known Russian Institute at Harvard. The result of this activity was the anti-Soviet book *Soviet Marxism,* Marcuse's "first best seller.") They also published detailed summaries of his books, stressing that in the 1920's, living in Germany, he renounced "communism and social democracy" and that later, already in the USA, he created his own "teachings" intended for young people who were "without a compass." [. . .] What is the essence of this "teaching?" [. . .]

It is characteristic that his "interpretation of the prophetic illumination for the unenlightened" has much in common with the praxis of the Mao Tse-tung group. And what is significant to an even greater degree is that although these [Maoist] groups are not niggardly with their insults directed against the imperialists, the governments of the capitalist states are very tolerant about the spread of their ideas. This holds equally with respect to the activity of Marcuse and his noisy youngsters. Recently, in a lead article in the *New York Times,* Sulzberger talked about this theme with the chancellor of the Federal Republic of Germany, Kiesinger. Sulzberger soothed him and explained that the activities of Marcuse's followers "had nothing to do with Soviet Communism" and that "they have their own gods."

Kiesinger stated that these people are drawn by the Maoist idea that in our age wars will take place in the underdeveloped "Third World" . . . This, he said, makes an emotional impression on the students of Marcuse "SINCE IT PRESENTS NO DIRECT THREAT TO THEM!" Let the war take place there while we argue here, so feel these R-R-Revolutionaries.

Attacks on the Working Class

The bourgeois ideologists understand that during the serious sharpening of the class struggle their old theories of "people's capitalism," "convergence" (the gradual converging of the two opposed systems) do not have the power to influence the fighting proletariat. Consequently, the "ultra-left," anarchist slogans are released, very frequently, saturated with the ideas of Mao Tse-tung. With their help it is attempted to spread confusion, to lead astray the impetuous but politically uneducated young people, split them up, and to convert those with whom this succeeds into blind tools of the provocateurs.

Marcuse is not alone. In the FRG [Federal Republic of Germany] there are people who speak along his lines, saying that the West German working class cannot be revolutionary as long as, together with the bourgeois, it "participates in the exploitation of the Third World." In Italy the socialist delegate Codignola supports the thesis of Marcuse on the necessity of an "uprising" against the "industrial society in general" since, and he explained this to a correspondent of *L'Express,* "the present society, whether it is capitalist or socialist, is becoming more and more like an industrial enterprise."

However, quite similar to the demonstrations which are now being called by the Peking leaders to support, apparently, the struggle of the French workers for their rights, but in which the main blow is being directed against the French Communist Party and the USSR, the noisy followers of Marcuse in West Europe use their little fists to threaten the working class and the Communists.

This same goal is served by the turbid arguments of Marcuse and his students on the struggle *against "industrial civilization" in general,* without any distinction as to whether this refers to capitalist or socialist order. At the Sorbonne followers of Marcuse announced this "programmatic declaration":

"The beginning revolution questions not only capitalist society but industrial civilization in general. The consumer society should die a violent death. The society of alienation (!) also should die a violent death. We want a new and original society. We reject a society in which the certainty that you will not starve to death is exchanged for the risk of dying of boredom." [. . .]

In this struggle the working class is striving for the creation of a united front with the intelligentsia in spite of the attempts of reactionaries, using any means in their interest, including the most refined provocative methods. [. . .]

Whom Do These "Insurgents" Serve?

The bourgeois press is now using bright colors to depict the "tricks" of a certain 23-year-old from the FRG: Cohn-Bendit, who until recently studied at the University in Paris and there engaged in divisive activities among the student body. When journalists asked him how he made a living, Cohn-Bendit answered: "I obtain a stipend from the German [West German] state as an orphan." He is now on tour in Western Europe calling for a "bloody (!) revolution."

On May 8 the weekly *Nouvel Observateur* published an interview with this "insurgent." He bragged that his friends disrupted the speech of the Communist deputy Pierre Juquin to the students and called out, *"Beat the chaps from the Communist Party."* "At present," he boasted, "only the students (!) are carrying on the revolutionary struggle of the working class. The worker, being the head of a family, does not want (?) to fight."

When, however, the French working class on May 13 organized a million-person demonstration in support of the legitimate demands of the students for a democratic reform of the university, this very same Cohn-Bendit with a handful of his followers—Trotskyites, anarchists, and "Maoists"—vainly attempted to confuse and divide the ranks of the demonstrators, hurling out the provocative slogan, "Let's storm the Elysée Palace!"

Speaking on May 27 to workers at the Renault automobile plant, Benoit Franchon described the unseemly role which the US Central Intelligence Agency and the French underground terrorist organization OAS tried to play in the events involving the French students. He added: "Now the whole gang of them are only concerned to see that it 'boils.' They praise in every manner the enthusiasm of young people, but really are preparing to ensnare and confuse us."

Recently two of his countrymen came to the help of Cohn-Bendit in Paris. They spoke at student meetings. The newspaper *Combat* helpfully published an interview with them, hiding their names behind the initials "J. S." and "P. B." This interview was quite frank. "P. B." stated that "throughout the entire history of the FRG the working class there has identified with the bourgeois system" and that "among you" in France the workers "also are doing nothing." While "J. S." added that "the working class is satisfied (?!) to such an extent that it cannot criticize the existing system."

Here the correspondent asked: "And is there consciousness among the students themselves?" "P. B." answered: "Yes, because they are among the privileged (!) groups. Revolutionary subjects are discussed in privileged groups, including the so called Marcuse groups."

Their Calculations

Blasphemously using the name of Marx, the werewolves are attempting to undertake a "de-communization of Marxism" to divide and bring internal quarreling to progressive forces, and thus carry out the quite explicit social imperatives of the enemies of the working movement, who are seriously concerned about the intensification of the class struggle in their nations. This struggle is led by the working class, which, as *L'Humanité* stresses, is "powerful and organized and knows where it is going. It is the decisive force and is, in the final account, the sole revolutionary class since it has nothing to lose but its chains."

The leading force has been, is, and always will be the Communists, drawing their force from the great teachings of Marx and Lenin. And no matter how much unrequested "advisors" from the *New York Times* now prophesy the "de-communization of Marxism," no matter how much the bourgeois press advertises the reflections of Marcuse and the activities of his students, the plans of the enemies of the working class will fail.

This, in particular, is convincingly demonstrated by the development of events in France. *"In France there cannot be left policy and social progress without the active participation of communists,"* said Waldeck Rochet, the General Secretary of the French Communist Party on March 28. *"It is all the more impossible to claim seriously to move towards socialism without the communists."* [. . .]

THE PROLETARIAT MUST LEAD!

On the eve of the events in France in May 1968, the major party organ of the Soviet Union, Kommunist, *carried a leading article. To counter Western students' demands for a leadership role, if not the leadership itself, the article employed outworn arguments and an old quotation from Marx. The following paragraphs convey the antiquated argumentation.*

Editorial, "Rabochiy klass: vedushchaya sila za sotsializm i kommunizm" [The Working Class: The Leading Force in the Struggle for Socialism and Communism], *Kommunist,* 8 (1968), 3–12. Here pp. 10–12, released to press May 31, 1968.

Marxist-Leninists are decisively opposed to any attempt to undermine the leading role of the working class and its Communist Party, against any revisions of Marxism-Leninism, and against any attacks on socialism.

Marxists-Leninists struggle for the purity of Marxism-Leninism, which is not a national but an international teaching. They, as the true spokesmen of the interests of the working class and socialism, will not permit anyone to deprecate the significance and role of this class, moving at the forefront of human progress.

The leading role of the working class is never based on some sort of exclusive privileges or rights obtained at the expense of other classes and strata of society, but always on its moral and political authority. To be the leading force in the revolution and in the construction of socialism and Communism is not only a right but also a responsible duty of the working class, arising from the very position of this class in society and from its honorable task and goal of the revolutionary transformation of society.

The leading role of the working class in all spheres of socialist society is determined by the leading position of socialist industry and by the socialist public ownership of means of production. Just as socialist industry unifies all sectors of the national economy into a single economic organism, the working class, linked to this industry, unifies and consolidates all social strata and groups of our society and leads them. [. . .]

The revolutionary struggle of the working class is spreading in the capitalist world. The imperialist bourgeoisie is striving with all its force to maintain its rule and to delay the world revolutionary process. It is attempting to direct the main blows against the worker and Communist movement.

The ideologists of the bourgeoisie, the leaders of the right-wing social democracy, and the revisionists of all shades are furiously attacking Marxist-Leninist teachings on the revolutionary role of the working class, trying to belittle its significance in every way possible, and striving to make it lose its faith in its power. They are directing their basic efforts in order to show that under contemporary conditions exploitation does not exist in the capitalist nations, and that the so-called revolution in incomes opens the possibility for every worker to become a capitalist. The ideological opponents of the proletariat are speaking in every way possible about the "deproletarization," that the concepts of "class" and "class struggle" have long become obsolete, that the relationship between the bourgeoisie and the proletariat is based not on the principle of the class struggle but on the principle of social partnership and cooperation.

All these false theories have been refuted by life. The facts indicate that in the capitalist nations exploitation has not only not disappeared but has intensified. Contemporary capitalist reality is increasingly affirming the correctness of the Marxist-Leninist analysis of the situation of the working class under capitalism and its revolutionary potential. The working class, linked to large-scale industry, is not being "deproletarized," it is constantly growing in number. In the capitalist nations it amounts to over 350 million workers. It is developing as a social force to an extent similar to the development of modern industry. In all the capitalist nations it has now become more obvious that the working class is the main productive force and, as Marx stated; "makes up the basic backbone of the entire people." [. . .]

The working class and all workers in the capitalist nations are opposed by monopoly capital, which is based on the state apparatus. Under these conditions there is a real possibility of uniting around the working class all social groups being exploited by capital—this amounts to 80–90 percent, the overwhelming majority of the population of the developed capitalist nations—into a joint struggle against monopoly rule. [. . .]

The working class is the most numerous and best organized class in the capitalist world. Its most important assets are the militant Marxist-Leninist parties, the international solidarity of which serves as an important source for the strength of the proletariat. In its struggle, the proletariat of the capitalist nations is based on the success of the world's socialist system and has a reliable and powerful ally in the national liberation struggles of the peoples of Africa, Asia, and Latin America. [. . .]

FOR IV: A PORTRAIT CHANGES (1969–1972)

THE STUDENTS ARE MORE COMPLICATED

At the end of 1969 appeared the essay of a younger Soviet author, A. Brychkov; it presented, for the first time, a more differentiated picture of Western students. The author saw the reasons for the development of the New Left not only in student protests against their economic situation, restrictions as to their studies, and decreasing career opportunities, but especially in their personal alienation (otchuzhdennost', sometimes rendered "alienatsiya" by translation of English "alienation"). The author also recognized that the alienation of the students differed qualitatively from that of the workers, with which Marx concerned himself above all.

A. Brychkov, "Ot bunta k bor'be . . ." [From Unrest to Struggle . . .], *Molodoy Kommunist*, 12 (1969) 44–50. Here pp. 48 ff.

Students [in the West] are entering the democratic struggle under special conditions. Making up a numerically sizable and ever increasing group of the population they are nevertheless not a separate, special class. Consequently, the mass of students taken as a whole has no economic, social, political, or even professional interests in common.

Students do not yet directly participate in the production process. Although an ever greater number of students must combine study with work and are subject to various forms of capitalist exploitation, to a considerable degree it is rather abstract to them. However, students are beginning to perceive the real contours of the situation which they must face after finishing higher educations. In addition, while still in the university they can really feel some aspects of their future situation. This, above all, applies to the indifferent attitude towards students on the part of society, which does not wish to solve the problems of the university, the subordination of the educational process to the narrow interests of monopolies, the restricted freedom of the individual, and the possibilities for creative individual development . . . Students have become conscious of their own type of alienation and uselessness to society, to which they personally

153

would like to be of use. Consequently, they are striving to find a way of overcoming this type of alienation. Initially many representatives of the radical student movement placed their basic stake in the alienated individual and not the exploited class. Don Hammerquist noted in the journal *Political Affairs* that, as a rule, this is not "the alienated individual in the Marxist understanding, whose alienation arises from the nature of the labor process under capitalism." Rather, it was closer to an existential understanding of the alienated individual as an individual "isolated," "alone," doomed to an absolute individual responsibility for his actions, but defenseless in his absurd struggle with the forces oppressing him.

There is good reason why the existentialism of Sartre occupied and continues to occupy an important role in a number of concepts popular in the radically-oriented student movement.

An understanding of the problem of alienation, even in an existentialist sense, leads to reflection on the injustice of a system which has no room for the individual, and on the necessity of its destruction and replacement by something new. Radical students initially attempt to develop their original, hitherto unknown model of a social system. Nothing results from this other than an eclectic conglomeration of the various conceptions of utopians, populists, ideologists of the French Revolution, of existentialism, etc. The natural way out of this blind alley can only be found in the theory of scientific socialism. It is just to this theory that larger and larger numbers of representatives of the radically-oriented student movement are turning as the obstacles of anti-Communism are overcome. However, coming from the middle stratum of society, from the petty bourgeoisie, from the situation of the "alienated individual," they are not in a position to immediately master the theory of scientific socialism. Their interests mainly turn to one facet of the problem, the unlimited potential which socialism opens for the development of the individual, democracy, and freedom. They initially totally reject the problems of the class struggle, socialist revolution, and dictatorship of the proletariat, which are linked to the struggle for the victory of socialism. This is the reason for the suspicious attitude towards Communist parties on the part of various student representatives who have joined the democratic movement.

OUT INTO THE ARENA!

It may be that the Session of the Presidium of the Academy of Sciences, which took place in Moscow at the end of February 1969, established the outlines for a more

intensive and less narrow discussion of the New Left. If this assumption is correct,
no doubt the talk given at the session by the great Russian physicist Pyotr L. Kapitsa
contributed to the decision. Part of a synopsis of his words follows; it concerns the
New Left and intellectual debate with that Left. (Emphasis added)

M. P. Gapochka, "Obsuzhdeniye na Prezidiume AN SSSR zadach i perspektiv raboty zhurnala *Voprosy filosofii*" [Discussion in the Presidium of
the USSR Academy of Sciences of Tasks and Prospects for the Work of
the Journal *Voprosy filosofii*], *Voprosy filosofii,* 5 (1969), 146–152. Here pp.
147 ff.

It is well known that in recent years in the capitalist nations a revolutionary movement of a mass nature has grown up, especially among youth.
This movement encompasses all the most developed capitalist nations, it
is growing, and its leaders are students. The forces causing this movement
are still not completely understood. However, it has already been established that it was not caused by dissatisfaction with people's material conditions in society. It is directed at changing those ideological conditions
under which people must live in a capitalist society. Thus, the progressive
public in the capitalist nations has, without outside influence, spontaneously raised the question of reexamining the ideology on which capitalist
society is based.

Along what lines is this reexamination going? Who has created the
program of reconstruction which the progressive part of society will accept and which will properly lead it towards human progress? Obviously,
this will be solved in the process of the ideological struggle between
various world views, which has now already begun and is rapidly expand-
ing.

Should we openly engage in this struggle? What should our role be in
it? Undoubtedly the ideas and principles which lie at the basis of the
development of Communist society, as they were given by Marxism, are
the sole ideas which can direct this struggle in the proper direction. This
is now acknowledged by the entire progressive part of humanity. The
search is now underway for concrete methods for the most effective development of this revolutionary movement. These searches are conducted
in the process of the struggles between ideologists of the new formation,
such as, for example, Marcuse. The struggle also includes Trotskyites and
others.

One should not be afraid to admit that at *present our ideologists are*
standing isolated from this revolutionary process and are having no prac-

tical influence. This is not normal. It contradicts the fact that the success-ful existence of our socialist society itself, as an example, cannot help but influence this revolutionary movement.

How can we most effectively engage in these revolutionary processes taking place in capitalist society? In order not to lag behind the develop-ment of progressive thought and to take into consideration the conse-quences of the scientific-technical revolution taking place in the world, we must now raise the standards of our social sciences. Therefore, we in the Academy of Sciences must highly approve of the efforts of the editorial board of the journal *Problems of Philosophy* (*Voprosy Filosofii*) to pro-mote the development of philosophy. One of the basic goals of this effort is to influence the development of social thought now taking place in the revolutionary movement in the capitalist nations.

In order to have such an influence we must more actively engage in the ideological struggle taking place there. In this struggle our philosophers must operate under conditions similar to those of our sportsmen. One must note that our ideologists will lose the privilege which they have in our nation, where they do not have to encounter opposing views. In the forthcoming struggle this will not occur. [. . .] Therefore, I suggest that the Presidium of the Academy of Sciences of the USSR support the pro-gram advanced by the new editorial board of the journal *Problems of Philosophy,* since it has given the journal the task of increasing its inter-national influence. Furthermore, the Presidium of the Academy of Sciences should give more time to the examination of philosophical problems con-cerning the ideological basis of socialist society. *Today in the Presidium this subject is practically absent from our learned papers.* This must be changed.

FOR V: READING THROUGH THE KEYHOLE

GREEN GROW THE REICHS . . .

Charles Reich's The Greening of America, *the 1970 American bestseller, made a strong impression in the Soviet Union. Pages of the book were quoted verbatim, among others in a mass periodical like* Literaturnaya Gazeta. *No doubt Reich's espousal of Utopia strongly attracts and fascinates the Soviet intelligentsia: his vision of a lovelier world of harmony and love, of victory over the rule of a too-powerful apparatus through a "higher consciousness," of a subsequent flowering of American culture (why only American culture, the Soviet intellectual might ask). But at the same time Reich's sins must be discovered and unmasked. Below, an example from the most detailed review of the book.* Bellamy's Looking Backward *appeared in 1888, and Henry George's* Poverty and Progress *in 1879.*

Ye. Arab-Ogly, "Molodezh i budushcheye Ameriki" [Youth and the Future of America], *Mirovaya Ekonomika i Mezhdunarodnyye Otnosheniya,* 10 (1971), 120–130.

The new generation in his [i.e. Reich's] opinion is a broad, stable social category, for its main characteristic is not age but above all a definite type of consciousness, common views of the world, and a unified style of life and culture. As a result of its inherent honesty and rejection of any type of violence against the individual, youth is the social medium which has given impetus to the "revolutionization" of the consciousness of wide strata of the American people, to their comprehension of the threat to human values and thus has helped in a formation of a definite social community. It is young people, "being guided more by intuition than by reason," who are breaking the path towards the transformation of America towards "a revolution through consciousness." Reich feels that the youth movement in its initial form was born of the "biological necessity" of self-preservation. However, cultivating the new life style, it moved beyond the framework of sectarianism and took the form of a "logical, purposeful movement to save humanity." It thus became the "sole means for sav-ing America itself."

By its life style, feelings, and even its exterior appearance the young generation is demonstrating a "sincere" consciousness, rejecting the in-human capitalist reality, assisting in liberating from "false" consciousness not only mány Americans from the lower strata but also creating a definite split in the ruling, highly-educated elite. [. . .]

In his description of contemporary American reality as a "corporate society," Reich is essentially repeating many of the propositions of left-radical critics. However, in describing the social political crisis in America, Reich exhibits greater objectivity. Frequently his model of "corporate society" quite clearly has the features of state monopoly capitalism and his critique is, to a great extent, similar to that made by Marxists.

At the same time, in contrast to the bourgeois left radicalism, his views are permeated by a spirit of optimism. He seeks the factors and forces of a transformation of American society. For him it is not the importance of the recognition of the fact of "total" subjugation that is important, rather the understanding of the mechanisms of the subjugation and the libera-tion from its power. He views the sharp leap in the consciousness of the masses as an omen of the fall of the "corporate society." [. . .]

Reich feels that youth is the most active social force capable of decisive action against the "corporate and consumer society." Encountering the cynicism and hypocrisy of their fathers, young people break traditional ties with the family and are ever more oriented towards their own cul-ture and life style, rejecting material success and calling for the resto-ration of "naturalness" in life, etc. The bonds of this "brotherhood" can become all the stronger the more society and the older generation reject youth. [. . .]

The book gives a major role to students in the implementation of this program. Upon finishing the university, they enter organizations and in the process of their labor activities strive to put the "new consciousness" into practice. Organizations, depending on students as qualified specialists, cannot effectively resist the introduction of the "new life style." What is more, they themselves will be forced to change. For Reich the life style goes beyond the framework of that individual problem, it becomes a socially and politically significant process.

Reich does not fear the possibilities of intensified repression and the fascistization of America. He quickly assures young people that they should not fear any sort of violence. First, young people are not struggling for power but for the minds of people, and second, their efforts lead to the elimination of war, hate, and civil strife. However, if repression is unavoidable then it, in his opinion, will be only useful; after all, "blood frequently is more convincing to people than ideology." Reich warns youth against the dangers of becoming "contemporary Luddites," and admonishes them not to destroy technology but to make its utilization more humane. In addition, he feels that in the new society technology will take on the task of material support for humanity, while people themselves will be involved in the development of the aesthetic and spiritual facets of their nature. For him the task of moral perfection, being the core of his model of "revolution," consists of the spiritual and aesthetic development of humanity and the development of a new feeling about the world on this basis. These shoots of the "new humanity," he writes, have already broken through the asphalt of the "corporate society" and announced the transformation of America into a "blossoming garden." [. . .]

Noting that the "maintenance of the status-quo is the most illusory of goals," he expresses confidence that in the somewhat distant future America will experience a further revolution in views and a renewal in the motives of individual behavior which will result in Utopian thinking. The externally oriented, [warped] individual of the "consumer society" will be replaced by the autonomous individual seeing the essence of life in the total development of his human qualities. [. . .]

Strictly speaking *Molodaya Amerika* is chiefly an Utopian work, not only in an objective sense but also rather by the intention of the author himself. [. . .]

That is why the stereotyped reproaches against Utopianism addressed to Reich by numerous reviewers miss their mark. Such a reproach, which is deadly to a public figure striving to appear as a realist and pragmatist, is not effective when directed against a person who consciously strives to be an Utopian. Of course, the intentional Utopianism of Reich is disguised in contemporary form. He does seek his Utopia in distant lands or on other planets, but in the consciousness of the people surrounding him, that is, no matter how paradoxical it may sound, in the very place of its location. Many pages of his book have their own sort of "parallel" with respect to the books of Edward Bellamy—*Looking Backward* and especially *Equality* —although they are written in the language of contemporary sociology. This comparison with Bellamy is a compliment to Reich, for the gifted American Utopianist of the end of the last century was incomparably more perceptive with respect to the future United States than the professional sociologists, economists, and jurists of his time.

Utopianism, however, is by no means a criterion of the truth of a judgment. Even when it is intentional this does not save it from criticism. Reich's concepts have many vulnerable spots. However, it would be incorrect to reject all his propositions on this basis. [. . .]

The critique of Utopian works consequently requires somewhat different criteria and evaluations than the critique of academic "positive" literary products. Utopian thought rests on methodological principles differing from those of social research. It is therefore absurd to reproach an Utopian author for the violation of academic canons, for the unrepresentative nature of his generalizations and his arbitrary conclusions. The characteristic feature of Utopias is not so much the unreality of their stated purposes and social ideas (although this is frequently the case) as their unattainability in practice with the help of those methods which have been recommended by their authors, and the political naïveté of the latter. As far as the Utopians' ideals themselves are concerned, many of them have been realized in the course of history, although by other methods than were suggested.

Under contemporary conditions the objective significance of an Utopia is not determined by the good intentions of its author but by whether or not the ideas of social justice formulated in it are really progressive and by whether or not, in the concrete historical situation, it promotes or hinders the practical achievement of these ideals. If, guided by these criteria, we turn now to *The Greening of America* of Reich, we see that the social ideas he has advanced are basically borrowed from Marxism, although they are burdened with the heavy freight of abstract humanism and petty-bourgeois radicalism. [. . .]

Reich is naturally no Marxist and does not pretend to be. However, with respect to a whole series of problems he stands closer to the young Marx than a number of petty-bourgeois radicals in the United States attempting to present themselves as Marxists.

Throughout the entire book Reich carries out a lightly veiled polemic with the views of John Galbraith and Herbert Marcuse, two ideologists of the American intelligentsia who have taken a stance in opposition to the "establishment" [the Soviet authors use the English word]. Reich's conventional compliments to them are simply a tactical method whereby the author hoped to make his concepts more acceptable to university circles, where both these authors enjoy great authority and have numerous followers. Naturally, neither of them were fooled by this. Galbraith and Marcuse were the first to appear in the press with formally restrained but unambivalent criticisms of Reich's concepts. [. . .]

Reich rejects the alternatives adhered to by many of the "New Left" in the U.S.A.—either armed struggle or capitulation. Calling for an armed struggle against the "corporate society" in the present situation is felt by Reich to be a bombastic, pseudo-revolutionary phrase intended to justify the refusal to search for other, effective forms of struggle. Those who put forth such perspectives, he notes, also reject them and come to pessimistic conclusions. The radicalism of the Marcusians, consequently, is directly proportional to their social pessimism and serves primarily as a plausible justification for them, Reich ironically concludes. They call their followers into the struggle not for the sake of victory, but to soothe their own consciousness along existential lines. It is no accident that the most consistent champions of such views finally end up being prepared to look for the model of the future revolution in China, Africa, and in Latin America; in short, anywhere they want, but not in their own nation. Thus, Reich considers both the "realism" of Galbraith and the "radicalism" of Marcuse as Utopian.[. . .]

Reich states that the future of America will not be solved in the universities although it germinated there. "The youth movement in itself cannot attain much on the road to political and structural changes." The hope of "Consciousness III" for social solidarity will be buried if workers and people of the older generation turn out to be opposed to it. Then there will be polarization which will lead to violence, repression, and perhaps even to the establishment of fascism for a time. "Consciousness III can either go beyond the limits of youth or will betray its expectations," writes Reich. However, the content of this consciousness appeals not only to youth. It reflects the deep, although not completely recognized interests of very wide strata of the population. Not only Negroes but also whites, not only students but also workers, are dissatisfied with their social position.[. . .]

No matter how dubious *Young America's* initial proposition on revolution through consciousness may seem at first view, it does contain a definite rational core.

The revolutionary shifts in the world view of people and in social values, of course, are not arbitrary. Reich thoroughly shows how they are determined by the social crisis of "corporate society," objective contradictions in "consumer society," and finally, the demands of the technological revolution. Reich's error, consequently, does not so much consist in the exaggeration of the role of consciousness, although this is the case, as much as it does in his reduction of the formation of revolutionary consciousness to a spontaneous process. This reduces the role of theoretical thought and political organization in the preparation and implementation of radical social transformations. Beginning at this point Reich, the realist, finally leaves the stage to Reich, the Utopian.

Reich's inconsistency and social narrowness is also shown by the fact that in his analysis the "corporate society" acquires the character of an impersonal mechanism, while in reality it reflects the class interests of the reactionary monopolistic bourgeoisie. Therefore, a consistent struggle against this system assumes a struggle against the class personifying it, and against its representatives. The principle difference between the Marxists and Reich shows itself just at this point. [. . .]

Revealing the bankruptcy of limited reforms for the transformation of a society to one based on social justice, Reich essentially opposes bourgeois liberal reformism not with social revolution, but with a unique ideological reformation, the nature and assumed historical consequences of which are similar to the expansion of Christianity during the transition from antiquity to feudalism and to the Protestant movement in the period of the rise of capitalism. This reformation, which is called upon to bring "Consciousness III" into life, will, in Reich's opinion, make political violence unnecessary and will lead to the assertions of new social values and new social relationships, thanks to the moral rejuvenation and spiritual rebirth of humanity. Both the oppressed and the privileged strata of the "corporate society" will be equally interested in this.

Obviously, historical analogies should not be taken literally. In *Young America* the discussion is not simply about the replacement of one religious world view by another. In our century such a call would be viewed as a flagrant anachronism. While in their time Huss and Luther, Calvin and Zwingli could venture, as Marx stated ironically, to wrap themselves in the clothes of Old Testament prophets, in the middle of the 20th century this would obviously not work in the case of Reich. Therefore, in his Sermons on the Mount to Americans he is ultra-modern, in jeans and a suede jacket. However, one should recall that Protestantism can in no way be simply reduced to the rebirth of early Christianity. It brought new social values into our world, a new ethic, the belief in the earthly predestination of man, in the unique value of the individual, and, as a result, in the principle of "natural law" without which capitalism would be unthinkable. It is just for these reasons that "Consciousness III," as well as the "counter culture" accompanying it, appear as a completely worldly version of a spiritual reformation, of a moral and ideological renewal of society, as the replacement of decaying social values and norms of behavior inherent in capitalism with others, responding, as Reich states, to a new historical epoch.

Several critical comments could be made with respect to this conception, stated in the first pages of the book. Any new social-economic formation is not only based on technological means of production and definite social relations specific to it, but also assumes a new complex of social values and moral norms of behavior as well as a new world view in general. These differing spheres of social behavior undoubtedly develop in a relatively independent manner. Transformations in technology can precede the consolidation of a new social order, as was the case with the industrial revolution in Germany, or they can follow it, as was the case in England. The Reformation could also have anticipated and completed the victory of capitalist relations in a unique historical form. However, the irrefutable historical fact remains that capitalism was consolidated in England, the Netherlands, and in the USA only after a bourgeois-democratic political revolution. Where such revolutions did not occur, or where they were suppressed, for example in Germany and in the Scandinavian nations, religious reformation coexisted for centuries with feudal relationships. This fact topples Reich's key proposition about the possibility of burying the "corporate society" by the conversion of the population to "Consciousness III" without turning to revolutionary violence in any form. [. . .]

The unique historical situation in the USA lies in the fact that in spite of wide-spread dissatisfaction, the majority of Americans are still prepared to carry on in the old way, while the ruling class is in no condition to govern as before. The swift course of events both inside and outside of the nation has clearly gotten out of its control. It cannot deal with the social results of the scientific-technical revolution, harness inflation, slow down the growth in crime, and curtail the use of drugs. In short, it cannot put order into its own house.

In the unique historical situation in the United States, Reich's ideas appear not only very attractive to democratically-inclined Americans, but also relatively progressive in comparison with the numerous competing liberal, reformist, and radical doctrines found among the intelligentsia and student youth, Negroes and other minorities. In comparison with the views of the "New Lefts" it has obvious advantages. It refutes Luddite inclinations, condemns technophobia and links the prospects of a liberating, democratic movement in the USA with the further course of the scientific-technical revolution. The main advantage of Reich's ideas is that they destroy the voluntary ideological ghetto in which the sectarian representatives of the "New Lefts" have attempted to incarcerate their followers. Generalizing the spontaneous dissatisfaction with state monopoly capitalism, Reich puts the views of the "New Lefts" in a form which makes the radical goals and social ideals of this movement incomparably more acceptable to the majority of the American people, who are striving to throw off the yoke of the state monopoly oligarchy.

In a short time Reich has gathered more followers in the USA than many theoreticians of the "New Lefts" have gathered in an entire decade. Obviously, he does not find his followers among Marxists, but selects them among liberals and reformists, as well as petty-bourgeois radicals similar to Marcuse. *The Greening of America* will not cause a revolution in the USA nor will it lead to a spiritual reformation, even if Reich, following Luther, who nailed the famous 95 Theses on the door of the Wittenberg Cathedral, were to paste all 395 pages of his book on all the doors of the Capitol. However, similar to the books of Edward Bellamy (*Looking Backward*) and Henry George (*Progress and Poverty*), it could have a deep impression on the consciousness of Americans and assist in the implementation of a program of democratic reforms directed against state monopoly capitalism. However, it could turn into yet another quasi-religious teaching of moral redemption, of which there are many on the American scene.

AGAINST ENZENSBERGER AND OTHER "GRAVEDIGGERS OF LITERATURE"

Ever since Stalin took a strong stand toward art, and Vladimir Mayakovsky, Russia's leading revolutionary poet, took his life in despair, Soviet politics and art have been equally conservative and anti-experimental. Here is a typical example of this attitude toward art, with regard to a member of the extreme German left. Enzensberger is a left-wing West German poet and magazine editor.

Yu. Archipov, "Kurs 'Kursbukha' i poetika bessmyslits" [The Course of *Kursbuch* and the Poetics of Nonsense], *Literaturnaya Gazeta*, 46 (1970), 15.

Recently, students at the "Free University" in West Berlin published a proclamation stating, in particular: "The interpretation of literature is a mindless occupation . . . It requires that we reproduce in the depth of our own individuality a long-dead bourgeois culture."

In light of the social situation in recent years in West Berlin and in the FRG, this act was quite natural. It is now the time of self-rejection, the literati reject literature, critics reject criticism, and those involved in the theatre reject the theatre. Some of the left intellectuals, ignoring the Marxist thesis on the existence of two cultures in class society, deprecate and reject any sort of traditional culture as bourgeois culture. A crude identification of "bourgeois" culture with power, of culture with capital is underway. "Culture is the sole and last bulwark of the bourgeoisie," states, for example, the poet Hans Magnus Enzensberger.

The "New Left" is singing the death chant of literature. Enzensberger feels that it is "one of the good signs of our times that the smartest minds between twenty and thirty would like to spit on fiction writing. They not only reject writing it but also buying it." [. . .]

Literature can still be of use in performing "informative" and "educational" functions. This justifies, for example, political journalism [Publististika]. All else is an unnecessary and harmful luxury.

Such theories and attitudes are expressed in the issues of *Kursbuch*, an irregularly appearing [German] journal. It is published by Hans Magnus Enzensberger, who found relatively wide recognition with his poetry in the 1950s. In the 1960s he devoted himself practically exclusively to political publications, to an arch-left platform which for him consists of a mixture of Trotskyism, anarchism, and Marcusianism. The journal he publishes also gives an impression of a strange mish-mash. Its pages advertise particularly works of Proudhon, Bakunin, Bernstein, and Trotsky, as well as publications of the "New Left."

The journal's editors try to publish issues devoted to a single theme. In the issue devoted to literature and art, the lead article written by Karl Markus Michel was entitled "A Wreath for Literature." Naturally, this implied a funeral wreath and no crown of laurels. Why are poets necessary in our era when the world is finally undergoing a transformation of its very foundations? This is the question presented by this gravedigger of literature. Referring to Freud, he asserts that in the past poetry, drama, and novels were only a sublimated source of sexual energy for young people, similar, say, to needlework for an old maid. In the era of the sexual revolution they have become an anachronism.

K. M. Michel places literature on the same shelf with magic, myth, and religion, calling it a "social putty." In complete agreement with the esthetics of the "New Lefts," he classifies all non-avant-garde literature as bourgeois. A characteristic sample of the artistic activities of this group can be seen in a pamphlet containing the text of a program of the rather well-known West German entertainer Wolfgang Neuss, "Bunter Abend für Revolutionäre" [Potpourri for Revolutionaries]. The aim of the pamphlet is the "revolutionarization of the bourgeois individual." Then follows a chaotically arranged and randomly chosen selection of newspaper articles with demagogic commentary accusing the socialist societies of "embourgeoization." These accusations have a simple-mindedness rare even for leftish dogmatists: the Soviet Union receives diplomats and business leaders from the FRG—aha, becoming bourgeois! Willy Stoph meets Willy Brandt—aha, becoming bourgeois, etc.

Enzensberger and his like-minded friends have become politically confused and in turn are confusing intellectuals listening to them, whom they attempt to tie to some sort of "general metaphysics of art." Such pretensions discredit them in the eyes of cultural figures and the working masses.

The movement of the "New Lefts" and its esthetic destruction of forms, and rejection of "traditional literary genres," has markedly increased Western society's interest in all sorts of avant-garde tricksters, who are also demanding a "total uprising" against all and everyone.

The neo-avant-gardists arose in the FRG in the beginning of the 1950s after a twenty-year break, caused by the tremendous historical events, the fatal times of which did not allow for tricks and stunts. Since then, they were firmly entrenched in the hinterlands of literature. They made up what one critic called its "dismal riffraff" until "New Lefts" advertised them with their pretentious attacks on "old" literature. Always fond of vivid labels and the gaudy esthetic programs, they called their creativity an experience in "concrete poetry." [. . .]

With the help of cleverly designed machines, Max Bense cleans all world literature of its living fabric for the convenience of consumers. [. . .] Destroying language, they assume that they can destroy the world it has created and which they make use of. [. . .] They are firmly convinced that the division of texts into phrases, phrases into words and words into letters indicates the irreconcilable struggle between experimental art and "conformist society." This linguistic idealism hides a complete moral atrophy. It is exactly this moral indifference, the rejection of the task which history has given to art, the task of being the conscience and prophet of a new epic, that disclose the link between "concrete poetry" and the old conceptions of "art for art's sake."

The idolators of language and its simultaneous destroyers have some-

thing in common with their antipodes, the total rejection of art and literature. [. . .] Actually both these are thinking only of driving vital life
from the world of "self-satisfied structures." The struggle with both these
types of "thought" is a pressing task which cannot be delayed.

FRANTZ FANON—"PETTY BOURGEOIS SOCIALIST"

*Frantz Fanon is one of the best-known black ideologists. Every black revolutionary
from San Francisco to Johannesburg knows his name and his writings, the most
famous being* The Wretched of the Earth, *one of the books most widely read among
the New Left.*

*But Moscow does not care for him. In contrast to Angela Davis he did not join any
Communist Party. The attempt is to neutralize his influence; the following document indicates how. In the truest sense of the word: The Moor has done his work.*

G. Usov, "Frants Fanon i ego revolyutsiya otchayaniya" [Frantz Fanon
and his Revolution of Despair], *Mirovaya Ekonomika i Mezhdunarodnyye
Otnosheniya,* 10 (1969), 133–142. Here p. 142.

As the goals of the national liberation movement are achieved, as the
proletariat is formed into an organized class and the class struggle de-
velops on the African continent, the progressive elements in Fanon's
theory move into the background and his utopian and reactionary ideas
become ever more perceptible. What is more, it is impossible to ignore the
fact that many ideologists of imperialism attempt to use his propositions
in the struggle against the Communist movement and the world system
of socialism.

A number of Fanon's critics have noted that although his ideas have
become comparatively widespread and quite popular, many of them have
not withstood the test of reality, for example in Algiers and in the nations
of Tropical Africa, to the peoples of which his call was primarily directed.

V. I. Lenin warned of the inevitability of such manifestations of the
insolvency of revolutionary petty-bourgeois socialism. This socialism is a
subjective one, which is born of a "sympathy" for the international anti-
imperialist movement, but lacks sufficient objective conditions for its implementation.

Every revolution is the combination of two basic factors: the destruction
of the old and the creation of the new. When the order of the day demands the uniting of the masses (both the proletarian and the non-proletarian) for the overthrow of the forces of the old order, petty-bourgeois

socialists and nationalists appear as allies, frequently very active ones, of the international working class and world socialism. The implementation of these goals in the revolutionary struggle and the shift of priorities to the problems of building the new society, reveal the incapacity of petty bourgeois radicalism to present and consistently implement a constructive program. After all, this inevitably requires disciplined organized work, which will be wholeheartedly protested by rabble rousers, deeply imbued with the ideology of revolutionary extremism and leftism.

DOES THAT HOLD ONLY FOR THE WEST?

To divert criticism of the Soviet state, Mamut, a scholar of constitutional law in Moscow, does not distinguish between anti-state anarchists and Hegelians, since both, so goes his argument, make a fetish of the state (p. 44): the first negatively, the others positively. Mamut's following words would presumably convince the Soviet reader less of the kinship between Hegel and Bakunin, than of the kinship between the absolutist state, which the anarchists attack, and the Soviet state.

Certainly Soviet readers know much that is negative about anarchism; it is part of their political education. But what they learn in the course of indoctrination— marginally, like so much of what they are told—takes on a different meaning when they suddenly discover that not only Bakunin, long dead, but also a part of the living, contemporary Western youth swears by the black flag of anarchism.

L. S. Mamut, "Kritika politicheskoy ideologii anarchizma" [Critique of the Political Ideology of Anarchism], *Sovetskoye Gosudarstvo i Pravo,* 5 (1971), 42–52.

The fetishization of the state takes place usually where there is a large and wide-spread state apparatus of the bureaucratic type, that encloses the nation like a net, and penetrates into all areas of the life of society, and subjects society to strict regimentation. The Prussian absolutism, Bona-partism in France, and the Russian autocracy were such states (with some differences between one another). [. . .]

The anarchists reject the political legal system both of capitalism and socialism. They accuse both of being equally guilty in suppressing the individual and violating the rights of the personality, and in reducing people to robots who are arbitrarily manipulated by a state apparatus which is alienated and separated from the people.

[Further on, citing the Yugoslav sociologist A. Krešić, perhaps because it was not wanted to cite Djilas, who expressed it more clearly:] "Ties with political power increasingly mean participation in the material privileges of power as the most important, perhaps the only way to the pos-session of wealth. [. . .] The privileges of power as such form the basis for power in general." [Then Mamut goes on:]

No one will deny the fact that compared to the previous century the role of the state in social life has increased greatly, its economic function has intensified, and the relationship between politics and economics has become more complex. However, as before, economics still remains the dominant factor in social processes. In a number of places authors have made quite transparent allusions to absolutism being a phenomenon ob-served on a global scale. A. Krešić writes that political absolutism disguises its actions, which are harmful to society, by referring to "general interests," "the interests of democracy," and even covers them with the term "dicta-torship of the proletariat." The sense of these reflections is clear: any (in-cluding also a socialist!) social-political system is fraught with the danger of the absolutism of power . . . Their anarchistic implications are just as clear. However, it is not possible to stop here: a brief comment is required.

The view is illusory and naïve which holds that the radical difference between socialism and capitalism, and the huge advantages of the first over the second, result from the new order not being familiar with the various situations reigning in bourgeois society. The essence of the radical oppo-sition between socialism and capitalism lies elsewhere. The situations aris-ing in both sides of the modern world are, in fact, analogous in some areas (for example, in organizational-institutional areas) and in some aspects: leadership of the state by political parties, interdependence between higher and local organs of power, relationship between centralized power of the state and self-management, growth of the state apparatus, and other as-pects. However, these are solved differently and have differing social and class significance.

FOR VI: THE THIRD M

PROLETARIANS OR "OUTSIDERS"—OR NEITHER?

The authors of the first articles on Herbert Marcuse sidestepped to secondary questions; finally, in the spring of 1969, W. Cheprakov dealt with one of Marcuse's central theses: not the workers, integrated into bourgeois society, but—Cheprakov uses the English word—the "outsiders" (the students, the "ghetto," the Third World) are the true revolutionary force of our time. The following excerpts show that Cheprakov (and Moscow along with him) believes in the revolutionary power of the "outsiders" no more than Marcuse believes in the power of the workers. What if both were right?

V. Cheprakov, "O sotsial'no-ekonomicheskoy kontseptsii Gerberta Markuze" [On the Social-Economic Concepts of Herbert Marcuse], *Mirovaya Ekonomika i Mezhdunarodnyye Otnosheniya,* 4 (1969), pp. 89–96. Here pp. 93–95.

[Neither the "Ghetto" ...]

According to Marcuse the "ghetto" and the middle strata intelligentsia, including the students, are an "explosive force." Notwithstanding the differences which exist between these strata, Marcuse feels that they are united by their rebellion against, and challenge to, society. In his words they stand for new requirements and values, and new social institutions. They also advocate the elimination of domination and exploitation no matter under what name. Striving to begin at once at the "second stage" (that is, with communism—V. Ch.), these forces express their mistrust of all ideologies, including a socialism which has become an ideology. They reject the pseudo-democracy of the West which supports the rule of state monopoly capitalism, and are opposed not only to the entire system as a whole but also to any transformation "maintaining the existing structure." They also speak of their readiness to fight for the creation of a new system qualitatively different from former systems.

There is of course some share of truth in these characteristics. They reflect the attitudes of those groups which have been driven to despair, which Marcuse combines in the conception of "ghetto." [. . .] A sizable stratum of "superfluous people" and "outsiders to society" is the direct result of the development of capitalism and the product of the disintegration of the social order. In a political and in an economic-statistical sense they are considered poor. The majority of this very diverse stratum consists of semi-poor artisans and craftsmen, ruined petty-bourgeois and tradesmen, peasants driven from the land who have not found work in the city, individuals with irregular employment, paupers, Bohemians who have gone to seed, and the victims of capitalist urbanization.

These "ostracized" members of society are very numerous. In the USA they amount to 30 million paupers, of which one-third suffer from constant malnutrition. In England there are 7.5 million (14 percent of the population), in France 2 million pauper families, and there are many of them in the FRG and especially in Italy. They amount to 10 percent of the population of the industrially-developed capitalist nations.

A certain part of this social category is formed by workers who have been released from jobs which have become unnecessary in view of new conditions, as well as chronically unemployed individuals who, however, have not broken their ties with the working class. The relative overpopulation, which is a condition of existence of capitalism and which will disappear only with the elimination of the exploiting stratum itself, is a serious economic and political problem for the Western nations.

During the period of the gigantic scientific-technical revolution all these diverse groups drag on a miserable existence. They experience acute dissatisfaction. However, being in themselves incapable of carrying an organized and strictly disciplined struggle to change the ruling order, they attempt to implement their not always clearly acknowledged goals by the methods of rebellion.

Their demands frequently have a narrowly consumerist nature. This has made it possible for Marcuse to state that they want to begin at the "second stage," that is, avoid socialism and immediately introduce a Communism which they see in a very primitive fashion. This group includes people overwhelmed by a hopeless feeling of uselessness, rapidly moving from apathy to despair. Under some conditions, especially as a result of the rapidly changing political situation, they can become dangerous disorganizers of the revolutionary ranks.

Utilizing the anti-monopoly attitudes of the dissatisfied, non-proletarian strata of the population, the proletariat and its Communist advance guard can channelize their revolutionary potential in the interests of a joint struggle. The putting forth of demands for the liquidation of poverty, the creation of jobs, professional training, etc., within the framework of a general program of struggle against monopoly capital is, as the experience of Communist parties in the capitalist nations indicates, a very pressing problem. [. . .]

[... nor Third World]

The "Third World" occupies a special position in the concepts of Marcuse. Marcuse is right when he states that the national liberation movement is an integral force in the potential socialist revolution. However, his assertion that the "Third World" was theoretically and strategically acknowledged only as the result, and after the Second World War, directly contradicts the theory and practice of Marxism-Leninism. Leninism is based on the fact that in the period of imperialism the international revolutionary process encompasses the immediate struggle for the victory of the proletariat in the industrially developed nations, the national liberation wars, and the uprisings against imperialism. One should note that in contrast to many other left-radical ideologists, who state that the center of struggle against capitalism has shifted to the "Third World," Marcuse speaks out against the present "very strong tendency to view the national-liberation struggle as the main, if not the sole revolutionary force of the present day." According to Marcuse, opposition in the imperial metropolitan centers (student movement, unrest among Negroes) is today attracting all the elements potentially able to undermine capitalism which exist in the "Third World" or which have an effect on them. True, it is still a puzzle how this opposition, in itself quite weak, possesses such a great attraction. Apparently in this case the "force of attraction" is the international proletariat. However, it is just this proposition which is not included in the theoretical arsenal of ideologists of the "New Lefts."

How does Marcuse view the national liberation movement? It turns out that a new historical factor has appeared which could be termed an alternative both to capitalism and to the old forms of development of socialist society. This is the struggle for a new way of socialist construction, specifically construction "from below" using new methods and rejecting the old system of values. By new values H. Marcuse understands cooperation and self-determination, which are created by individuals in accordance with their needs and goals.

Marcuse himself recognizes the unconvincing nature of his line of argument and therefore states that the fate of the revolution (as a global transformation) can only be ensured in the metropolitan centers and only if the strongest link in the chain becomes the weakest. Only then will the liberation movement be able to assume a tempo enabling it to grow into a global revolutionary force, and enabling the potentially existing alternative to become reality.

MARCUSE—"PSEUDO-REVOLUTIONARY PHRASEMONGER"

Bykhovsky begins an essay with the words: "Marcuse? Herbert Marcuse? You would search philosophical dictionaries and encyclopedias in vain for information about this German-American philosopher." In the article Bykhovsky tries to push Marcuse's critique of Soviet Marxism to absurdity. After long detours explained in the chapter "The Third M," he turns to three accusations, made by Marcuse against the Soviet Union and reprinted below. (In view of the existence of several editions of Marcuse's Soviet Marxism, quotations from this book are cited by page number as well as chapter.) The argumentation of Bykhovsky's article, for which one had to wait so long, is not overwhelming, even less so because he has selected some especially weak spots from a book over 250 pages long.

Bykhovsky gives his annihilating final verdict on Marcuse at the very beginning of his article; here it is presented at the end, after the asterisk.

B. Bykhovsky, "Filosofiya melkoburzhuaznogo buntarstva" [The Philosophy of Petty Bourgeois Rebellion], *Kommunist,* 8 (1969), 114–124. Here pp. 122 ff., 114.

In order to give his slandering of socialism some semblance of the truth, Marcuse makes use of three basic fabrications. The first is that the nationalization of the means of production does not yet in all cases and in any social order signify their socialization. Marcuse "forgets" that Marx and Engels, in the "Manifesto of the Communist Party," wrote that "Communists can express their theory in one proposition: the elimination of private property." Could any sensible person deny that as a result of the Great October Revolution this basic problem, defining the transition from capitalism to socialism, was solved finally and indisputably, and that the socialization of the means of production and the overthrow of the ruling class and the expropriation of the expropriators, which was carried out on this basis, lead to the elimination of capitalists as a class, that is to the construction of the socialist society? In this regard Marcuse ignores the very essence of the matter: the class nature of the social order carrying out the nationalization.

Marcuse continues to pull himself out of the swamp by his own hair in claiming that the Soviet society and state is not a socialist society, since the ruling class in the Soviet State is some sort of "class of bureaucrats." This is his second slanderous fabrication. We will not undertake to determine who has priority in the discovery of this "new class," Herbert Marcuse or the renegade Milovan Djilas, who was recently awarded a prize in the USA for anti-Communist activity. Neither of them have even an elementary understanding of what a social class is. With professorial seriousness Marcuse explains that he uses the concept "class" in a special sense: "We here use the term 'class' to designate a group which carries out governmental functions (including the function of economic management) as 'special' functions in the social division of labor—with or without special privileges [*Soviet Marxism,* on the first page of Chapter 5, p. 89]. In accordance with Marcuse's logic all factory directors, heads of shops, foremen, kolkhoz brigade leaders, store directors, policemen on the beat, not to mention the thousands of deputies of city and local soviets and the members of public control committees, should be included in the ruling class of bureaucrats since they carry out their "special" functions in the social division of labor, although the sole privilege which they enjoy is the respect and trust of the people. [Here Bykhovsky gave free rein to his imagination; none of this was claimed by Marcuse.] As if wanting to lessen the thankless work of refuting his "theory," Marcuse is forced to acknowledge that [. . .] "Soviet bureaucracy is not the owner of the nationalized means of production" [Ibid., in the middle of Chapter 5, p. 93]. Consequently, the problem does not lie in a special form of property defining the "class."

However, could it be possible that within the framework of the social division of labor the employees of the state apparatus carry functions dictated by general social interests? Marcuse objects that this can in no way be possible. General interests are a fiction. This concept, according to Marcuse, ignores the antagonistic contradiction of interests . . . between husband and wife, between urban and rural inhabitants, and between skilled and unskilled workers [Ibid., toward the end of Chapter 5, p. 100]. To this one could add . . . the antagonistic contradictions between "physicists" and "lyricists" and between fans for various sports. Just where are there "general interests!"

Finally, the last trump card which he plays in the reckless game against Marxism-Leninism is the badly tattered card of "individual and society." In the same metaphysical manner in which Marcuse contrasts negative-positive, freedom-necessity, particular-general, he places the development of the individual in opposition to social development. Speaking as a firm opponent of collectivism, he preaches a "new form of individualism" [. . .] which is alien to the understanding that only in social activity can a person develop his individual gifts and capabilities. The direction Marcuse is taking here is shown by his laughable critique of the obligatory education, social insurance and social welfare carried out in the USSR as . . . a violation of individual freedom. [Such argumentation by Marcuse is actually to be found toward the end of Chapter 9, p. 191.] [. . .]

* In his social-political convictions Professor Marcuse is an ideologist of petty-bourgeois rebellion, issuing forth ultra-left slogans and presenting himself as a "true" socialist, "genuine" Marxist, and an irreconcilable critic of capitalism not adhering to any political party. In actuality his followers (even with the most sincere intentions) play a disorganizing role in the revolutionary movement, accepting the truth of Marcuse's pseudo-revolutionary phrasemongering and not understanding his anti-Marxist essence and his lack of historical perspective.

This "socialist" negates the role of the working class in the revolutionary transformation of society. With the same hostility he expresses in criticizing bourgeois society, he condemns the socialist system, which stands in opposition to the capitalist world. This "revolutionary" does not see the real scientifically-based revolutionary prospects in the contemporary world. Playing on the spontaneous instinctive feeling of dissatisfaction which young people have for the mustiness, falsity, and emptiness of the bourgeois way of life, and pandering to their anarchistic attitudes, Marcuse leads them from the revolutionary struggle of the working masses and pushes them along the fruitless path of petty inflammatory actions.

THE FERTILE SOIL FOR THE NEW LEFT REMAINS

In a revealing book on Marcuse, which appeared in early 1971 in an edition of 19,000, its three authors warn against the hope of an early end to the New Left. True, the "monopoly" had been torn from the "left-radical anarchists," a monopoly which they once "held in regard to posing and solving the problems of youth, and which had allowed the Marcusians to speculate on the insufficient working up—by the Marxists [i.e. the pro-Soviet Communists]—of a few current problems which interconnect with the change in the actual position of youth and the intelligentsia in bourgeois and socialist *society."* (Emphasis added.) *However . . .*

E. Ya. Batalov and others, *Pokhod Markuze protiv Marksizma* [Marcuse's Campaign Against Marxism], (Moscow, 1970), pp. 141 ff.

The first successes of [pro-Moscow] Communist forces in the field of battle against the followers of Marcuse should not give rise to illusions of the "end" of the left-radical "Utopia." The objective conditions prompting the rise and relatively wide dissemination of Marcuse's concepts continue to exist both within the developed capitalist nations and in the international arena.

The scientific-technical revolution continues, causing major rapid shifts in the class structure of the developed capitalist nations. Consequently, there will continue to be modifications in this structure itself, inevitably causing definite breaks between the "new" social existence of various sectors of the working classes and their "old" group consciousness. Such a break can serve as fertile soil for the growth of New and the rebirth of Old Left radical concepts.

Inasmuch as the transformation of the proletariat from a "class in itself" to a "class for itself" is a permanent process, then at some historical stages of its development it is possible to have a temporary decline in the social activity of the proletariat in various concrete forms. This is easily subject to left-radical falsification, for example to the theory of the "disappearance" of the proletariat as an "agent of historical action."

In view of the growth of integrative processes in the contemporary world, the revolutionary activity of the working class in the developed capitalist nations can have not only a direct manifestation (within the "developed society"), but also an inverse manifestation (within the world system of socialism and the "Third World"). This can again be interpreted as a rejection of scientific analysis, as a "deproletarianization" of the working class of developed capitalist society.

The activities of schismatic groupings within the Communist movement, putting forth their left, radically-oriented ideological programs, can promote the infiltration into the consciousness of the workers of left-radical theories, which are similar in spirit to the worker's ideas but which have been formed within the framework of bourgeois society. This is especially a problem when these schismatic forces are in power and thus have the possibility of putting these programs into practice.

The uneven development of socialism makes it necessary for various socialist nations to give priority to differing solutions to social problems. This can create the illusion (with respect to a consciousness functioning in a different context) of the "convergence" with capitalism and the loss of revolutionary spirit. Under these conditions the struggle against Marcusianism itself and against other spiritually similar left-radical theories continues to be a vital factor in the ideological struggle, and an orientation point for further positive development of Marxist-Leninist theory.

FOR VII: THE INTELLIGENTSIA—
WHERE DOES IT STAND?
WHERE IS IT GOING?

LENIN: IT IS IMPORTANT BUT TROUBLESOME

Soviet authors often treat the subject of the students and the intelligentsia together. Many quotations are available to demonstrate Lenin's attitude toward the intelligentsia. This reassures the Moscow ideologists, since it provides a firm basis for their conceptions; but it also discomfits them, since Lenin did not and probably could not give them clear directives. About one question, however, the class position of the intelligentsia, Lenin's opinion is unequivocal; therefore it is cited in almost every essay on the intelligentsia (quotation I). On another, equally important question—the attitude of the party toward the intelligentsia—Lenin espoused two opinions that are difficult to reconcile: On the one hand the intelligentsia is useful since it produces ideologists, something of which the worker, in Lenin's often repeated conviction, is incapable (quotations II and III); on the other hand intellectuals are willful and undisciplined (quotations IV and V). The intelligentsia, in other words, is enormously important but at the same time troublesome. This has remained essentially true, and probably will remain so. For even if, as Moscow hopes, the proletarization of the Western intelligentsia should finally occur, the net gain would be minimal since a proletarized, even a radicalized intelligentsia would not automatically tend toward Soviet Communism. Even Hitler exploited this circumstance, and others, like Marcuse and Djilas, have demonstrated it anew.

I. The bourgeois intelligentsia [. . .] is not an *independent* economic class and therefore is not an *independent* political force. (V. I. Lenin, "Concerning an Article Published in the Organ of the Bund," in *Collected Works,* English translation of the 4th Russian ed. [Moscow, 1962, and London], XI, 380).

II. All those who talk about "overrating the importance of ideology," about exaggerating the role of the conscious element, etc., imagine that the labour movement pure and simple can elaborate, and will elaborate, an

177

independent ideology for itself, if only the workers "wrest their fate from the hands of the leaders." But this is a profound mistake. [. . .] There can be no talk of an independent ideology formulated by the working masses themselves in the process of their movement. [. . .] This does not mean, of course, that the workers have no part in creating such an ideology. They take part, however, not as workers, but as socialist theoreticians, as Proudhons and Weitlings; in other words, they take part only when they are able, [. . .] more or less, to acquire the knowledge of their age and develop that knowledge. But in order that working men *may succeed in this more often,* every effort must be made to raise the level of the consciousness of the workers in general. (V. I. Lenin, *What Is to Be Done?* in *Collected Works,* English translation of the 4th Russian ed. [Moscow, 1961, and London], V, 383–384.)

III. The history of all countries shows that the working class, exclusively by its own effort, is able to develop only trade-union consciousness, i.e., the conviction that it is necessary to combine in unions, fight the employers, and strive to compel the government to pass necessary labour legislation, etc. The theory of socialism, however, grew out of the philosophic, historical, and economic theories elaborated by educated representatives of the propertied classes, by intellectuals. By their social status, the founders of modern scientific socialism, Marx and Engels, themselves belonged to the bourgeois intelligentsia. (V. I. Lenin, *What Is to Be Done?* in *Collected Works,* English translation of the 4th Russian ed. [Moscow, 1961, and London], V, 375.)

IV. Lastly, the opposition cadres have in general been drawn chiefly from those elements in our Party which consist primarily of intellectuals. The intelligentsia is always more individualistic than the proletariat, owing to its very conditions of life and work, which do not directly involve a large-scale combination of efforts, do not directly educate it through organized collective labour. The intellectual elements therefore find it harder to adapt themselves to the discipline of Party life, and those of them who are not equal to it naturally raise the standard of revolt against the necessary organisational limitations, and elevate their instinctive anarchism to a principle of struggle, misnaming it a desire for "autonomy," a demand for "tolerance," etc. (V. I. Lenin, "To the Party," in *Collected Works,* English translation of the 4th Russian ed. [Moscow, 1961, and London], VII, 455–456.)

V. No one will venture to deny that *the intelligentsia, as a special stratum* of modern capitalist society, is characterised, by and large, *precisely by individualism* and incapacity for discipline and organisation. (V. I. Lenin, "One Step Forward, Two Steps Back," in *Collected Works,* English translation of the 4th Russian ed. [Moscow, 1961, and London], VII, 269.)

WHO LEADS—THE PROLETARIAT OR THE INTELLIGENTSIA?

To arrive at a long-term assessment of the New Left, as a manifestation of unrest among intellectual youth, Moscow considers it important to answer the question: what future role will intellectual youth, and the intelligentsia as a whole, play in the West? In their two-part essay Mel'nikov and Sonov conclude, first, that the answer given by Western Marxists is not uniform (they cite a Frenchman and an Australian, respectively). Then they give their own answer, which probably corresponds to Moscow's official opinion, and in which the concept "intelligentsia" almost always means "Western intelligentsia." To anticipate their result: In a number of highly developed capitalist states "the intelligentsia assumes the role of the most important ally of the working class."

A. Mel'nikov and S. Sonov, "Rabochiy klass i ego soyuzniki" [The Working Class and Its Allies], *Mirovaya Ekonomika i Mezhdunarodnyye otnosheniya,* 2 (1971), 67–78. Here pp. 72–74, 76.

The intelligentsia, the size of which is growing extremely rapidly under the influence of the scientific-technical revolution and the effect of other factors, is becoming an ever more important ally of the working class. The basic mass of the intelligentsia now consists of individuals working as wage laborers (in the USA about 90%) and their share is constantly increasing. Individuals working for wages belong to professional groups of the intelligentsia which play an important role in social production and which are very large. They include scientists and engineers, economists, instructors at higher educational schools, and teachers, doctors, press, radio, and television workers, and others.

All Marxists unanimously agree that the rapid proletarization of the basic mass of intellectual workers is underway. This entails the ever greater convergence of their social-economic position with the position of the basic ranks of the working class. As extensive strata of the intelligentsia lose their independence and are being converted into wage laborers [which are] the object of capitalist exploitation, and they lose their social and material privileges, the objective base for their union with the working class in a joint struggle against state monopoly capitalism is strengthened. In characterizing the reasons pushing the intelligentsia along this path, one should stress that the intelligentsia is not only an object of capitalist exploitation, but that it also, in view of the specific nature of its work, especially acutely feels the spiritual oppression of the monopolistic bourgeoisie encroaching on the basis of intellectual work: the freedom to create. Robbed of its creative drive, intellectual labor is transformed into a sort of assembly line for the production of ideas, recommendations, and decisions, entirely adapted to the pragmatic purposes of strengthening the class rule of capital.

The objective condition of the intelligentsia as a creative force, developing, accumulating, and applying scientific-technical knowledge, as well as theoretically generalizing practical experience in all areas of social life, cannot but help force an ever greater number of intellectual workers into the struggle against capitalism, which prevents the use of the scientific-technical revolution in the interests of all humanity, and converts it into a means for intensifying class and national oppression, and into an instrument of militarism and aggression.

Changes in the organization of labor and in its social origins have also helped bring the intelligentsia into the anti-monopolistic struggle. In the past century and even in the pre-war period of our century the intelligentsia carried out its activities in isolation. Individualism was a characteristic feature of intellectuals. It was primarily a result, as V. I. Lenin noted, of the conditions of their work. Work in isolation or in very small collectives could not offer possibilities for the extensive unification of forces. It made the forms of their labor organizations similar to the scattered petty-bourgeois entrepreneur. Character and forms of the organization of intellectuals' work changed sharply in the second half of the 20th Century. The centralization of capital in the nonproductive sphere, and the intensified necessity of utilizing the achievements of the scientific-technical revolution, led to the concentration of "enterprises" of intellectual labor. This resulted in the rise of complex cooperation of intellectual workers. Although even now specialists in some professions work individually, for the majority of technical professions, medical workers, and many representatives of the scientific and creative intelligentsia, work is characterized by large and frequently multi-stage collectives. They are combined into large scale research centers of industrial companies, scientific laboratories, engineering firms, legal "factories," and serve in large clinics and gigantic universities. The work of specialists has become increasingly collective and there is extensive labor cooperation. Although individualism is still characteristic of many intellectuals, the objective conditions have now arisen for the consolidation of efforts and the unification of individuals involved in intellectual labor. It is for this reason that there is a rapid increase in the membership of trade unions which combine specialists of various types. Their actions are assuming a mass nature.

The middle of the 20th Century has seen major shifts in the social origins of the intelligentsia and in the extent to which it has developed direct ties with the working class. Previously, the intelligentsia was made up of sons of the ruling classes. Now, in contrast, a considerable percentage of the intelligentsia originates from working class families. This circumstance has undoubtedly facilitated the convergence of intellectual laborers and industrial workers.

The enlistment of extensive strata of intelligentsia into the anti-monopoly struggle is not a prediction but a real fact. This is witnessed by such immediately visible processes as the growth of the political activity and the intensification of the democratic wing of the working intelligentsia, its expanded practical cooperation with the working class and its organizations, and finally the growth of the influence of the ideas of scientific Communism in its ranks. Under the specific conditions of a number of developed capitalist nations, the intelligentsia is assuming the role of a very important ally of the working class in the anti-monopoly struggle. [. . .]

The main mass of intellectual toilers is becoming part of the working class, or becoming similar to it, naturally bringing its knowledge with it. [. . .] In the final account this will lead to an increase in the role of the working class in the life of capitalist society, and will assist in the implementation of its historical mission—the revolutionary transformation of social relations, the elimination of class exploitation, the construction of socialism and Communism.

FOR VIII: IS THE WEST DECAYING?

LOVE, DRUGS, AND HYSTERIA IN SODOM AND GOMORRAH

In the Soviet Union, the land of law and order and cast-iron conformity, the Wood-stock Festival, the last great happening of the Hippie Era, could only arouse un-comprehending amazement mixed with revulsion: it was a Walpurgis Night, a Witches' Sabbath, madness without method. Yet the picture drawn from life, from which several excerpts are presented below, contains a vein of sympathy for this astonishing and spontaneous eruption. It also makes clear that the hippies are a phenomenon of the affluent society. Aside from the incidental and pious wish that American youth join the Communist Party, the article could have appeared in the West without appearing unusual.

V. Vul'f, "Vokrug Vudstokskogo festivalya" [Around the Woodstock Festival], *Teatr,* 8 (1970), 147–156.

The "Woodstock Festival of Music and Art" could have led one to suppose that America had given itself over to carnival buffoonery. Bedecking themselves with beads, feathers, and flowers, bearded young men and long-haired girls set themselves up among the hemp fields in an area of slightly more than 1,000 acres of pastureland rented from a local dairy farm, and camped for three days, singing songs and listening to singers, smoking and swallowing drugs, walking around nude, becoming acquainted with one another, doing whatever came to mind, affirming their belief in the values of Love, Friendship, and Simplicity, and their right to do what they wanted without obeying any set rules.

The Woodstock festival differs sharply from ordinary festivals. It was a forum of the followers of rock 'n' roll and of love as the goal of life. [. . .]

Upon conclusion of the performances and concerts, the indefatigable members of the gathering sent up canine howls and did frenzied dances in the light of the revolving searchlights. Inarticulate wails rang out all night long. [. . .] Although those who smoke marijuana were not arrested (there would not have been enough jails for them in all Sullivan County and in the neighboring three counties), dozens of hippies were taken into custody for being found in possession of LSD. A fresh wind carried streams of the sweetish marijuana smoke around. Four hundred people became ill from overdoses of LSD. Sick persons appeared at medical aid points, complaining of colds, broken bones, and cuts and punctures from touching the barbed wire. An additional fifty doctors were flown in from New York City to resolve the critical situation. On the last day of the festival a tractor ran over a young man in a sleeping bag on the shoulder of a road. But the enthusiasm was undiminished. It was as if the communes of hippies consolidated their members at Woodstock. While differing greatly from one another in regulations, length of existence, and ways of spending the night, they all brought to the festival their amateur art and a yearning, they felt, to develop warm human relations. Jazz music was followed by dialogue from dramatic scenes. A succession of rock performing groups—there were 24 of them—followed the "kings" and "queens" of blues and twist. The songs of Melanie and Arlo Guthrie seemed to summarize what the festival (as the hippies firmly believe) was organized for: "love and not war. Love and only love." [. . .]

Crowds gathered around displays of multi-colored fabrics, embroidery, craft articles, and depictions of bodies joined in love. For three days and three nights the fantastic gathering stunned America. "What is this," the magazine *Newsweek* asked, "a revolutionary act or just a picnic with marijuana and LSD instead of beer?" An "event of planetary scope" (as it was called by the Beatnik poet Allen Ginsberg) or a "swampy nightmare?" Different people interpreted it differently, as was also the case with the entire hippie movement.

Some feel that the hippies are worshippers of mystic love, while others call them loafers and drug addicts. [. . .]

One thing is clear: the hippies are a protest movement even though they do not have the features typical of such a movement. The hippies are not organized and they do not use force. Rejecting force, they put love at the center of existence.

Young people who have decided to go off to the hippies are looking for a society in which it is possible to love and be loved. They have declared that the idols of this cult of love are Jesus, Buddha, Gandhi, and Francis of Assisi. Flowers are their emblem. They symbolize beauty and brightness, wildness and primitivism, openness and naturalness. They are worn in the hair and behind the ears. The body is ornamented with depictions of flowers, and in this way they give their rebellion the pathos of free human individuality. [. . .]

This leads to alienation and conflict with everything that is understood historically as "individuality." All this gives rise to the fury of the young generation, which carries within itself a fund of devastating protest against "atomization" of the individual, his alienation, and against the decrepit spiritual principles of the capitalist civilization which is in its death throes. The critical inspiration of young Americans is extreme nihilism. The hippies represent an infantile rejection of the existing way of life. (Its infantile nature is one of the factors which brought about the end of the myth about the strength of flowers.) [. . .]

Raised on love for immediacy and "self-expression," a certain part of American youth suddenly showed an attraction for "communication" in the bosom of nature. This assumed the form of establishing communal settlements in rural areas, on the outskirts of some cities, and on Indian reservations. In the middle of a society of abundance, the hippies raised the banner of poverty. Purposely rejecting any comfort and agreeing to work only enough to insure a minimum level of prosperity, they came out against efforts to achieve material success. [. . .]

The assembling of hippie communes (there are a hundred in California alone) testifies to innumerable attempts to find desired idyllic relationships among people, but the hypocrisy of the society they have rejected pursues them here too. Furious fits of race hatred reside alongside rivalry for the possession of women. The attempt to change skin and be born anew has clearly failed.

The members of the organized communes (many of them have names such as Hog Farm, Black Narcissus, and so on) have one uniting feature: a desire to forget themselves, to lose their sense of reality, to enter into ecstasy, revel in drugs, and find some kind of justification for life. From this comes a yearning to establish their own subculture, that is, the culture of their immediate social environment as distinguished from the culture of the adult members of society. The specific nature of the hippie culture is emphasized with special sharpness in its music, manner of dress, and language. [. . .]

The attempts to flee from social reality differed; turning to the mystical teachings of Asiatic cultures (Buddhism, Taoism, Lamaism, and Confucianism), which attracted by their lack of scientific rationalism and the possibility of probing the depths of one's own soul through intuition alone, testified that the hippies hoped to find comfort in a "different reality." [. . .]

The hippie journeys into their own depths were promoted by the use of drugs. But the return from these "trips" showed that the time spent by the hippies in the "new world" was very brief and the inhuman world of capitalism continues to control their behavior when they return to "reality." This leads to apathy and rejection of the struggle against the world around. Interest in the mystical philosophy and art of the East turns into social inertia. [. . .]

Identification with the East is interpreted as a simple opposition to the West. In recent years the number of hippies from the United States, England, Sweden, and West Germany who have traveled the route between the West and Nepal through Turkey, Iran, Afghanistan, and Pakistan goes into the tens of thousands. It is no surprise that it was precisely the Indian guitarist Ravi Shankar who was given a unanimous ovation by the hippies at Woodstock. He was dumbfounded by their fanatical devotion to and worship of his native country.

"What made you become a hippie and come to the festival?" a correspondent from the magazine *Newsweek* asked an 18-year-old girl student from Michigan. "I came to be with others who think and feel the way I do," she answered. "In order to feel good it is important for us all to be together, or else each of us will be very lonely. I ran away from the loneliness of my home." [. . .]

The young people came here with their babies, cats, dogs, and bird cages. Hungry participants at the festival made raids on neighboring farms to get vegetables from the gardens and tear down the fences to fuel their fires and build improvised toilets. Growing tired, they looked for chances to sleep in tents between empty Coca-Cola boxes. Married couples and children were constantly losing and then finding one another. The noise did not die out for a second. Two cows suffered noise shock and gave birth. But there was not a single rape or robbery, and the chief of police of the city of Beverly Hills stated that he had "never seen so many people in such a small area who were in such a peaceful mood." [. . .]

But is it possible to find "God and love" in Sodom and Gomorrah? The Woodstock festival gave a negative answer to this question. The path chosen by the hippies to find a happy world proved mistaken and led them into an even greater chaos than the one they wanted to avoid. [. . .]

At the festival in Woodstock there was debate on the problem of group marriage, marriage for three, and love between men, between women, and between old people and juveniles. On the stage of the Living Theater, which is directed by Julian Beck and his wife Judith Melina, the sexual act was performed without shame and the hippies who live in Greenwich

Village, the American Montmartre, applauded ecstatically this ultimate attempt at theatrical "innovation." [. . .]

The newspapers and magazines are full of discussions of "sexual freedom." Sex has become a kind of "last boundary" (in the definition of the American sociologist David Riesman) on which young people hope to affirm their individuality. The hippie press is filled with advertisements such as "Do you want to? Just call and we'll do it right there," "I am looking for a fat, ugly girl," "Come to the partner exchange club," and so on. The newspaper *Horse Shit* ran an ad which read "I am looking for an affair." There is no longer any talk of love. "We used to think about him, but now we think about many; he used to think about love, but now he thinks about orgasm. The result is loneliness. Sex and not love means a broken heart, but there is still no happiness," concludes Vanessa Redgrave. [. . .]

The Woodstock festival revealed that the hippie colonies are not "communities of love," but rather gatherings of drug addicts and egotists. All the talk of love for one's neighbor has degenerated into empty chatter and unrestrained sexuality, into an imaginary and harmful, for spiritual and physical health, retreat from society into drug addiction. [. . .]

The infatuation with religious teachings led to frenzied praying which gave an illusory feeling of retreat from reality. Prayers became part of the daily schedule. Formerly they had only sung rock songs, but now many switched to evangelical psalms. In hippie shops where beads, buttons, chains, and rosaries are sold, one may find an old coffin or skull. This is a sign that prayers are held there in the evenings. Fortune tellers come and predict the future. A certain Bob, called Lucifer, calls up a spirit. Around twenty people hold one another by the hand, extinguish the candles, and when the spirit appears all begin to scream hysterically, tremble, and beat their heads on the floor. Ecstasy changes into an orgy. A suicidal mixture of sex and religion. In the "Society of Satan" (and there is one such society in San Francisco) the service is conducted by a nude girl. A group of hypnotists alleges that there is "something beyond this life." In one shop a local prophet predicted that California would perish, and thousands of hippies left Hollywood believing this prophesy. In the paper *Sunday's Child* the "witch" Melanie Black, who is popular in hippie circles, gives daily advice, and a good-looking 20-year-old pastor, whose photograph is published by the newspaper, calls on people to go away with him into medieval times. During the day the "pastor" begs but in the evening he buys marijuana and enters the so-called "Blue Grotto," where "visions" occur. [. . .]

Blinded by the idea of "withdrawing from society," the hippies in practice remain within it. What is more, the idea of awaking a sleeping and inert society by means of shock tactics leads to unforeseen results. The tactical function is not fulfilled and everything remains in its place. Adventurers, unemployed persons, parasites, and criminal elements join the movement. It becomes less and less ideological and acquires a purely antirational character.

All these "bourgeois in hippie garb" are strongly influenced by anarchist ideas. Freely organized communes and mass actions marked by looting and fires constitute the reality of their behavior today. It seems to some groups that with their provocative actions they are strengthening the antiauthoritarian camp and mobilizing all elements of social discontent. In fact their activity is perceived simply as barbarism. [. . .]

The young people who have passed through the evolution from professing the "cult of love" to professing the "cult of violence" have opened the way for forces which may lead to authoritarianism of a worse type. This is particularly dangerous under conditions where neo-fascism has clearly become active.

The hippies gave a definite style to the rebellion of young people against capitalist society. "They turned the question of style into a political question," writes Stewart Hall. Finding pleasure in a semitheatrical existence (groups of barefooted, long-haired people who purposely dress in a bright and sloppy manner, gather on street corners, and sing psalms and songs to the accompaniment of banjos, guitars, and flutes; speeches and dances, turning the sidewalk into "live theater"), the hippies have combined in themselves a search for pleasures with a militant resistance to the "society of abundance" they hate. The state, the police, war, and authority—all of these structures (from the hippie point of view) are backed up by violence, and those who try to bring these structures down are opposing one form of violence by another. This view led the hippies to the position of passive resistance. Along with social inertia and apathy, however, the stratification of the hippie movement has also engendered extremist groups which commit actions of unjustified vandalism.

The extremist nucleus is small, comprising some 6,000–7,000 people in the United States. Most of them are from economically secure families whose social status is significantly higher than the average level. Opposition to the authorities serves as a functional equivalent of the ability to establish themselves in a professional area. In their criticism of capitalism hippies frequently use Marxist phraseology, but actually the extremist groups have little interest in the situation of the working class and deny its revolutionary role, placing their hopes on the "unintegrated elements" of society, which at bottom contradicts the spirit of Marxism. [. . .]

While recognizing the full complexity of the palette, one should not consider the hippies as people who have sensed—be it sometimes intuitively—the need for a new type of social relations; rather they should be viewed as nothing but pathetic victims of bourgeois civilization and for the most part incapable of political activism. [. . .]

The fantastic festival ended, and even its participants were amazed that it was held and carried through to the end.

And once again the absurd and outcast, confused and befuddled long-haired young people set off to roam the roads of America, looking for happiness.

THE HIPPIES IN THE FOREST CAMP

The liveliest and not exactly hostile description of a hippie was written by a Soviet correspondent in Geneva in summer 1971. Whether everything happened as he says, and whether a hippie named Barry, whom the author picked up hitchhiking, took him to this nocturnal forest camp by Lausanne, is unimportant. What Rozental' describes occurred hundreds of times during the flowering of the Hippie Era. To anticipate the author's verdict: the hippies "have declared war on parasitic society. . . . In reality they themselves are parasites on the body of society."

E. Rozental', "Khippi i drugiye" [Hippies and Others], *Novyy Mir*, 7 (1971), 182–204.

Learning that I was a journalist, Barry suddenly suggested, "Do you want to visit a hippie camp? It's in the woods not far from Lausanne. Generally we don't like it when outsiders try to work their way into our confidence. But we put up with it."

So I found myself by the fire at night.

About fifty people were assembled in a clearing in the woods. They were sitting and half-lying, hardly moving. Like Africans during the siesta. Some couples were kissing. And they would freeze that way for a long time. Now and then someone would get up to throw branches on the fire. From time to time a boy and girl would go away from the fire into the darkness. Later they would silently return. A blonde little hippie about four years old was sleeping in the arms of a young woman. Before he went to sleep I saw him crawl around at the feet of the silent boys, pulling on their trousers and calling them all "Dad."

Someone was strumming a guitar mournfully. When the musician grew tired he was replaced by another. Only the melody did not change. A monotonous set of sounds. The impression was that the guitarist was tuning his instrument and would really start to play in just a minute. But he just continued to tune and tune.

At first I felt out of place, but no one paid any attention to me, and soon I became accustomed to this strange situation. However, I tried not to get separated from Barry. In the flickers of the fire he looked something like a Biblical elder. But in fact he was about 30, and during the day he had young, deep blue eyes.

Barry took off his tasseled boots and put his feet in a blanket.

"What you see here are real hippies. There aren't that many of them in the world. Those two over there," he pointed at a girl and boy who were kissing, "have even been in Katmandu. For us that is something like Mecca. Lots of people today have let their hair grow and play at being hippies. But in the evening some return home to their mamas and others have travelers checks. They get their money at the bank and spend the night in fine hotels. Those are not real hippies, they're fakes."

"Then what are real hippies?"

"You see, they are not so much individuals or even a movement as much as a philosophy. Not a theory, but a philosophy of life itself. Or, to be more precise, a life philosophy. Life in isolation from society. The philosophy of withdrawal from a sick society." Barry nodded at my notebook, "You are wasting your time to write it down. I won't be able to say what I feel in words, and what you write about us will just be nonsense. We are not like others. . . . It is not a matter of external features. . . . We have a different internal world and we live, if you like, in a completely different dimension."

Barry was choosing his words with difficulty.

"Your Pavlov called speech a secondary signal system. But we hippies communicate with one another by means of a tertiary signal system."

At that moment, obviously, my face also assumed a "different" expression. Barry laughed, "You see, I said you wouldn't understand. But listen to me."

I listened. The crickets were chirping and the guitarist continued to tune the guitar. Barry closed his eyes.

"Music. It is the tertiary signal system. You weren't at the festival in Woodstock. But I was. With their music Joe Cocker, Arlo Guthrie, and Jimi Hendrix brought half a million hippies who didn't know each other together. You should have seen that. Magnificent!"

I quietly began to be "turned on." I won't dispute that pop music can be pleasing; everything depends on education, culture, and so on. But no music, whether it is Bing Crosby or Beethoven, can replace words for human beings.

"You don't want to tell me that you understand one another by means of such music."

Honestly, he looked at me with pity.

"I said that the music brings us together. But I did not say that we understand one another. We don't even understand our own selves. I myself don't know what I want. I know what I don't want. I don't want to participate in all this capitalist swinery. And each of us is withdrawing or trying to withdraw from this pig-sty."

Barry made a broad, sweeping gesture toward the camp.

"You think that all of us here know each other. You're wrong. I only know these two right here. I know that we have Americans, French, and Scandinavians. But we do not know each other. And we do not have any desire to get to know each other. But still we communicate with each other. That is the point; we don't know each other but we love each other. Yesterday in Basel someone told me where the camp was and I came here. Others also came. Alone, in couples, and in communes. And tomorrow we'll wander off the same way. Maybe we'll never meet again. That isn't important. In order to love it is not necessary to be acquainted. The main thing is to be free."

. . . It had become cool. There was heat coming from the fire, but my back was cold. I huddled up from the chill. A girl who was sitting not far away came over and threw a plaid rug on my knees. Without a word. Then she returned to her place. I wrapped up in the rug.

"Barry, how did you become a hippie? And when?"

He frowned.

"I have asked myself that. And I can't answer exactly. Just like I don't know how I became bald. Just like that, hair by hair. I remember that my father used to tell me that he had dreamed of becoming a geographer—and our house was full of maps and globes, but he became a businessman. And he doesn't regret it. He taught me that the main thing in any profession is business, dollars. And my mother, as far as I remember, repeated over and over again that the main thing is cleanliness. She was always sniffing me and sprinkling me with some substances. My teachers in college talked about the greatness of American democracy and the beauties of the Grand Canyon.

"I drank in all this abracadabra. Then came the university with all its variety. During vacations I hardly rested, I did extra work. Either I washed dishes in restaurants or helped the mechanic at the garage. And it wasn't because I needed money. I was simply ashamed to waste time. I was making my way, that's how I was brought up. Many people do that."

Barry smiled ironically:

"But then I understood that all that is garbage. Why make money? In order to set up a home and family, sire snot-nosed kids and teach them business and cleanliness? To talk about the beauties of the Grand Canyon? I'm sick of it. Maybe everything would have been different if my father hadn't rejected his globes. I don't know."

Barry stretched and yawned.

"When we are kids we all think that we are born for something great. Everyone is confident that great deeds await him. But then we suddenly note that the years are passing and there isn t a sign of great deeds. Our grandfathers, when they were young, naïvely consoled themselves with the thought that everything still lay in front of them. But we have to hurry before the megatons fall on our head. That is why we rebel. I also started to rebel. I made some speeches and ran away from the police. But then that passed too. I sent it all to the Devil, and here I am."

It was already late but I didn't want to sleep. I found Barry very interesting. He started to talk again.

"You'll ask why I'm here. I don't know. Neither the Louvre nor the ruins of Rome excite me. Only nature does. Only it is natural. Although they are poisoning it too, as well as they can. It'll get colder and we'll move south. But for now it's not bad in Helvetia. The Swiss have been lucky with nature; it's beautiful, that's all you can say.

"No great deeds tempt me any more. I am free, and that's the main thing. I don't want to work, so I don't work. I am free to choose whether to build or reject. I have taken the second choice because I don't see the point of building. To stuff yourself with calories and wear yourself out sitting behind the wheel is not a goal. We are often reproached for begging. But so what? After all, we don't demand, we ask. And they don't give us very much, you know. We get by as well as we can. Some sell their passports to criminals, and some give their blood to laboratories— that pays well. There is sometimes stealing too. And sometimes people do die of typhus and other infections."

Barry waved his hand tiredly.

"In general, we hippies are a dying tribe. But we are proud that we were the first in history to refuse to participate in the rat race for material well-being. We reject meaningless consumption which destroys everything living. This society cannot offer anything else. We have begun a revolution which, unfortunately, no one understands. It's okay, some day they'll understand." He suddenly stopped short. "It seems that I have given a speech . . ."

I realized that the conversation was coming to an end. But there was still a great deal I wanted to hear. Just at this minute another couple returned from the darkness and began to arrange themselves by the fire. I took advantage of this.

"Barry, you said that love does not require familiarity, that it needs freedom. Like that?" I nodded in the direction of the couple.

Barry raised himself and motioned with his hands, "Hey, red-head, I don't know your name. Can you come over for a minute?"

She got up without hurrying and came over. Tall as a pole. She held out her hand: "My name is Ula."

Barry mumbled something indefinite, then said, "This journalist wants to know about your attitude toward love."

Ula was not surprised. "If a boy is 'sexy' and I like him, I sleep with him."

"Do you like me?"

"No, I don't like you."

I intervened. I asked Ula if her understanding of love was not too simplistic.

She looked at me carefully.

"Why make it complicated? I was liberated from my bourgeois complexes long ago."

"Begging your pardon, how old are you?"

"I'll be 19 soon."

"But now, that little boy who is sleeping on his mother's knees. He probably isn't even four yet. But he sees everything. What will he be like at 19?"

"He will never have to be liberated from complexes. And he will never be boring."

The last remark probably referred to me. The conversation was exhausted. Ula nodded drily to us and returned to her "sexy boy," a gloomy fellow in glasses with pink cornelian beads around his neck.

In the meantime Barry went to work. He unlaced his bag. From it he took some rags, a roll of thread, a worn book by Ghandi, and finally a small aluminum box. He winked at me:

"Let's take a better trip."

In hippie language this meant to take drugs.

I had several more questions ready, but I refrained. Hippies are not ill-tempered people, but there is one sure way to make a hippie angry—to distract him when he is preparing to "trip out."

Barry was acting like a priest. He raised the lid of the box with a finger-nail and took a pressed green cube out of it.

"This is Moroccan kif. It's not much, but it's better than nothing." He chipped a small piece off the cube and ground it into powder with his fingers. He poured the greenish dust into a small piece of paper, licked it, and rolled a long cigarette. Its tip was bent upward. Then he hid the box in the bag, got some matches, and lit up. He held it out to me. For pro-priety's sake I took a couple of puffs of the slightly bitter smoke and returned the cigarette to him. He pressed it with the palms of both hands and slowly inhaled. Again. And again. He closed his eyes.

"Now the legs will get heavy and the head light. And the colors will be brilliant." He inhaled again. "Very brilliant." Then he fell silent. For a long time.

"The trip" had begun.

. . . The stars were disappearing in the eastern part of the sky. The musicians were silent. The camp was deep in sleep. I looked at the glow-ing coals of the fire, and in my memory other nights and other images came alive: the crackle of dry wood, sparks rising to the sky, flushed young faces. And a feeling of happiness that could not be contained, an expecta-tion of something enormous which would come in life. And the ringing Russian song "Soar like campfires, blue nights . . ."

They were not to know this youthful happiness. Essentially good boys and girls, they threw down a challenge to the parasitic society. It seems to them that they have rejected this society and withdrawn from it. But in fact they themselves live as parasites on its body. However, many of them will repay their debts to this society. Rarely does anyone stay a hippie until 25 or 30 years of age. I know several respectable young bourgeois who are former hippies and Beatniks. Snuggling their feet in a rug, they love to sit in the warmth of their home and recall their former adventures. And with such condescending bravado.

"LEFT" SEX IS WRONG

Sex education within the Soviet Union hardly exists. Soviet readers discover more about sexual behavior in foreign countries than about behavior at home. The soci-

ologist I. Kon wrote the most comprehensive essay, "Sex, Society, and Culture," the basic conceptions of which are presumably shared widely by Russian intellectuals. His critique of the views of Western sexual revolutionaries is of primary interest for us. It hardly differs from the criticism of such views in bourgeois circles in the West. The official Soviet position is in fact rather more conservative than Kon's, which is given below. And Soviet marriage laws, despite some change since the thirties, are among the most conservative in the world.

I. Kon, "Seks, obshchestvo, kul'tura" [Sex, Society, Culture], *Inostrannaya Literatura,* 1 (1970), 243–255. Here pp. 253 ff.

Things are no better, however, with those fairly numerous "left" theoreticians who propose that the general liberation of mankind be begun with sexual liberation. Underlining the negative aspects of capitalist sexual morality, they demand its complete annihilation. The repressive sexual morality which is instilled in a person from early childhood, they argue, deprives him of internal freedom and prevents him from developing his creative potential, not just in the sexual sphere but also in any other activity. The journals of these groups—the West German *Konkret,* the English *It,* the American *Evergreen* [*Review*]—are adorned with such gaudy titles as "Sexuality, Politics, and the Subconscious," "Sexuality and the Class Struggle," "The Sexual Revolution," and so on. These articles argue that "sexual repression" plays an important, if not decisive, role in "maintaining the existing society" and that "struggle against the masters of society is impossible without sexual liberation." [. . .]

Like the extreme right wing, the ultra-leftists criticize the existing situation harshly, but from the opposite side. Emmanuel Petrakis, editor of the journal published by the "Movement for Sexual Emancipation" [London, since 1964], writes in his program article: "On the one hand we are constantly sucked in by the sexual stimulation carried on by films, books, magazines, advertising, and so on, while on the other hand the law and hypocritical social morality, which is ignored in private life, prohibit us from openly expressing this fundamental inclination. If society is like a schizophrenic in this respect, is it any wonder that people are driven to show themselves in pathological ways, since less morbid ways of self-expression are closed to them?" But exactly what kind of "revolution" are [René] Hauser, Petrakis, and others calling for? In their criticism of capitalist sexual morality they rely on some facts. It is true that repressed sexuality is usually associated with general emotional constraint and an inability to have warm and open relationships with people in general. But in their conclusions the ultra-leftist "revolutionaries" turn the question upside down. "It is easier to nudge disillusioned, isolated people into war and racial conflicts and subject them to economic manipulation than it is to do this with groups of people who are united and loving," Petrakis writes. But what has caused this disillusionment and this isolation? Petrakis answers, "Conflicts in personal, professional, racial, and political life can often be derived from the damage done to many people by sexual inhibitions. People often fail to recognize that it is precisely the fact that they are unloved and have no one to love that causes their bitterness and resentment, which they take out on others."

To avoid this, Petrakis recommends that nudism be practiced wherever possible, that communication with others be intensified, touching them "with nude skin," and, of course, that there be complete freedom of sexual relations. But this religion of sensual love looks naïve at best. Sociological and sexological research invariably shows that psychosexual troubles are the result of social troubles much more often than they are their cause.

The very slogan of "sexual freedom" is just as indefinite as it is eye-catching. Concealed behind it one usually finds anarchistic petit bourgeois inertia, without a realistic program, drawing young people away from effective social struggle. Of course this hullabaloo will "épater le bourgeois." In its campaign against the student "communes" in the FRG and France, the press played on the theme of "sexual licentiousness" with special intensity. But wasn't this simply a calculated (and very correctly calculated) propaganda trick for the purpose of discrediting the leftist youth movement? Given the lack of clarity in the political program of certain student organizations, the slogan of "sexual freedom" can also be used as a safety valve which reduces overall tension: follow your own "rules," sleep with whoever you want however you want, but don't encroach on the socio-economic foundations of the existing order! The capitalist system in the Scandinavian countries has not been weakened as a result of the abolition of moral censorship and legalization of pornography, just as the hippie movement does not represent a serious threat to it.

When we look at the large-scale *political* question, the "left" hullabaloo about "sexual revolution" not only fails to go beyond the framework of capitalist ways, but actually plays the role of a kind of "distracting agent." In such theories, as Lenin remarked, "questions of sex and marriage are not perceived as parts of the main social question. On the contrary, the big social question itself begins to appear as a part, an appendage to the problem of sex. The main thing retreats to a secondary place. This not only makes this question less clear, it confuses thinking in general, it confuses class consciousness." Furthermore, the purveyors of pornography are getting rich on it. Needless to say, the "ideologists" condemn commercial eroticism. "Arousing without satisfying is a good way to sell commercial goods," Petrakis writes. But what about the advertising for pornographic pictures in *It* or *Konkret*? Their suppliers do not look like altruists, they are simply making money. And probably the journals don't print these advertisements for nothing. So who is serving whom?

Extremes touch each other. For all their outward antagonism, the ultra-rightists and the ultra-leftists are doing the same thing.

FOR IX: IS THE SOVIET UNION
REALLY IMMUNE?

SELF-PORTRAIT OF A SOVIET CITIZEN GROWING UP

Soviet journalism emphasizes again and again that the youth of its country grows up far removed from any consumer mentality, and is wholly dedicated to the service of socialist society. At the same time, in a study of the young generation, one finds the following poem of an anonymous youth, as a typical, not a shocking example.

Vadim V. Makarov, *Chem ty zhivesh, rovesnik? Zametki sotsiologa* [What Are You Living for, Contemporary? Remarks of a Sociologist], Volgograd, 1968, 110 pp.

Some day, for sure, I will be old and gray,
Will be as bald as any worn-out coin,
And get accustomed having milk to drink,
And cure my colds, and watch my diet too.

Who knows how it will be then? But so far
I still am young, with fire in my blood.
All joys I want to savor to the end,
Embrace a girl and win a game of chess.

I want my team to win at volley ball,
Outrun a friend at hundred meters dash,
I want to kick the ball right in the gate.
I want them all, the joys of skillfulness.

I want to read into the dead of night,
Admire heroes, strong and pure and bold,
And listen, while the silence is so tense,
To powerful melodious tunes of Lizst.

At evening time I want to roam the streets,
Dream, think, and watch the curious ways of men.

I want to be at sunrise on the beach,
And laugh, and play, and also fall in love.

UNROMANTIC WEDDING NIGHT

Not only poems like the one above, but satire too can reveal moods and tendencies. Like all Soviet journalism, satire is a purposeful instrument of indoctrination. Naturally such satire exaggerates, especially the sketch below, but it does not invent. The satire here chastises what we would call the consumer mentality of Soviet young people. To understand the second sentence: From time immemorial it has been the custom, at Russian wedding feasts, for guests to call out at intervals, "Bitter! Bitter!" The bride and groom answer, "No, sweet," and for the amusement of the spectators they must kiss.

M. Dymov, "Brachnaya noch'" [Wedding Night], *Literaturnaya Gazeta,* 43 (1972), 16.

A wedding. The groom looks absent-mindedly at the bride. The guests constantly shout "bitter!" The newlyweds hastily kiss each other. Glasses tinkle until late in the night. Songs, noise and dancing . . .

Finally, the weary guests scatter to their various homes. The young couple is shown to their room and the mother of the bride locks the door behind them. Both of them run from the doorway of their bedroom to a table and start calculating.

The groom whispers, "Here are two sets of china, about 25 rubles each —fifty. A feather quilt worth 60 rubles, that's already 110. Now a crystal vase—20, makes 130! What else have we been given? Pillows, linen, shirts —add another 50."

"And what about the chandelier?" she asks.

"Twenty."

"Six wine glasses; true, one has been broken."

"The bastards! All the same, it is still worth ninety."

"What else . . . ?"

"Towels, a thermos, bucket, and flowers, add another 11 rubles, also a ball point pen, three bottles of wine and two tortes . . ."

Let us leave them alone, reader! . . .

"YOU TOO ARE SOMEHOW ALONE"

Under this heading a selection of letters to the editor appeared in Moscow, letters which deal with the subject of marriages arranged by electronic data processing (EDP). According to the editors, letters arrived in great numbers, and with one exception all favored such an arrangement, not yet available in the USSR. All letter writers considered the problem urgent; in her letter one woman used the distress signal SOS. (In the Soviet Union there are 65 million unmarried men and women between the ages of 18 and 60.) Here are quotations from the letters selected by A. Volodin; some writers asked that their names not be used.

A. Volodin, "Ty tozhe gde-nibud' odin" [You too are somewhere Alone], *Literaturnaya Gazeta,* 8 (1970), 13.

". . . It is considered improper to make acquaintances in the street, in the metro or cinema," writes B. Medvedev. "Young girls are supposed to look for husbands at dances, but middle-aged women, not wishing to meet the onset of old age alone, must find their life companions in parks of culture and recreation. Here, however, one encounters individuals searching for amorous adventures. Women must defend themselves from drunks, and hear dubious compliments, and sometimes insults as well. It turns out that even cemeteries are turned into meeting places. Many people who have recently lost a husband or wife go to the grave in hopes of finding some happiness to replace that which they have lost. Some of them succeed in this. Single people diligently search for information on someone similar to themselves. Isn't it possible to help them in this?"
[. . .]
". . . What do you do if you do not want to lower your requirements of a person who should be a friend for life, when you belong to the class of predominantly female teachers? What would a super moralistic hypocrite suggest in such a case? Run to dances and stand there next to one's own students. For whom it's the proper time to fall in love? It's inane, isn't it? It is a paradox: to love children and give them [in the school] your heart and mind and not have what is most dear—ones own children!"
"I am 22 years old and work in a female collective. I don't know how to get acquainted with someone in the street, and I do not yet date anyone. I know such young women at my place of work. We are already called old maids. I no longer believe that there is any love in the world; if there is it has passed me by. I am neither a monster nor a fool, but I can't do anything. What do you think, should one hope and wait? Or should one get married without love, as a neighbor advises me, in order not to remain alone? It would be horrible to marry without love. I don't want to do that. However, neither do I wish to become an old maid."
"There are enterprises and even industrial cities where there is a high

percentage of men. There are also those where there are many single young women who have passed 30 years of age. It thus appears that the problem of loneliness lies primarily in the impossibility of meeting people. After making acquaintances one can select, fall in love, and get married. Here EDP could play the role of fate, although only in the first stage. It would be unfortunate if this polemic were to continue as long as the discussion about the dotted line on the birth certificate [the place for the name of the father in cases of illegitimate children] because then many people would not be able to make use of EDP . . ." [. . .]

"Today people in love are similar to [newborn] blind cats. Potentially they have been in love for a long time; way before they meet a person they carry within their hearts the features, characteristics, habits and interests of the person they would like to love (and here a machine [EDP] could be of help). However, one must be satisfied with whatever comes along. The years fly by and one does not know where to look."

"Every person has his ideal in love, which is all the harder to find the higher the ideal is. It is not always among one's acquaintances, one must hope for a chance meeting, but this possibility is very small. The machine could considerably increase the probability of meeting such a person."

HIS PERSONAL LIFE IS EVERYONE'S OWN BUSINESS

An essay by Professor B. Urlanis, which favored the three-child family and compared a childless family to a vase without flowers (LG 39, 1972, 13), resulted in a "flood of letters." Here are three excerpts.

"V sem'ye odin rebenok?" [One Child in the Family?], *Literaturnaya Gazeta*, 46 (1972), 13.

Professor B. Urlanis's article is based on unproven axioms. For example, it talks about the properly understood interests of the family. However, each one sees them in his own way.

For some, the "properly understood interests of the family" is a

By chance the New York Times *almost simultaneously carried an article which describes, and comments on, the aversion of young American couples to have children. Comparison of the two quotations shows a startling similarity.*

Rita Kramer, The No-Child Family. Going against 100,000 years of biology, New York Times, *December 24, 1972.*

The main reason we enjoy our lives together is because we are together. I am not in the kitchen washing baby bottles while he thinks of an excuse to get out of the house because the baby is screaming.

pile of children not very well taken care of, with a minimum of tenderness, toys, and enjoyments. In my family this means having a comfortable home, eating well, fashionable clothes for my wife, trips to theatres, museums, cinema, a well-raised happy child, and vacations in the Crimea. One child is enough in order to experience the joys of being a father or mother.

Who can prove to me that my position is less convincing?

It is difficult to combine the first with the second: to have three children and also free time and money.

With respect to the interests of the state, the increase in the national product and the strengthening of its power can be obtained through other more effective and modern methods—putting all the potential of scientific-technical progress into action, thorough mechanization and automation, scientific organizations of labor, and so on . . .

Finally, in addition to academic coefficients there is another very concrete concept in demography: personal life. In it everything is voluntary. The desire to marry, to love a blonde or a brunette, to have many children or not to have any.

N. Kol'tsov, Leningrad

I am totally in agreement with the point of view of Professor B. Urlanis. I also have one child, a

The thing I find amusing is there are people our age with two or three children, struggling along, and they tell us we are missing something. Meanwhile we ride in a new car, own our own lakefront home, spend our summers on our boat, go away every weekend, and spend every Christmas holiday skiing in Europe. And they tell us we are missing something.

I'm sure there are some very happy families with children, but the unhappy ones far outnumber the happy ones. I don't want to take that chance.[. . .]

There are those of us who stop to think about the big fantastic world out there waiting to be explored. I feel that most people are so busy washing diapers and trying to balance the budget that they merely exist and look around them, but never see. They're too busy wiping runny noses.

After five years, both sets of parents are putting on the pressure for us to have kids. They have taken to calling our cat and two dogs their "grandchildren."

A man's life isn't anywhere near as greatly altered as a woman's once the baby arrives. He may need to increase his earnings, but there is still the job, a productive life outside. The woman will have to sacrifice many things. I would feel trapped in that role.

daughter. We have everything necessary to bear and raise a large number of children (a good apartment, a sound, secure income, and a kindergarten in the courtyard of the building, as well as other things). However, my wife is against it. Our women are more and more departing from the ways of their mothers and grandmothers in this regard, without any sort of serious reasons for it.

V. Burylov, Chemical
Engineer, Gorky

My husband wants to have three children. I have told him that I will not have so many children, even under the threat of being shot. One or two is sufficient. We already have one daughter.

Our child is now one year and four months old. I am glad that there are only four more months and I will cease to be a domestic worker. I will be around people, I will have many interests, and independent work for which I will be paid money. I will also dress well.

Don't judge me harshly: there is now another life and I am still young. In such times, can one completely deny the private life?

G. Aleksandrova

It's depressing how crucial my sister and I are to my mother—she more or less lives for us. I will never let that happen to me.

I want to live my life while I'm young. My parents were always telling me that after my younger brother and I were out of school they would do all the things they wanted to do. My father will be 60 by the time my brother's out of college.[. . .]

When we say we don't want kids, people ask us, "What if everyone felt the way you do?" What a silly question.

RAISED BY WEAK WOMEN

"It was for good reason that Marx valued strength in a man and softness in woman," says an article which notes with horror how male Soviet citizens are raised almost entirely by women. One might add that in the Soviet Union, aside from military academies, girls and boys attend the same schools. Even for the armed forces, according to the article, Feminisatsiya was a serious problem. Here are some passages.

K. Grigor'yev and B. Khandros, "Muzhchina ukhodit iz shkoly" [Men Leave the School], *Literaturnaya Gazeta,* 11 (1969), 12.

At the same time that we were working on this article, both the central and the republic press ran, as if specially planned, a whole series of articles on an educational theme. There were alarming articles of the type "The Price of Lack of Character" to exhortations: "Be a Man!," "Nevertheless: Become a Man!" One starts to feel somewhat uncomfortable in reading such a series of articles. . . . Has a masculine character really become such a scarce thing? This, in a nation where we have, as a norm of life, not simply individual heroes but mass heroism. Every day we see new affirmations of the courage of Soviet man. Where, therefore, does this infantile attitude, inertia, and lack of character come from?

A boy is born. From his very first days he sees his mother's tender eyes. And feels the warmth of her arms. Later the little person is sent to a nursery where he meets another good fairy—the nurse. Then our somewhat older person meets his educator, also a good aunt. Still later the lucky day, the very first September First [Beginning of school] arrives and he meets a new aunt, Yelena Vasil'yevna, who perhaps will be his beloved teacher all through his life. In any case, she will instruct and educate him. Later he will be taught by other female teachers . . . [. . .]

". . . The quite insufficient masculine influence on young boys in and out of school is now a serious problem. Among teachers and Pioneer leaders [the Pioneers are a Communist children's organization] the majority are females. In the family it is primarily the mother who raises the children . . . We do not propose to resurrect Spartan education. We are living in another epoch and have other goals. However, a young boy who does not receive the essential male upbringing during his childhood years is prematurely condemned to a listless, weak development and to excessive breaks and fissures in his character in the adolescent years. This is unavoidable." [Quotation from a statement by a member of the Academy of Pedagogical Sciences of the USSR] [. . .]

At many schools the Komsomol organizers and the heads of councils for Pioneer detachments, in other words, the entire active core of the class and school, consists entirely of women. Then later we wring our hands in surprise that boys are inert and without initiative. [. . .]

A sense of responsibility forces us to remember that today's youngsters are tomorrow's soldiers. The Soviet people are the most dedicated advocates of, and fighters for, peace. However, the time has not yet come to beat our swords into plowshares. Therefore the schools should raise a generation which, if necessary, can defend our achievements with weapons in hand. [. . .]

It was for good reason that Marx valued strength in man and softness in woman. [. . .]

It is thus clear that the schools need men. It is also a fact that men are leaving the schools. What about the replacements? We already know about the present contingent of students at pedagogical colleges. It is difficult to predict the shifts in the immediate future. Researchers at the Institute of Psychology have conducted a massive poll of senior class students and have demonstrated that in the list of professional interests pedagogical work comes last. Of 1,200 male students questioned, only 9 choose this profession. The same poll was conducted in Kiev before the war, in 1936. A comparison is very revealing. At that time the number of potential teachers among young men was at least 10 times higher.

FOR X: CONCLUDING REFLECTIONS

FROM THE KREMLIN ON HIGH

In June 1969 a Communist World Congress dealt for the first time with the New Left, when the "International Meeting of Communist and Workers' Parties" convened in Moscow, exactly one year after the May uprising in Paris. Brezhnev, Secretary General of the Soviet Communist Party, alluded to the unrest of youth (quotation I), and the "Main Document" of the conference also referred to it (II). In the following two years Brezhnev mentioned the problem two more times: in his talks before the Sixteenth Komsomol Congress (III) and before the Twenty-Fourth Party Congress (IV). Ponomarev, the Central Committee member responsible for relations with foreign Communist parties, spoke in 1971 (V), and in 1972 the party organ Politicheskoye Samoobrazovaniye *gave an official definition of the "left" (VI).*

Although this study carries only through the end of 1972, it is concluded with a quotation from the year 1973 (VIII). Five years after Zhukov's outcry against Marcuse (see the document, "The Three M's"), it suggests the deeply rooted bitterness of Moscow's orthodox Communists toward their unorthodox and radical rivals. M. Basmanov, a historian by training, is a leading specialist in leftist heresies, known especially for his writings against Trotskyism.

Throughout key words are set in italics, to show the development in the reaction of the party leadership to the New Left: Brezhnev's talk before the "International Meeting" contained a number of hostile words; the subsequent "Main Document" sounded rather more cautious, perhaps under the influence of Western Communist parties with a closer understanding of the New Left. Brezhnev's remarks before the Komsomol Congress were brief and emphasized the more positive aspect of youthful unrest, his words before the Party Congress were longer and more negative. Ponomarev spoke with considerable hostility, the official definition from spring 1972 contained nothing positive or even charitable about the New Left, and Basmanov's article only angry criticism. In short: The party leadership in Moscow, as the years went by, grew more rigid in its rejection of the New Left, while the intellectual writers, as this study has shown, became increasingly understanding.

I. There are now many new problems of work with the intelligentsia, especially with that part of it which, together with the working class, is engaged in industry and subject to ever greater exploitation. Professions

205

requiring intellectual labor are becoming ever more massive. The engineering-technical intelligentsia in the capitalist nations is now formed not only from representatives of the bourgeoisie but also from the middle strata, in particular from workers. All this makes significant changes in the relationship of the intelligentsia to the capitalist order and brings its interests close to the interests of the working class.

Communist parties cannot ignore these changes. As experience indicates, the intensification of their work with the intelligentsia increases its activity in the anti-imperialist struggle.

The extensive attention which fraternal parties are now giving to work among youth is natural. After all, it is a fact that the young generation in the capitalist nations, including the students, has been seized by revolutionary ferment. Youth is actively struggling against imperialistic wars, against the militarization of bourgeois society, and against attempts of the bourgeoisie to curtail the democratic rights of working people.

True, the actions of youth frequently indicate *lack of political experience and of ties with the advance guard of the revolutionary struggle.* Therefore, its actions are frequently of a *spontaneous nature* and are expressed in politically *immature* forms. *Extremists,* elements essentially *hostile to Communism,* and frequently *simply agents of the imperialists,* attempt to make use of this. However, it cannot be doubted that, having mastered the theory of scientific socialism and armed with the experience of class struggles, the young fighters against imperialism will accomplish great deeds (June 7, 1969, in *Kommunist,* 9 [1969], 57).

II. In our epoch, when science is being transformed into a direct productive force, the intelligentsia is increasingly entering the ranks of wage labor. Its social interests are intertwined with the interests of the working class, and its creative efforts collide with the interests of owners-monopolists, for whom profit is most important. Although there are substantial differences in the situation of various groups of the intelligentsia, an ever greater part of it is entering the conflict with the monopolies and with the imperialist policies of the governments. The crisis of bourgeois ideology and the attractive force of socialism help put the intelligentsia on the path of the anti-imperialist struggle. The alliance of intellectual and physical workers is becoming an ever more significant force in the struggle for peace, democracy, social progress and for democratic control over production, institutions of culture and information, and for the development of education in the interests of the people.

The convergence of the interests of the peasantry, the urban middle strata and the intelligentsia with the interests of the working class, their growing cooperation will restrict the social base of monopoly power, sharpen its internal contradictions and assist in the mobilization of broad masses into the struggle against monopolies and imperialism.

[. . .] The growing number of young people and the intensification of their political activity have become important factors in the social life of Western Europe, America, Japan, Turkey, and other nations.

The actions of youth reflect the deep crisis of contemporary bourgeois society. Working people, above all working youth, who are subject to super exploitation and who see no prospects for themselves under capitalism, are ever more actively engaging in the class struggle, and joining trade unions, Communist and other democratic organizations. Broad masses of students are engaging in actions not only against the shortcomings of the lagging educational system, not only for the right to have their organizations and to participate effectively in the management of educational institutions, but also they are opposing the policies of the ruling classes. Ever more young people, inspired by the struggle of the Vietnamese people and other examples of heroic struggle against imperialism, are participating in large-scale public protests against imperialism, for democracy, peace and socialism.

Communists highly value the upsurge in the youth movement and actively participate in it. They disseminate the ideas of scientific socialism throughout its ranks and explain the danger of various types of pseudo-revolutionary ideas which could influence youth. Communists strive to help youth find the proper path in the struggle against imperialism and in the protection of its own interests. *Only close ties with* the workers' movement and *its Communist advance guard* can open for youth truly revolutionary perspectives (June 17, 1969, in *Kommunist,* 9 [1969], 19 ff.).

III. We are witnesses of an upsurge in the youth movement in the nations of capital. This is a *major symptom of the intensification of the general crisis of capitalism.* Youth will not tolerate an exploitative order and the bloody adventures of imperialism. The massive demonstrations of young workers, peasants, and students, as well as the mass nature and militant spirit of their actions, have become a *serious factor of the political struggle* in the capitalist nations in recent years (May 26, 1970, in *Molodoy Kommunist,* 7 [1970], 10).

IV. However, comrades, we cannot ignore the fact that *negative phenomena have not been overcome everywhere*. This above all means the pressing struggle against right and "left" revisionism, against nationalism. It is precisely on nationalist tendencies, and in particular on those which assume the form of *anti-Sovietism,* that bourgeois ideologists and bourgeois propaganda most eagerly place their stakes in the struggle against socialism and the Communist movement. They push the *opportunistic elements in the Communist parties* into a sort of ideological bargain. In a way, they say to them: Show that you are anti-Soviet and we will be ready to announce that it is you who are the genuine "Marxists" and have a completely "independent position." Incidentally, the course of events indicates that such people also take the path of struggle *against the Communist parties* in their own nations. Examples of this are the renegades such as Garaudy in France, Fischer in Austria, and Petkov in Venezuela, as well as individuals in the "Manifesto" group in Italy. The fraternal parties view the *struggle against such elements* as an important factor in strengthening their own ranks. Thus, these examples, and one could cite many more, are evidence that the *struggle against revisionism* and nationalism *remains an important task for* Communist parties (Applause) (March 30, 1971, in *Kommunist,* 5 [1971], 17).

V. [. . .] The movement of the so-called New Lefts is one of the indicators of the shift leftward. Its main base consists of *radical strata of the intelligentsia, and of youth, primarily students.* The movement is not distinguished by homogeneity nor by ideological or organizational integrity. It is widely led by various types of *adventurist* elements, including *Maoists and Trotskyites.* Participants in the movement are *easily influenced by revolutionary phraseology.* They *lack the necessary restraint and capability of soberly evaluating the situation. Some of them are clearly infected by anti-Communist prejudices.* However, they undoubtedly have a general anti-imperialistic orientation. Overlooking this part of the mass movement would reduce the intense heat of the anti-imperialistic struggle and hinder the development of a unified front against monopoly capital.

Of course, in itself, the *shift to the left does not guarantee success.* Everything depends on whether the progressive forces of the workers' movement, above all the Communist parties, can unify the anti-monopolist front, consolidate new positions, and defeat all varieties of revisionism (*Kommunist,* 15 [1971], 51).

VI. As is known, there are individuals and various groups claiming that they are even more "left" and even more "revolutionary" than genuine Marxist-Leninists. *Such heroes of the ultra-revolutionary phraseology are called "lefts" in quotation marks. They should be distinguished from the genuine revolutionaries*—Communists, and Marxist-Leninists who are in the advance guard of the forces of democracy, freedom, and social progress, and at the front line of the struggle against imperialism.

Denying the necessity of a broad, general democratic program of anti-imperialist struggle, and the combination of general democratic and proletarian class goals and interests, *"left" opportunists thus create the danger of isolating the revolutionary advanced guard from broad strata of workers, condemn it to a passive waiting or leftist and adventurist actions. They are opposed to fusing the main revolutionary forces of the present day into a single stream,* absolutize the armed form of struggle for power, and deny or pervert the principles of peaceful coexistence of states with different social systems. As a rule, "left" opportunism is combined with dogmatism and inevitably leads to sectarian rigidity. [. . .]

One of the very favorite theses of revisionists, which, incidentally, they have taken directly from bourgeois literature, is the thesis that the working class of the developed capitalist nations has lost its revolutionary potential and has "integrated itself" into bourgeois society. [. . .]

Opportunists attempt to oppose the working class with the intelligentsia as the main moving force of social development. Thus, the fairly well-known apostate of Marxism, R. Garaudy, in his book *The Great Turning Point of Socialism,* suggests replacing the concept "working class" with the concept "new historical block of workers performing mental and physical labor." However, according to the assertions of this renegade, only scientists and researchers "are at the present time the bearers of the decisive force for the transformation of the world." The *working class thus ceases to be hegemonic and the leader of the contemporary revolutionary process.*

"Left" revisionists—*anarchists, Trotskyites, Maoists, "New Lefts,"* and others—go to the other extreme with respect to the question of the role of the working class. They are armed with the ideas of bourgeois scholars on the "dying out" of the revolutionary attitudes of the working class, on the advancement, as it is said, of lower urban elements, of *unemployed, declassé elements, students, "left" groups of the intelligentsia,* and others to the forefront of the anti-imperialistic struggle. Striving to attract *insuffi-*

ciently experienced young men and women who are not versed in politics, the "left" entices them with *ultra revolutionary phrases and slogans* amounting to a call for an immediate, world-wide uprising.

"Lefts" frequently hide their disbelief in the revolution, their "disappointment" in the working class, under *pseudo-revolutionary and pseudo-class phraseology about "bourgeois nations" and "proletarian nations."* Adherents of this concept, among whom the Maoists occupy a prominent position, state that the main contradiction of our era does not arise from the opposition between capitalism and socialism, but from the difference between the "world city," that is, the industrial powers, and the "world village," the economically backward nations of Asia, Africa, and Latin America. *Thus, the radical opposition of two social systems is replaced by pseudo-scientific geopolitical theories.*

The concept of "bourgeois nations" and "proletarian nations" is disseminated by its adherents both among the new national states and the developed capitalist nations. On the one hand, the concept "proletarian nations" is used to serve the idea of *"cooperation" between the bourgeois and working class* of the developing nations. It is a call to break all contacts with the working class of the more developed nations. On the other hand, the concept "bourgeois nations" is used in the attempt to "prove" that the workers of the developed capitalist nations have lost their revolutionary potential and are not interested in the struggle against capitalist society. [. . .]

Wrapped in ultra-revolutionary phrases, the "left," above all the "Maoists," deprecate the decisive role of the world socialist system in the anti-imperialist struggle, and carry out divisive policies within the international Communist movement. *They fan hatred against the socialist countries and Communist parties,* attacking above all the USSR and CPSU. They slanderously accuse the latter of "revisionism" and "plotting with imperialism" (I. Golovatyy, "Ponyatiya 'pravyye' i 'levyye' v politicheskom Leksikone" [The Concepts of "right" and "left" in the Political Lexicon], *Politicheskoye Samoobrazovaniye,* 3 [1972], 108–112. Here pp. 110 ff.).

VII. On the road [on which move the adherents of quick solutions] there is a fork: to the right or to the left. The road to the right leads to fascism. [. . .], If, however, one takes a sharp "left" turn, then one can encounter the most diverse variants of anarchism and petty-bourgeois "revolutionaryism," which resembles anarchism or borrows much from it. [. . .]

The advocates of "only direct actions" win a sizable number of their followers from among that section of radically oriented youth which is characterized by ideological turmoil, a low political "inflammability," a readiness to respond to the most adventurist calls, and which in addition is not capable of self-control, organization, or discipline. The unstable, overheated revolutionary attitude of such people is, as is known, accompanied by an overestimation of their own forces and potentials by a neglect of the working class and by prejudice against its parties. As a rule, such attitudes are characteristic of young people who have not directly experienced capitalist exploitation [i.e. of students from bourgeois families].

Extremist groups have a motley make-up. There are political adventurers, fanatics, and simply people who are psychologically disturbed. [. . .] To them the working people are only an object to "stir up," a gray faceless mass which must be "ignited" and "led." This requires "strong personalities," heroes and "groups with initiative," set above the masses and called upon to give them a "strong shove." [. . .]

Extremists do great harm in that they discredit the very idea of revolutionary force. [. . .]

In addition it is quite obvious that without force the revolution is impossible.

(M. Basmanov, "Bessil'nyye bomby. Komu na ruku 'revolyutsionnyy' ekstremizm?" [Powerless Bombs. Whom Does 'Revolutionary' Extremism Serve?], *Literaturnaya Gazeta,* 14 [1973], 13).

MATERIALS

MATERIALS

Experience with Soviet periodicals for almost half a century, more exactly since my university studies began in 1925, prompted me to research primarily the *journals* and *periodicals* for this study, and only in exceptional cases the *daily press,* for example for reportage on the May 1968 events in Paris.

On examining the last twelve years of Moscow's weekly index of Soviet articles (*Letopis Zhurnalnykh Statei*), I found that twenty-five periodicals and monthlies warranted closer inspection. This inspection in turn revealed that most of the pertinent articles on the New Left had been published in a few organs, while the rest discussed the subject only sporadically. A sampling of periodicals, beyond the twenty-five studied closely, showed that their meager commentaries followed the lines of the leading periodicals and contained no new insights.

Before the May 1968 eruption in Paris, Soviet journalism took almost no notice of the New Left. Therefore I looked through most of the selected periodicals only from 1967–1968 on, and through a few earlier periodicals, some from 1960: those especially concerned with Western youth, or those of which I expected results. In each case I have noted the years I checked.

The four hundred articles used in this study should provide a fairly complete picture of the subject. They are listed alphabetically in the appended bibliography. If a reader knows additional articles that illuminate Moscow's views, I would be happy to have such references.

The matter of books and pamphlets is less satisfying. It is relatively simple to obtain Soviet periodicals, but often difficult to obtain books and especially pamphlets; thus a researcher is partly dependent on accident. The bibliography lists almost exclusively books and pamphlets that I have actually seen. Emphasis in this study was clearly on periodicals; they are more frequently printed, more easily obtained, and in large part contain what is later published in book form.

Of the twenty-five periodicals examined, let me briefly describe these: In quality *Voprosy Filosofii* is the leader, quantitatively *Literaturnaya*

215

Gazeta, followed by *Molodoy Kommunist.* *MEiMO* is the leader in observation of Western countries generally, *SShA* specializes in America, *Inostrannaya Literatura* in literature outside the Soviet Union. *New Times,* the English-language edition (which I used) of *Novoye Vremya,* carries many, but brief articles. Despite a disappointing yield, *Kommunist* is also among the leaders. The official humor magazine *Krokodil* is more interesting for negative than for positive reasons.

To give the reader an idea of the relative meagerness (or fulness) of pertinent essays in individual periodicals, I have included the number of contributions, by years if there are many.

Agitator

Organ of the Central Committee of the Soviet Communist Party; it appears monthly in 64-page issues; circulation: 1,350,000. The six years examined: 1967 through 1972; pertinent articles: 4.

Azia i Afrika Segodnya (Asia and Africa Today)

Organ of the two institutes for Asian Studies (*vostokovedeniye*) and African Studies of the Soviet Academy of Sciences; appears monthly in 56-page issues; circulation not listed. The four years examined: 1968 through 1971; pertinent articles: 2.

Inostrannaya Literatura (Foreign Literature)

Organ of the Writers' Union of the USSR; appears monthly, at 288 pages; circulation not announced. The five years examined: 1968 through 1972; pertinent articles: 1968, 1; 1969, 5; 1970, 1; 1971, 6; 1972, 1; total: 14.

International Affairs

Organ of the society "Znaniye" ("Knowledge"); appears every month in 120-page issues; circulation not listed. The five years examined: 1968 through 1972; pertinent articles: 5.

Kommunist

Organ of the Central Committee of the Communist Party of the Soviet Union; eighteen issues yearly at 128 pages; circulation: 859,000. The five years examined: 1968 through 1972; pertinent articles (including leading articles): 1968, 3; 1969, 3; 1970, 3; 1971, 1; 1972, 3; total: 13.

The party's central organ, before any others, would seem the logical place to comment on the new rivals on the left and to set down the rules of discussion. But *Kommunist* spoke out only after a series of other periodicals had risked taking positions (see Chapter II). Only Minayev's February 1970 article really commented on the subject; the other authors treated secondary questions, especially the "scientific-technological revolution," a relatively neutral, favorite topic. The difference between the slow-moving *Kommunist* and the lively *Voprosy Filosofii* can probably be explained by the ideological ossification of the first.

Kommunist Vooruzhennykh Sil (Communist of the Armed Forces)

Organ of the central political administrators of the Soviet Army and Navy; appears monthly at 96 pages; circulation not given. The eight years examined: 1965 through 1972; pertinent articles: 5.

Krokodil

Organ of *Pravda,* daily paper of the Central Committee of the Communist Party of the Soviet Union; appears weekly in 16-page issues; circulation: 5,580,000. The eight years examined: 1964 through 1971.

The examination of almost a decade of this magazine proved very disappointing. One would have thought that the colorful, scurrilous life style of the Beatniks, hippies, commune dwellers, street demonstrators, and university occupiers would give Soviet humorists endless material for their brushes and typewriters. But that was not the case. Anyone drawing only on *Krokodil* for knowledge on Western youth's unrest would never know what was going on.

Below are listed topics which *Krokodil* caricatured; its criticism is directed almost exclusively not against Western youth, but against the Soviet imitators of Western youth: long-hairs doing the twist (14, 1964, 15); "modern-chic," a hippie as monkey (17, 1964, 7); loafers (8, 1965, 4); solemn opening of a "drying-out" facility (8, 1965, 7); a Russian girl copying insane Western hair styles (29, 1965, 7); aping of the West (17, 1967, 7); when Soviet children reach hippie-age the parents say: "My son doesn't shave anymore, my daughter already wears short skirts" (22, 1967, 13); Russian hippie (1, 1968, 9); Western dances in the USSR (3, 1968, 3); Russian hippie wants to join the merchant marines. Why? Because they wear bell bottoms (5, 1968, 14); "Save me from boredom," is the plea of a Soviet drunk (22, 1968, 5); finally something political on Western youth: In America they burn induction notices! (25, 1968, 7), but nothing on May in Paris or on the invasion of Czechoslovakia; long-hairs in Russia (12, 1969, 7); good-for-nothing daughter raids the refrigerator (23,

1969, 13); Russian boys and girls—indistinguishable, since both wear pants and long hair (26, 1968, 1); "communal language" of youth: the radio (14, 1970, 7); Soviet girls with very brief skirts (25, 1970, 5); juvenile vandalism (32, 1970, 2); uncouth young people mock the law (35, 1970, 1); hippies are not interested in culture (9, 1971, 5); youth loves hot music more than classical (14, 1971, 9); young Russians racing motorcycles (15, 1971, 1); hippie hair styles (31, 1971, 6).

Literaturnaya Gazeta (*Literary Gazette*)

Organ of the Writers' Union of the USSR; appears weekly in 16-page issues; circulation not listed. The five years examined: 1968 through 1972; pertinent articles: 1968, 3; 1969, 20; 1970, 20; 1971, 21; 1972, 25; total: 89.

Despite its unlisted circulation *Literaturnaya Gazeta* must belong to the most widely read weeklies in the world. It is read far beyond the limited circle of those interested in literature, partly because of its literary section, but not least because it reports on foreign countries, often from where events take place. As a weekly *Literaturnaya Gazeta* comments on the latest topics faster than the monthlies; it is also livelier, more awake, more controversial, and therefore less didactic than the others.

The Soviet citizen who wants to know something of new political developments and events in the West reads the *Literaturnaya Gazeta,* not the tedious and boring newspapers of the Western Communist parties, like *Neues Deutschland. Literaturnaya Gazeta* is valuable for the Russian reader because it discusses—though one-sidedly and often inaccurately— subjects on which other organs are silent, or give a delayed response starched with ideology. Although it has attacked me more frequently than other publications (I mentioned one such case in the preface), its liveliness makes it my favorite Soviet paper.

If millions of people in the Soviet Union have some idea of important, contemporary Western thinkers, ideas, and books, they owe this primarily to the *Literaturnaya Gazeta.* A disadvantage is that it is hard to obtain outside the large cities except by subscription, and sometimes not even then, as readers' letters indicate. I hardly ever saw it in provincial newsstands. The large number of articles from *Literaturnaya Gazeta* used in this study is partly because, in the chapters "Is the West Decaying?" and "Is the Soviet Union Really Immune?", I used essays that do not comment directly on the New Left, but on sociological and psychological topics related to our subject.

Mirovaya Ekonomika i Mezhdunarodnyye Otnosheniya (MEiMO) (World Economy and International Relations)

Organ of the identically named Institute of the Academy of Sciences of the USSR; appears monthly in 160-page issues; circulation: 42,000. The thirteen years examined: from 1960 through 1972; pertinent articles: 1960–1965, 0; 1966, 1; 1967, 0; 1968, 2; 1969, 4; 1970, 6; 1971, 12; 1972, 4; total: 29.

As indicated by its title, MEiMO deals with international studies generally, and as part of this, with ideological and sociological issues. Hence the New Left also belongs to its area of concern. Its stance toward the New Left is more austere than that of Literaturnaya Gazeta or Molodoy Kommunist; it shows little interest in the colorful, extravagant, disorderly aspect of Western youth.

Significantly, MEiMO carried its first essay on the Western youth movement in 1966, years after Molodoy Kommunist, and in the following year again fell practically silent. From 1960 through 1967, MEiMO published a number of essays on social conflict in countries with radical student groups (Japan, Latin America, Italy, West Germany, America), and articles on ideological subjects (petty-bourgeoisie, national liberation movements, class struggle, bourgeois ideologies). But it used none of these opportunities to comment on the role and the ideas of the students. Even after May 1968 in Paris it continued to report on similar issues without commenting on the New Left. Such essays are not included in the bibliography or in the figures above. Finally, from 1969 on, essays on the New Left did appear in greater numbers.

Molodaya Gvardiya (Young Guard)

Organ of the Central Committee of the Communist Youth Organization (Komsomol); appears monthly at 320 pages; circulation: 367,000. The five years examined: 1968 through 1972; pertinent articles: 3.

Molodoy Kommunist (The Young Communist)

Organ of the Central Committee of the Communist Youth Organization (Komsomol); appears monthly in 124-page issues; circulation: 785,000. The thirteen years examined: 1960 through 1972; pertinent articles: 1960, 2; 1961, 7; 1962, 3; 1963, 3; 1964, 1; 1965, 0; 1966, 3; 1967, 4; 1968, 3; 1969, 13; 1970, 10; 1971, 4; 1972, 10; total: 63.

Despite its large circulation, this periodical is no mass medium, but an organ of the Komsomol leadership. Of course it deals primarily with internal issues of the Komsomol and the Soviet Union, and only tangentially with foreign countries. But it reported on foreign youth before other periodicals, although at first, as we saw in Chapter II, very traditionally and without hints that something new, the New Left, was in the offing. *Molodoy Kommunist's* intense concern with Western youth must be due to its maintaining connections with many Communist, semi-Communist, and one quarter-Communist youth organizations abroad. Quite a few of its usually young editorial staff thus have intermittent opportunities to meet with Western youth—in the Soviet Union or abroad, during youth festivals or conferences—and to gather livelier impressions than those obtained from foreign newspaper clippings by reporters at home, at their desk in Moscow. This more intimate view of the nature of Western youth resulted in greater understanding of the New Left, and a generally more positive attitude toward it, than is to be found in other periodicals.

Narody Aziy i Afriki (*The Peoples of Asia and Africa*)

Organ of the two institutes for Asian Studies (*vostokovedeniye*) and African Studies of the Academy of Sciences of the USSR; appears six times annually at 260 pages; listed circulation: 4000. The two years examined: 1971 through 1972; pertinent articles: 2.

New Times (English Edition of *Novoye Vremya*)

Publisher: *Trud*; appears weekly in six languages, at 32 pages; circulation not listed. The six years examined: 1967 through 1972; pertinent articles: 35.

The quotations in this study are from *New Times*, the English-language edition of *Novoye Vremya*. The periodical's role is to inform both Soviet and foreign readers about Soviet and foreign events. Its staff of foreign correspondents is large. Since the weekly issues deal with many subjects, often in very short articles and notes, *New Times* can be topical and current but its contributions are too brief to penetrate deeply. A special issue on the "American crisis" (29, 1971) avoids discussing youthful unrest in America in its six brief individual articles.

Novyy Mir (*New World*)

Organ of the Writers' Union of the USSR; appears monthly at 288 pages; circulation: 157,000. The six years examined: 1967 through 1972; pertinent articles: 7.

Among the "thick journals" *Novyy Mir* for many years enjoyed the best reputation in the Soviet Union and abroad, above all in a literary way but also in publishing in general. Many significant works of the new Soviet literature first appeared in it, among them Solzhenitsyn's first stories. Even after the unfortunate January 1970 departure of chief editor Aleksandr Tvardovsky, since deceased, it still merits the reader's attention. And that obtains to its few essays pertinent to our subject.

Oktyabr' (October)

Organ of the Writers' Union of the RSFSR; appears monthly at 224 pages; circulation: 159,000. The four years examined: 1969 through 1972; pertinent articles numbered 3, in addition to Kochetov's novel.

Politicheskoye Samoobrazovaniye (Political Self-Education)

Organ of the Central Committee of the Communist Party of the USSR; appears monthly at 144 pages; circulation: 1,731,000. The five years examined: 1968 through 1972; pertinent articles: 5.

Sovyetskoye Gosudarstvo i Pravo (Soviet State and Law)

Organ of the Institute for Constitutional Law of the Academy of Sciences of the USSR; appears monthly in 160-page issues; circulation: about 33,000. The two years examined: 1971 and 1972; pertinent articles: 1971, 2; 1972, 1.

SShA (Soyedinyonniye Shtaty Ameriki = USA)

Organ of the Institute for American Studies, Moscow; appears monthly at 128 pages; circulation: 32,000. I examined it from the first issue through 1972; pertinent articles: 11.

This organ of the recently-founded SShA Institute published eleven articles on our subject, mainly concerning America, in its first three years—less than Molodoy Kommunist, for which America is but one country among many. SShA moves with some caution as if, being relatively new, it lacks sufficient confidence. The best essays are by Kon and by Yulina and Zenushkina, although Kon's, compared with his other essays, brings hardly anything new. Gil Green, very favorably reviewed in September 1972, is an American Communist.

Teatr (Theater)

Organ of the Writers' Union and of the Cultural Ministry of the USSR; appears monthly at 192 pages; circulation: 20,000. The five years examined: 1968 through 1972; pertinent articles: 3.

Vestnik Vysshey Shkoly (*The Academic Messenger*)

Organ of the Ministry for Higher Education and Trade Schools; appears monthly at 96 pages; circulation: 10,865. The three years examined: 1968 through 1970; pertinent articles: 2.

Voprosy Filosofii (*Problems of Philosophy*)

Organ of the Institute of Philosophy of the Academy of Sciences of the USSR; appears monthly at about 190 pages each; circulation: 40,000. The six years examined: 1967 through 1972; pertinent articles: 1966–67, 1; 1968, 5; 1969, 6; 1970, 2; 1971, 3; 1972, 6; total: 23.

This journal deserves praise, if for no other reason, because it is one of few that documents every (or almost every) quotation, and in every case identifies its contributors on the next-to-last-page. Some of the most thorough essays on our subject appeared in it, among them two by the husband-and-wife team Zamoshkin and Motroshilova. Zamoshkin belongs to the periodical's editorial board and is also a department head at the Institute of the International Workers' Movement; his wife Ninel Motroshilova (Ninel is "Lenin" spelled backward, a favorite girl's name in the USSR) is a researcher and associate at the Institute of Philosophy of the Academy of Sciences. Two essays are by the famous physicist Kapitsa, two by the specialist in French affairs, Mrs. Myalo, from the Institute of the International Workers' Movement. The essays by Ostrovityanov (acting chief editor of *MEiMO*), the sociologist Kon, and the ideologue Batalov (lecturer at the Institute for the Social Sciences) are also important.

In the spring of 1969 the essay by Maya Novinskaya, research fellow at the Academy of Sciences' Institute of the International Workers' Movement, was to introduce, according to an announcement, a series "on the theme of youth and social progress"; for unknown reasons, however, this series never materialized. Perhaps the editors recognized that, at the time, the theme was too touchy for a whole series. An alternate series appeared, on the "scientific-technological revolution"; it was introduced by Meleshchenko, then head of the Leningrad branch of the Institute for Natural History and Technology of the Academy of Sciences. This series continued for months, indicating the significance of the subject for the ideologists.

Two authors writing on our subject were foreigners, the American Howard Parsons and the East German Dieter Ulle. As we know, Parsons' essay grew from a lecture; he had been invited, as early as 1967, to give it in Moscow. This suggests that *Voprosy Filosofii* was the first of the major Soviet periodicals to consider the New Left worthy of study.

Voprosy Literatury (*Problems of Literature*)

Organ of the Writers' Union of the USSR and of the A. M. Gorky Institute for World Literature of the Soviet Academy of Sciences; appears monthly at 256 pages; circulation: 20,000. The five years examined: 1968 through 1972; pertinent articles: 2.

Yunost' (*Youth*)

Organ of the Writers' Union of the USSR; appears monthly at 112 pages; circulation: 2 million. The six years examined: 1967 through 1972; pertinent articles: 2.

Za Rubezhom (*Abroad*)

Organ of the Journalists' Union of the USSR; appears weekly at 32 pages; circulation: 1,000,000. The three years examined: 1970 through 1972; pertinent articles: 6.

AUTHORS

AUTHORS

Three institutes, above all, treat our subject; all three belong to the Soviet Academy of Sciences.

Among the co-workers of the "Institute for World Economy and International Relations" (MEiMO) are—or were—Brychkov (special interest, USA), Diligensky (France), Yaropolov (Italy), Ostrovityanov, Reutova (West Germany), Shlikhter (USA); at the "Institute of the International Workers' Movement" (Institut Mezhdunarodnogo Rabotshego Dvizheniya), among others, Batalov, Bykov, Kantor, Myalo, Novinskaya, Zamoshkin, Vul'f; among the associates at the—now changed—"Institute for Concrete Sociological Research" (Institut Konkretnykh Sotsiologicheskikh Isledovaniy) Kon is most prominent.

At the *Literaturnaya Gazeta,* which contributed a great deal to knowledge of the New Left and of its sociological and psychological background, Arab-Ogly is one of the important authors, also the America-correspondents, Borovik and his successor Gerasimov, as well as the France specialist Molchanov. *Molodoy Kommunist* found its authors at various institutes; like Brychkov and Reshetov, some had previously worked for Komsomol. The authors of pertinent essays in *Voprosy Filosofii,* published by the "Institute of Philosophy," also came mainly from the outside.

Two authors have treated our subject most extensively: Brychkov and Kon. Aleksandr Rodionovich Brychkov, who is in his late thirties, contributed the most essays, in number and extent, and was also among the first to recognize the subject's significance and to begin its intensive treatment. A decisive contributing factor is probably this: After his university studies in Moscow, during which he worked in the Komsomol and in student organizations, he was active for several years (until 1963) in the Moscow-oriented International Student Council in Prague; then, at the MEiMO Institute, he concentrated on the problem of the New Left, especially the American New Left. His years in Prague brought him contacts with the youth of many countries, even non-Communists, and broadened his outlook; he also spent time abroad, kept his eyes open and worked hard. Of course the results of his studies are put into the framework of official ideology, but he was above all interested in the facts. His pamphlet *Uprising at the Alma Mater* (1971) was, after Lomeyko's the second work on the subject; his book *Young America* was the first of its kind. This book was typeset in 1970, though not on the market until 1972; the pamphlet appeared in 87,370 copies, the book in 65,000. It was followed by a book in English, *American Youth Today,* certainly the best English-language summary (only for foreign consumption) of enlightened Soviet views on the New Left.

The first pamphlet on restless youth, *Left of Truth,* was written by Vladimir Borisovich Lomeyko. In age and temperament he resembles Brychkov; he, too, spent some time abroad, for example as correspondent for the news agency APN in Bonn until 1971. But in contrast to Brychkov, he did not specialize in our subject and, perhaps for this reason, discussed it in traditional Moscow fashion. Lomeyko's pamphlet and Brychkov's book have been published in a new series of the *Molodaya Gvardiya* (*Young Guard*) press. The series includes plans for additional works on our subject. The latest pamphlet of the former diplomat S. Salychev, "The New Left," received its imprimatur in September 1972, indicating that interest is still strong.

Igor Semyonovich Kon, doctor of philosophy and department head in the sociological institute, regards the New Left less as a notable historical event (as does Brychkov), rather he sees it in the sociological-psychological context. He is interested in modern phenomena of civilization, East or West, among other phenomena related directly or indirectly to the nature and developmental tendencies of youth, in other words questions of family, sexuality, education, or of the intelligentsia. Kon tries to communicate his knowledge in readable form. Like Brychkov, he does not try to press all phenomena into a dogmatic Procrustean bed.

Eduard Arturovich Arab-Ogly, 48, does much for the dissemination of news about Western youth's problems, which he observes with keen interest. Above all he helped introduce the Soviet public to Charles Reich's *Greening of America.* Despite his Turkic (Azerbaijan) surname he is considered a Russian; among other posts, he held that of lecturer at the "Academy of Social Sciences of the Communist Party's Central Committee"; his wife, Lilya Nikitina, is also listed in the bibliography.

The bibliography in fact contains several married couples. Besides Arab-Ogly and Nikitina there are Diligensky (MEiMO Institute) and Novinskaya (Institute of the International Workers' Movement); Salychev (MEiMO Institute) and Salycheva (area of interest, USA); and finally Zamoshkin (Institute of the International Workers' Movement, one of the editors of *Voprosy Filosofii*) and Motroshilova (Institute of Philosophy).

Two more names deserve mention. Pyotr Leonidovich Kapitsa, the ex-émigré, is one of the most important Soviet physicists. At eighty, he can afford to speak openly even about touchy ideological questions. Y. Gnedin is held in high esteem among the younger generation of writers, probably in part because he spent years in Stalin's camps. He deserves praise, especially at his age, for his sympathetic understanding of the New Left; yet significantly—for him and others—he was able to write that "the [students'] breakthrough from passivity to revolt" began "only at the beginning of the seventies."

Despite membership in various institutes and editorial boards, many of the journalists above have known each other for a long time, some since their student years. But although they discuss the New Left, they form no closed group, as we have seen, and are of unequal importance. A *Pravda* article by Yuri Zhukov, an essay by the France-expert Molchanov, even a few words by Pyotr Kapitsa have much more influence than homework by many almost unknown writers. But in this study the influence of individual authors was not the issue, rather the sum of their knowledge about the New Left. This knowledge is greater than I expected when starting out, and greater than Soviet readers know, unless they are particularly interested in the New Left.

BIBLIOGRAPHY

BIBLIOGRAPHY

This bibliography lists all pertinent articles and books by Soviet authors that I have examined for this study. As expressly noted, a few books have become known to me only through reviews. Some non-Russian articles and books mentioned in the text are also listed. When essay titles leave their subject matter unclear, I indicate the subject by a key word (in parentheses).

Abbreviations

IL	*Inostrannaya Literatura*
K	*Kommunist*
Koms. Pr.	*Komsomol'skaya Pravda*
KVS	*Kommunist Vooruzhennykh Sil*
LG	*Literaturnaya Gazeta*
MEiMO	*Mirovaya Ekonomika i Mezhdunarodnvye Otnosheniya*
MK	*Molodoy Kommunist*
NT	*New Times*
PS	*Politicheskoye Samoobrazovaniye*
SShA	*Soyedinyonniye Shtaty Ameriki*
VF	*Voprosy Filosofii*

Afanas'yev, V. G. *Nauchno-tekhnicheskaya revolyutsiya, upravleniye, obrazovaniye* [Scientific-Technical Revolution, Management, Education]. Moscow, 1972, 431 pp. A review in *VF*, 1 (1973), 247–248.

Aldridge, James. "Mnimyy avangard: komu on sluzhit?" [The Pseudo-Avant-garde: Whom Does it Serve?]. *K*, 18 (1969), 103–112. A letter from London, especially on modern art.

———. "Tuman v upakovke" [Fog in Wrapping]. *LG* (1971), 14 ff. A negative interpretation of Charles Reich.

Aleksandrova, O. "Studenchestvo v sisteme vysshego obrazovaniya SShA" [The Student Body in the System of Higher Education in the U.S.]. *MEiMO*, 6 (1971), 112–118.

Alekseyev, V. "Za kolyuchey provolokoy" [Beyond the Barbed Wire]. *MK*, 10 (1969), 100–107. A short report on Greece.

Alferov, M. "Studencheskiye 'bezporyadki' v zapadnom Berline" [Student "Disorders" in West Berlin]. *Vestnik Vysshey Shkoly*, 1 (1968), 90–92.

Ambartsumov, Ye. "Mozhno li potushit' etot pozhar? Studencheskoye dvizheniye i burzhuaznyye ideologi" [Can the Fire Be Extinguished? The Student Movement and Bourgeois Ideology]. *LG*, 30 (1969), 1 and 14.

———. "Utrachennye illyuzii professora Gelbreyta" [The Lost Illusions of Professor Galbraith]. *LG*, 16 (1971), 14. A critique of his theories.

———. "Dedal ili Tesey?" [Daedalus or Theseus?]. *LG*, 11 (1973), 13.

Amelin, P. P. *Intelligentsiya i sotsialism* [Intelligentsia and Socialism]. Leningrad, 1970, 149 pp.

Anatol'yev, A. V. "Na novykh rubezhakh borby" [On New Frontiers of the Struggle]. *SShA*, 4 (1970), 79 ff.

Andzhaparidze, G. "Bogachi-filantropy i belyye 'Mercedes'" [Rich Philanthropists and White "Mercedes"]. *LG*, 4 (1971), 13. Against the publication of Western thrillers in Soviet periodicals.

Aptheker, Herbert. "The American Peace Movement." *NT*, 46–47 (1967), 20 ff.

———. "Voyna protiv razuma" [War Against Reason]. *LG*, 38 (1969), 8. On sadism, pornography, etc., in the West.

Arab-Ogly, E. "Sotsialisticheskaya revolyutsiya i psevdorevolyutsionnoye mifotvorchestvo" [The Socialist Revolution and Pseudorevolutionary Myth Creation]. *MEiMO*, 7 (1967), 4–16.

———. "Zloklyucheniya psevdomarksizma" [The Mishap of Pseudomarxism]. *MEiMO*, 7 (1960), 136–141. On R. Aron.

———. ". . . shatkaya futurologiya" [(Unstable America . . .) and Unsteady Futurology]. *LG*, 45 (1970), 13. A negative critique of Bell's concept of postindustrial society. See Daniel Bell in *LG*, 45 (1970), 13.

———. "Otkroveniye ot Revelya" [The Revelation of Revel]. *LG*, 18 (1971), 13. A negative commentary on Jean-François Revel.

———. "Molodezh' i budushcheye Ameriki" [Youth and the Future of America]. *MEiMO*, 10 (1971), 120–130. Commentary on Charles Reich's *The Greening of America*.

———. "Otrecheniye ot svobody i dostoinstva" [Renunciation of Freedom and Dignity]. *LG*, 49 (1972), 15. On B. F. Skinner's *Beyond Freedom and Dignity*.

——, and A. Zhiritsky. "Tupiki asfal'tovoy Tsivilizatsii" [Dead Ends of Asphalt Civilization]. *LG*, 41 (1971), 13. On Charles Reich.

——. " 'Neprikayannyye' brosayut vysov 'isteblishmentu' " [The "Unattached" Challenge the "Establishment"]. *MK*, 1 (1973), 93–104. Relates to an unidentified article by K. Keniston.

Archipenko, V. "Deviz molodezhi: uchit'sya i sozidat' " [The Slogan of the Young: Learn and Create]. *K*, 13 (1968), 88–97.

Archipov, Yu. "Kheppening: Oruzhiye v bor'be ili triumf absurda?" [The Happening: Weapon in the Struggle or Triumph of the Absurd?]. *LG*, 26 (1970), 13.

——. "Kurs 'Kursbukha' i poetika bessmyslits" [The Course of *Kursbuch* and the Poetics of Nonsense]. *LG*, 46 (1970), 15.

Baskina, A. "Ne zver' ne angel" [Neither Beast nor Angel]. *LG*, 48 (1968), 13. On the sexual revolution.

Basmanov, M. "O sovremennom Trotskizme i ego podryvnoy deyatel'nosti" [On Contemporary Trotskyism and its Subversive Activity]. *K*, 7 (1969), 98–108.

——. "Sovremennyy Trotskizm i ego proiski v molodezhnom dvizhenii" [Contemporary Trotskyism and Its Intrigues in the Youth Movement]. *MK*, 5 (1971), 92–98.

——. "Bessil'nyye bomby. Komu na ruku 'revolyutsionnyy' ekstremizm?" [Powerless Bombs. Whom Does "Revolutionary" Extremism Serve?]. *LG*, 14 (1973), 14.

——. *Antirevolyutsionnaya sushchnost' Trotskizma* [The Antirevolutionary Essence of Trotskyism]. Moscow, 1971, 230 pp. See the review in *MEiMO*, 9 (1972), 145 ff.

Batalov, E. Ya. "Voobrazheniye i revolyutsiya" [Imagination and Revolution]. *VF*, 1 (1972), 68–80.

——, L. A. Nikitich, and Ya. G. Fogeler. *Pokhod Markuze protiv Marksizma* [Marcuse's Campaign Against Marxism]. Moscow, 1970, 138 pp.

Bell, Daniel. "Elektronnaya Tsivilizatsiya" [Electronic Civilization]. *LG*, 17 (1969), 12. See Ostrovityanov, Yu.

——. "Neustoychivaya Amerika . . ." [i shatkaya futurologiya] [Unstable America . . . (and Unsteady Futurology)]. *LG*, 45 (1970), 13. Excerpt from an article of Bell's about postindustrial society. See Arab-Ogly, E., *LG*, 45 (1970), 13.

See also Yu. Ostrovityanov. "Postindustrial'naya tsivilizatsiya . . ."

Belskaya, A. "Carnaby Street and the British Youth." *NT*, 31 (1968), 27 ff.

Bereshkov, V. "After the Siege," *NT*, 46 (1968), 32–34. On protests against the Vietnam War in the U.S.

Besonov, B. "Nesostoyatel'nost' 'kriticheskoy teorii' G. Markuze" [The Weakness of H. Marcuse's "Critical Theory"]. *PS*, 9 (1971), 72–79.

Besymensky, L. "Gunshots on Kurfürstendamm." *NT*, 16 (1968), 12–14. The assassination attempt on Rudi Dutschke.

Biarnes, P'yer. "Sotsial'nyy krizis: Studenty i vlast'" [The Social Crisis: Students and Power]. *Za Rubezhom*, 23 (1970), 19 ff.

Bochkarev, Yu. "After the Spring Storm." *NT*, 42 (1968), 12–14. On France.

Bodamer, Joachim. "Jugendlichkeitswahn und Altersverachtung" [Cult of Youth and Horror of Age]. Edited version in *LG*, 24 (1972), 15. *Die Politische Meinung*, XVI: 137 (1971), 37–42.

———: "Kuda idet molodezh' zapada?" [Where Are the Youth of the West Going?]. *MK*, 7 (1969), 59–66. Excerpt, commentary by A. Borshchagovsky.

Bolkov, G. "Opasnost' beschelovechnosti" [The Danger of Inhumanity]. *LG*, 10 (1969), 13.

Bolshakov, V. "Erzatsy vmesto idealov: O 'dukhovnykh tsennostyakh' kotoryye predlagayut v SShA molodomu cheloveku, vstupayushchemu v zhizn'" [Substitutes for Ideals: On the "Spiritual Values" Offered in America to Young People Beginning Life]. *Agitator*, 9 (1968), 10–13.

———. "Soyuz molodezhi Yugoslavii i ego problemy" [The Yugoslav Youth Organization and its Problems]. *MK*, 7 (1969), 59–66. A brief report on Yugoslavia.

Bol'shov, D. "Bez pozitivnoy programmy: O nekotorykh tendentsiyakh v molodezhnom buntarstve" [Without a Positive Program: On Some Tendencies in the Unrest Among Young People]. *Novyy Mir*, 8 (1970), 198–220.

Borisov, A. "Narastayet volna klassovykh bitv" [The Wave of the Class Struggle Grows]. *Krasnaya Zvezda*, January 14, 1969, p. 3.

———. "'Leviy' radikalizm i rabocheye dvizheniye razvitykh kapitalisti-cheskikh stran" ["Left" Radicalism and the Workers' Movements in the Developed Capitalist Nations]. *PS*, 2 (1970), 47–54.

Borovik, G. "Pokhozhdeniya violoncheli: Zametki ob Amerikanskom 'avangardizme'" [The Adventure of the Violoncello: Remarks on

American "Avant-gardism"]. *LG,* 7 (1970), 13, and 8 (1970), 15.

———. "Smyateniye i gnev Ameriki" [Confusion and Anger of America]. *LG,* 20 (1970), 15. On the struggle against the Vietnam War.

———. " 'Lordy' vykhodyat na ulitsu" [The "Lords" Go into the Street]. *LG,* 32 (1970), 14. On a youth group in New York.

———. *Odin god bespokoynogo solntsa* [One Year of a Restless Sun]. Moscow, 1971, 565 pp. Reviewed in *Novyy Mir,* 1 (1972), 275–279. Impressions from France.

———. "Ispoved' " [A Confession]. *LG,* 42 (1972), 15. On Hippies.

Borshchagovsky, A. "Vrag: budushcheye" [The Enemy: the Future]. *LG,* 20 (1969), 14 ff. and 21 (1969), 14. On Western ideologies.

———. "Lukavyye pastyri" [Sly Pastors]. *LG,* 39 (1971), 14; 40 (1971), 14 ff.

———. " 'Provo'—Tak nazyvayut Frantsuzskiye proletarii provokatorov-Maoistov" ["Provo"—That Is What the French Proletariat Calls the Maoist Provocateurs]. *LG,* 14 (1972), 15.

Breytburd, G. "Asfal't i bulyzhnik" [Asphalt and Cobblestones]. *IL,* 12 (1968), 215–223. On May 1968 in France.

Brychkov, A. "Est' i drugaya Amerika . . ." [There is also Another America . . .]. *MK,* 1 (1967), 108–111.

———. "Ot bunta k bor'be: Nekotoryye problemy sovremennogo studencheskogo dvizheniya v razvitykh kapitalisticheskikh stranakh" [From Unrest to Struggle: Some Problems of the Contemporary Student Movement in the Developed Capitalist Nations]. *MK,* 12 (1969), 44–50.

———. "Universitet v osade" [The University Under Siege]. *MK,* 7 (1970), 104–112. On the United States.

———. "V bor'be i poiskakh" [In Struggle and Search]. *MEiMO,* 2 (1971), 98–107.

———. *Bunt v Al'ma-Mater* [Uprising at the Alma Mater]. Moscow, 1971, 47 pp.

———. *Molodaya Amerika* [Young America]. Moscow, 1971, 254 pp.

———. *American Youth Today* (English), Moscow, 1973, 208 pp.

Buchholz, Arnold. "Wissenschaftlich-technische Revolution und Wettbewerb der Systeme." *Osteuropa,* 5 (1972), 329–390.

Burkov, G. and V. Shchetinin. "Ot N'yu Yorka do Los Anzhelosa" [From New York to Los Angeles]. *MK,* 3 (1961), 92–104.

Burlak, V. "Vse sily—bor'be" [All Effort for the Struggle]. *MK,* 9 (1969), 106–107.

Bykhovsky, B. "Filosofiya melkoburzhuaznogo buntarstva" [The Philosophy of Petty Bourgeois Rebellion]. *K*, 8 (1969), 114–124.

Bykov, V. "Puti 'razbitogo pokoleniya' Ameriki" [The Paths of the "Beat Generation" of America]. *MK*, 10 (1969), 22–28.

———. "Idei buntuyushchego pokoleniya Ameriki" [Ideas of the Rebeling Generation of America]. *MK*, 10 (1969) 22–28.

———. "Trudnyye dorogi bor'by. Zametki ob ideynoy evolyutsii Amerikanskoy molodezhi" [The Difficult Paths of the Struggle: Notes on the Ideological Evolution of American Youth]. *MK*, 7 (1970), 102–112.

Bzhilyansky, Yu. "Adam ne budet poslednim" [Adam Will Not Be the Last]. *LG*, 40 (1971), 11. On the low birthrate in the USSR.

Chekhonin, B. "Kogda ozhivayut smertniki" [When the Dead Awake]. *Molodaya Gvardiya*, 12 (1971), 233–248. The psychological manipulation of Japanese youth by the right.

Chelyapov, I. "Mirovoy revolyutsionnyy protsess v nashe vremya" [The World Revolutionary Process in Our Time]. *MK*, 11 (1969), 98–105.

Cheporov, Ye. "Violence: Symbol of the American Way of Life." *International Affairs*, 7 (1972), 74–78.

Cheprakov, V. "O sotsial'no-ekonomicheskoy kontseptsii Gerberta Markuze" [On the Social-Economic Concepts of Herbert Marcuse]. *MEiMO*, 4 (1969), 89–96.

———. "Sovremennyye liberal'no-burzhuaznyye i levoradikal'nyye teorii s tochke zreniya Leninskikh idey revolyutsionnogo protsessa" [Contemporary Liberal-Bourgeois and Left Radical Theories from the Viewpoint of the Leninist Ideas of the Revolutionary Process]. *Vestnik Moskovskogo Universiteta, Seriya VII, Ekonomika*, 1 (1970), 89–91.

Cherkasov, I. I. "Diskussiya o 'novykh levykh' sredi Marksistov SShA" [Discussions about the "New Lefts" Among Marxists in the U.S.]. *VF*, 8 (1969), 178–180.

Chernykhov, V. "Wakening America." *NT*, 19 (1971), 14.

Chernyshev, A., and V. Pronin. "Blagopoluchnyye ubiystva Agaty Kristi" [The Successful Murders of Agatha Christie]. *LG*, 36 (1970), 15.

Churbanov, V. "Novoye levoye dvizheniye" [The New Left Movement]. *MEiMO*, 1 (1968), 94–98.

———. "Mir studentov i studenty v mire" [The World of Students and Students in the World]. *MK*, 12 (1969), 51–57.

Cogniot, G. "Youth in Modern Society." *NT,* 22 (1969), 9–11, 23 (1969), 8–11. The author is director of the Maurice Thorez Institute in Paris.

———. "From Tub-Thumping to Violence: The 'Ultra-Left' in France." *NT,* 27 (1971), 22 ff.

Cohn-Bendit, Daniel. *Obsolete Communism: The Left-Wing Alternative.* New York, McGraw-Hill, 1968.

"Communists in the Youth Movement in Capitalist Countries." *World Marxist Review,* 1 (1972), 109–128, and 2 (1972), 31–48. Minutes of a seminar held in Prague, September 28–29, 1971.

Connor, Walter, D. *Deviance in Soviet Society.* New York, 1972, 327 pp. First edition 1969.

Danelius, Gerkhard. "Nasha partiya i Zapadnoberlinskaya molodezh' " [Our Party and the Youth of West Berlin]. *K,* 16 (1970), 102–108.

Danilov, V. "Golos Turetskikh studentov" [The Voice of the Turkish Students]. *Aziya i Afrika Segodnya,* 12 (1970), 12 ff.

Davydov, Yu. "Kritika 'novykh levykh' " [Critique of the "New Lefts"]. *Voprosy Literatury,* 2 (1970), 68–99.

———. "Syurrealisticheskiy revolyutsionarizm Gerberta Markuze" [The Surrealistic Revolutionaryism of Herbert Marcuse]. *Voprosy Literatury,* 9 (1970), 62–95.

———, and V. Gaydenko. "Kul'tura i bunt" [Culture and Uprising]. *IL,* 2 (1971), 212–217.

Daymond, Elen. "Myatezhnaya sovest' Ameriki" [The Mutinous Conscience of America]. *MK,* 6 (1967), 96–99. On youth against the Vietnam War.

Degtyarev, V. "Partiynyye organizatsii i nauchno-technicheskiy progress" [Party Organization and Scientific-Technical Progress]. *K,* 14 (1972), 12–24.

Deykin, A., and V. Linnik. "Universitet i voyenno-promyshlennyy kompleks" [The Universities and the Military-Industrial Complex]. *MK,* 5 (1972), 94–99.

Diligensky, G. "Molodoy proletariy 60kh godov: Zametki o molodezhi zapada" [The Young Proletariat of the Sixties: Remarks on the Youth of the West]. *Novoye Vremya,* 19 (1969), 13–15.

———, and M. Novinskaya. "Studenchestvo zapada i anti-monopolisticheskaya bor'ba" [The Students of the West and the Struggle Against Monopolies]. *MEiMO,* 2 (1969), 81–89.

Dobkin, S. "Posledniy bereg" [The Last Shore]. *MK*, 8 (1970), 104–111. On Australia.

Dolmatovsky, Ye. "Ruki Gevary" [The Hands of Guevara]. *LG*, 40 (1972), 15.

Dombrovsky, K. "Eti talantlivyye nevrotiki . . ." [These Talented Neurotics . . .]. *LG*, 43 (1972), 12 ff. Are there no neuroses in the USSR?

Douglas, William. "Points of Rebellion." *SShA*, 9 (1970), 91–96. On the U.S., a short excerpt with a foreword by S. Vishnevsky.

Drachkovitch, Milorad. "The New Left in the United States." *Western Politica*, 1 (1966), 3–21.

Drucker, Peter. "Budushcheye pred'yavlyayet schet" [The Future Calls to Account]. *Za Rubezhom*, 43 (1971), 22–24. Excerpts from an article by Peter Drucker in *Harpers Magazine*, with initial comments by A. Brychkov about students in the U.S.

Dymov, M. "Brachnaya noch'" [Wedding Night]. *LG*, 43 (1972), 16. About the consumer mentality of young Soviet citizens.

Dyuken', Zhak. "V sumerkakh mistiki" [In the Mists of Mysticism]. *LG*, 33 (1971), 15. On the witch cult in the West.

[Editorial] "Filosofiya v sovremennoy bor'be idey" [Philosophy in the Contemporary Struggle of Ideas]. *VF*, 7 (1968), 3–12.

[Editorial] "Politicheski vozhd naroda" [The Political Leader of the People]. *K*, 10 (1968), 3–13. About the proletariat.

[Editorial] "Rabochiy klass: vedushchaya sila za sotsializm i kommunism" [The Working Class: The Leading Force in the Struggle for Socialism and Communism]. *K*, 8 (1968), 3–12.

[Editorial] "Voprosy Filosofii" [Problems of Philosophy]. *VF*, 1 (1972), 3–17. About the editorial policy of the journal *Voprosy Filosofii*.

Emelyanov, V. "Meeting the Younger Generation." *NT*, 44 (1969), 8 f.

Ezhov, V. "Watch on the Main." *NT*, 9 (1968), 18–20.

Finkelshtayn, S. "Geniy ili fokusnik?" [Genius or Juggler?]. *LG*, 3 (1969), 13. A negative judgment on McLuhan.

Fischer, Ralph. "Pattern for Soviet Youth." See review in *MK*, 1 (1961), 98–104. See also Yu. Verchenko and A. Chubaryan.

Freeman, Harry. "American Youth and the Vietnam War." *NT*, 17 (1969), 9–12. Freeman is an "American journalist."

———. "Student Rebellion: U.S." *NT*, 37 (1969), 13–16.

————. "American Youth in Revolt." *NT*, 22 (1970), 6–8.

————. "New Levels of Confrontation." *NT*, 20 (1971), 4 ff. On demonstrations against the war.

Fremontier, J. "La Forteresse Ouvriere: Renault." Paris 1971. See review in *MEiMO*, 3 (1972), 139–143, and N. Komin.

Friedrich, Heinz. "Ubiystvo pod voskresen'ye" [Murder on the Eve of Sunday]. *LG*, 34 (1970), 14. The intellectual decline of the West.

Fyedorov, K. "Western Youth and Ideological Struggle." *International Affairs*, 9 (1968), 76–82.

Gapochka, M. P. "Obsuzhdeniye na Prezidiume AN SSSR zadach i perspektiv raboty zhurnala *Voprosy Filosofii*" [Discussion in the Presidium of the USSR Academy of Sciences of Tasks and Prospects for the Work of the Journal *Voprosy Filosofii*]. *VF*, 5 (1969), 146–152.

Garin, V. "Sniskhoditel'nost' opasna" [Forbearance Is Dangerous]. *LG*, 23 (1972), 13. On juvenile delinquency in the USSR. A reader's letter calls for sharper punishment.

Garofalo, Jack. "Chada isusa i ischadiya satany" [The Children of Jesus and Satan's Fiends]. *LG*, 30 (1971), 14. From Paris *Match*.

Genri, E. "Novyye perspektivy: Semidesiatyye gody—vremya soyuzov levykh sil?" [New Perspectives: The Seventies—a Time for the Union of Left Forces?]. *LG*, 27 (1970), 14; 28 (1970), 14; and 29 (1970), 14.

Gerasimov, G. "Brak po-Amerikanski" [Marriage, American Style]. *LG*, 41 (1972), 15.

Geyevsky, I. A. "Chernaya pantera" [The Black Panthers]. *SShA*, 1 (1970), 115–118.

Gil'bukh, Yu. "Bez nadezhdy na budushcheye" [Without Hope for the Future]. *Narodnoye Obrazovaniye*, 6 (1970), 108–111.

Gnedin, Ye. "Masshtaby i kharaktery: Zametki o sovremennom burzhuaznom obshchestve" [Measure and Character: Remarks on Contemporary Bourgeois Society]. *Novyy Mir*, 10 (1968), 211–235. After p. 229 covers contemporary Paris, as well as other areas.

————. "Utrachennyye illyuzii i obretennyye nadezhdy: Problemy molodezhnogo dvizheniya na zapade" [Lost Illusions and Recovered Hopes: Problems of the Youth Movement in the West]. *Novyy Mir*, 10 (1970), 173–194.

Golding, William. See S. A. Yelistratova.

Gorenkova, N. "Zhiv li Freyd?" [Does Freud Still Live?]. *MK*, 9 (1971), 87–93.

Granov, V. "Nature and Specific Features of Petty-Bourgeois Anti-Communism." *International Affairs*, 9 (1970), 12–19.

Green, Gil. See Yu. V. Yurin.

Gribachev, N. "Khippi vo Khriste" [Hippies in Christo]. *LG*, 1 (1972), 14.

Grigor'yev, K., and B. Khandros. "Muzhchina ukhodit iz shkoly" [Men Leave the School]. *LG*, 11 (1969), 12. The feminization of the school.

Gruliow, Leo. "Russia Eyes Hunt Gun Curb." *Christian Science Monitor*, January 24, 1973, p. 4.

Grushin, B., and V. Chikin. *Ispoved' pokoleniya* [Confession of a Generation]. Moscow, 1962. The answers of 17,446 young people to 12 questions.

Guevara, Ché. See Ye. Dolmatovsky and Juan Kobo.

Gur'yev, I. "Pasynki dyadyushki Sema" [Uncle Sam's Stepsons]. *MK*, 2 (1963), 119–122.

Gvosd'yev, Yu. "Student Revolt in Brazil." *NT*, 28 (1968), 7 ff.

Hall, Martin. "The Peace Movement After the Spring." *NT*, 25 (1971), 21.

Henrotte, J. "Yoga: nichego sverkh'estestvennogo." [Yoga: Nothing Supernatural]. *LG*, 36 (1970), 13.

Higgins, J. "Ob' 'yedineniye v bor'be" [Unity in Struggle]. *Za Rubezhom*, 47 (1971), 18 ff.

Hofstadter, R. "SShA: krizis dukha" [U.S.: Crisis of the Spirit]. *LG*, 35 (1970), 14.

Igitkhanyan, M. "Revizionisty v roli 'deideologizatorov'" [The Revisionists in the Role of "De-ideologizers"]. *MK*, 8 (1972), 89–95.

Ikonnikova, S., and V. T. Lisovsky. *Molodezh' o sebe, o svoikh sverstnikakh* [Young People on Themselves and Their Elders]. Leningrad, 1969, 131 pp.

Indursky, S. "Razreshite, predstavit': klub pokupateley" [Allow Me to Introduce: the Consumer's Club]. *LG*, 41 (1969), 11. On consumer society in the USSR.

Ivakov, B. "Sons and Fathers." *NT*, 17 (1969), 28–30.

Ivanova, Z. P. *Nauchno-tekhnicheskaya revolyutsiya v SShA* [The Scientific-Technical Revolution in the U.S.]. Moscow, 1971, 159 pp. After a review in *MEiMO*, 9 (1972), 135.

Ivashkevich, Ya. "Markuze: vkhod i vykhod svobodnyy" [Marcuse: Entrance and Exit Free]. *LG*, 41 (1970), 14.

Jacobs, Paul, and Saul Landau. *The New Radicals. A Report with Documents*. New York, 1966, 333 pp.

Johnson, Richard. *The French Communist Party Versus the Students Revolutionary Politics in May-June 1968*. New Haven, London, 1972, 215 pp.

Kagramanov, Yu. "O metamorfoze 'Amerikanskoy mechty', ili novyye zloklyucheniya 'bludnogo syna'" [On the Metamorphosis of the "American Dream," or the New Mishaps of the "Prodigal Son"]. *IL*, 8 (1972), 245–253.

Kantor, K. M. "Mirovoy revolyutsionnyy protsess i mezhdunarodnoye rabocheye dvizheniye" [The World Revolutionary Process and the International Workers' Movement]. *VF*, 12 (1972), 77–88, and 1 (1973), 96–111.

Kapitsa, P. "Obsuzhdeniye na Prezidium AN SSSR zadach i perspektiv raboty zhurnala *Voprosy Filosofii*" [A Discussion at the Presidium of the USSR Academy of Sciences of the Tasks and Problems of the Work of the Journal *Voprosy Filosofii*]. *VF*, 5 (1969), 146–152.

———. "Nekotoryye printsipy tvorcheskogo vospitaniya i obrazovaniya sovremennoy molodeshi" [Some Principles of Creative Education and Development of Contemporary Youth]. *VF*, (1971), 16–24.

Kapler, Aleksey. "Sluchay v dachnom poselke" [Incident in a Dacha Settlement]. *LG*, 9 (1973), 12.

Karushin, B. "Angliyskiye studenty segodnya" [English Students Today]. *MK*, 8 (1961), 102–106.

Kar'yev, D. S. *Izucheniye i preduprezhdeniye pravonarusheniy sredi nesovershennoletnikh* [The Study and Prevention of Crime Among Adolescents]. Moscow, 1970.

Kashlev, Yu. "'Molchalivoye pokoleniye Ameriki' obretayet golos" ["The Silent Generation of America" Acquires a Voice]. *MK*, 5 (1962), 112–118.

Kaufman, A. "V poiskakh puti: O melkoburzhuaznykh sotsialisticheskikh teoriyakh v razvivayushchikhsya stranakh" [On the Search for a Way: On Petty Bourgeois Socialist Theories in the Developing Nations]. *Aziya i Afrika Segodyna,* 11 (1971), 19 ff.

Keniston, Kenneth. *Young Radicals. Notes on Committed Youth.* New York, 1968, 290 pp.

Keyzerov, N. M. *Bor'ba dvukh ideologiy i molodezh'* [The Struggle of two Ideologies and Youth]. Leningrad, 1970, 36 pp.

Khanzhin, S. "Studenty i professora" [Students and Professors]. *MEiMO,* 8 (1972), 115–120.

Kharchev, A. "Tak li vse prosto . . ." [Is It Really So Simple . . .]. *LG,* 29 (1971), 10. Against computer dating.

Khatskevich, D. "Zashchishchayet li filosofiya ekzistentsializma lichnost' " [Does the Philosophy of Existentialism Protect the Personality?]. *MK,* 11 (1969), 16–23.

Khristov, Venko. "Ot Freyda i Shpenglera . . . k Markuze" [From Freud and Spengler to Marcuse]. *IL,* 12 (1969), 228–234.

Khromushin, G. "Ideologicheskaya bor'ba mezhdu sotsialismom i kapitalizmom na sovremennom etape" [The Ideological Struggle Between Socialism and Capitalism at the Present Stage]. *PS,* 3 (1972), 24–31.

———. "Nauchno-tekhniicheskaya revolyutsiya i ideologicheskaya bor'ba" [The Scientific-Technical Revolution and the Ideological Struggle]. *Novyy Mir,* 3 (1972), 160–174; 5 (1972), 179–206; 7 (1972), 146–175.

Kim, G. G., and A. S. Kaufman. "Ob ideologicheskikh techeniyakh v stranakh 'tret'ego mira' " [Ideological Currents in Nations of the "Third World"]. *Narody Azii i Afriki,* 5 (1972), 39–49.

Kleemann, Susanne. *Ursachen und Formen der amerikanischen Studentenopposition* [Causes and Forms of the American Student Opposition]. Frankfurt am Main, 1971, 228 pp.

Klyamkin, I. "Chelovek na rabote" [Man at Work]. *Koms. Pr.,* April 10, 1968, pp. 2 and 4.

Klyuyev, V. "Teatr Zapadnoy Germanii i 'novyye levyye' " [The Theater of West Germany and the "New Lefts"]. *Teatr* [Theater], 7 (1970), 137–146.

Ko, Jean. "Kakuyu 'moral' propoveduyet g-n Testrup?" [What "Morals" is Mr. Testrup Preaching?] *LG,* 41 (1969), 15.

Kobo, Juan. "Che Gevara: soldat revolyutsii" [Ché Guevara: Soldier of the Revolution]. *LG,* 41 (1969), 15.

Kochetov, Vsevolod. *Chego zhe ty khochesh?* [Just What Do You

Want?]. *Oktyabr'* [October], 9 (1969), 11–136; 10 (1969), 41–138; and 11 (1969), 107–172.

Koestler, Arthur. "Chelovek: oshibka evolyutsii?" [Man: A Mistake of Evolution?]. *LG,* 20 (1971), 13. A section of a negative critique.

Kogan, L. N. *Molodezh', ee interesy, stremleniya, idealy: Vsesoyuznaya nauchno-teoreticheskaya konferentsiya "Sotsializm i Molodezh'"* [Youth, its Interests, Aims, and Ideals": All-Union Scientific-Theoretical Conference on "Socialism and Youth"]. Moscow, 1969, 429 pp.

Kolbanovsky, V. "Vslukh na 'intimnuyu temu'" [A "Personal Subject" Discussed Aloud]. *LG,* 24 (1969), 96–100.

Komin, N. "Govoryat rabochiye 'Reno'" [The "Renault" Workers Speak]. *MEiMO,* 3 (1972), 139–143. A review of the book by J. Fremontier, *La Forteresse Ouvrière: Renault.*

Komlosh, Ya. "Zaviduyu ikh molodosti" [I Envy Them for Their Youth]. *MK,* 7 (1972), 106–110.

Kon, I. "Razmyshleniya ob Amerikanskoy intelligentsii" [Reflections on the American Intelligentsia]. *Novyy Mir,* 1 (1968), 173–197.

———. "Capitalist Society and the Youth." *NT,* 15 (1968), 5–9.

———. "Seks, obshchestvo, kul'tura" [Sex, Society, Culture]. *IL,* 1 (1970), 243–255.

———. "Muzhestvennyye zhenshchiny? Zhenstvennyye muzhchiny?" [Masculine Women? Feminine Men?]. *LG,* 1 (1970), 12.

———. "Studencheskiye volneniya i teoriya 'konflikta pokoleniy'" [Student Unrest and the Theory of the "Conflict of Generations"]. *SShA,* 3 (1971), 27–39.

———. "Studenchestvo na zapade kak sotsial'naya gruppa" [Students in the West as a Social Group]. *VF,* 9 (1971), 67–77.

———. "Obmanutyye nasledniki. Studencheskoye dvizheniye v zerkale zapadnoy sotsiologii" [Cheated Heirs: The Student Movement in the Mirror of Western Sociology]. *Zvezda,* 2 (1971), 143–165.

———. "Zachem nuzhny otsy?" [Why Are Fathers Necessary?]. *LG,* 9 (1973), 11.

Konstantinov, L. "Nravstvennye sumerki" [Moral Twilight]. *MK,* 7 (1970), 113–117. On Sweden.

Konstantinovsky, I. "Viennese Encounters." *NT,* 30 (1967), 30–32. On aimless youth.

Kosenko, Ye. "Molodezhnoye dvizheniye v SShA" [The Youth Movement in the U.S.]. *MEiMO,* 10 (1969), 126–132.

Kosolapov, R., and Pechenev, V. "Kuda vedet molodezh' filosofiya Mar-

kuze?" [Where Does Marcuse's Philosophy Lead Young People?].
MK, 1 (1969), 17–25.

Kovalev, S. M. "Chuzhdaya ideologiya v revolyutsionnom dvizhenii" [Foreign Ideology in the Revolutionary Movement]. *Znamya*, 2 (1971), 151–170 and 3 (1971), 187–199.

Krasin, Yu. "Revolyutsionnyy klass i ego kritiki" [The Revolutionary Class and its Critics]. *Pravda*, September 16, 1972, p. 4. On Marcuse.

Kravchenko, I. "Maklyuen i ego apologetika kapitalizma" [McLuhan and his Apology of Capitalism]. *MEiMO*, 4 (1971), 143–147.

Kugel', S. A. "Izmeneniye sotsial'noy struktury sotsialisticheskogo obshchestva pod vozdeystviyem nauchno-technicheskoy revolyutsii" [Changes in the Social Structure of Socialist Society under the Influence of the Scientific-Technical Revolution]. *VF*, 3 (1969), 13–22.

Kulikova, L. "Ugol padeniya" [Angle of Inclination]. *MK*, 7 (1972), 96–99. On alcoholism.

Kurylev, A. K. "Marksizm-Leninizm o sotsial'noy prirode intelligentsii i ee roli v postroyenii sotsializma i kommunizma" [Marxism-Leninism on the Social Nature of the Intelligentsia and its Role in the Construction of Socialism and Communism]. *Voprosy Istorii KPSS*, 7 (1969), 106–116.

Lakshin, V. "Gerbert Markuze na karnavale" [Herbert Marcuse at the Carnival]. *IL*, 9 (1971), 252–257.

Lapitsky, I. "Why the Black Panthers?" *NT*, 2 (1970), 23 ff.

Lebedev, A., and Tulayev, D. " 'Bunt' studentov: protiv kogo i pochemu" ["Uprising" of the Students: Against Whom and Why?]. *MK*, 4 (1969), 32–37.

Lenin, V. I. *Collected Works*. 45 vols. London: Lawrence & Wishart, and Moscow: Progress Publishers, 1960–1970. With the exceptions of No. 16 cited, in chronological sequence, after this translation of the 4th Russian edition prepared by the Institute of Marxism-Leninism. Many works cited here are contained in the anthology *On Youth*. Moscow: Progress Publishers, 1967, 306 pp.

  1. "The Drafting of 183 Students into the Army" (January 1901), IV, 416–421.

  2. "Demonstrations Have Begun" (December 1901), V, 322–325.

  3. *What Is to Be Done?* (1902), V, 347–529.

  4. "Signs of Bankruptcy" (February 15, 1902), VI, 79–85.

  5. "The Autocracy Is Wavering . . ." (March 1, 1903), VI, 348–353.

6. "On the Subject of Reports by Committees and Groups of the R.S.D.L.P. to the General Party Congress" (December 1902-January 1903), VI, 290–300.

7. "Draft Resolution on the Attitude Towards the Student Youth" (The Second Congress of the Russian Social-Democratic Labour Party, June-July 1903), VI, 471.

8. "Plan of Letters on Tasks of the Revolutionary Youth" (August-September 1903), VII, 41–42.

9. "The Tasks of the Revolutionary Youth: First Letter" (September 1903), VII, 43–56.

10. "A Letter to A. A. Bogdanov and S. I. Gusev" (February 11, 1905), VIII, 143–147.

11. "The Political Strike and the Street Fighting in Moscow" (October 1905), IX, 347–355.

12. "The First Results of the Political Alignment" (October 31 [18], 1905), IX, 396–404.

13. "To the Combat Committee of the St. Petersburg Committee" (October 16, 1905), IX, 344–346.

14. "The Lessons of the Moscow Events" (October 24 [11], 1905), IX, 376–387.

15. "The Student Movement and the Present Political Situation" (October 3 [16], 1908), XV, 213–219.

16. "The Question of Party Affiliation Among Democratic Minded Students," *On Youth* (November-December 1912), pp. 106–112.

17. "The Role of the Social Estates and the Classes in the Liberation Movement," in *Collected Works,* 4th ed. (August 1913), XIX, 328–331.

18. "To Inessa Armand" (January 17 and 24, 1915), XXXV, 180–185.

19. "The Youth International" (A Review, December 1916), XXIII, 163–166.

20. "Lecture on the 1905 Revolution" (January 1917), XXIII, 236–253.

21. *"Left-Wing" Communism: An Infantile Disorder* (April 1920), XXXI, 17–104.

22. "The Tasks of the Youth Leagues" (Speech Delivered at the Third All-Russia Congress of the Russian Young Communist League, October 2, 1920), XXXI, 283–299.

23. "To the Third Congress of the Young Communist International, Moscow" (December 5, 1922), XXXIII, 446.

"Leninskaya teoriya imperializma i revolyutsionnyye sily sovremennosti. Sotsial'nyye protivorechiya v mire kapitala" [The Leninist Theory of Imperialism and the Revolutionary Forces of the Present Day: Social Contradictions in the World of Capital]. Conference, January 1970, Report in *MEiMO*, 3, 4, 6, 7, 8, 10 (1970). Especially 8 (1970); a summary of a report by A. Brychkov.

Leroy, Roland. "Molodezh' i budushcheye Frantsii" [Youth and the Future of France]. *MK*. 10 (1964), 100–106.

———. "Pseudo-Socialism and Real Socialism." *World Marxist Review*, 4 (1972), 88–92.

Levin, B. "Sotsial'nyy portret alkogolika" [Social Portrait of an Alcoholic]. *LG*, 11 (1970), 12.

———. "Devushki, yunoshi, i vino" [Girls, Boys, and Wine]. *LG*, 2 (1971), 13. Alcohol among young people in the USSR.

Lightfoot, Claude. "Osvoboditel'naya bor'ba Amerikanskikh negrov" [Liberation Struggle of the American Negroes]. *K*, 14 (1969), 95–105.

Likhanov, A. *Labirint* [Labyrinth]. Moscow, 1970. After a review in *Oktyabr'*, 11 (1971), 221.

Lindsay, John. "Dolzhnost' mera N'yu-Yorka poroy vyzvayet otchayaniye" [The Position of the Mayor of New York Causes One to Despair at Times]. *LG*, 1 (1973), 14. An interview with John Lindsay.

Linnik, V. "Otrecheniye" [Refusal]. *MK*, 7 (1971), 104–112. On young Americans against the war.

Lisenkov, A. "Studenchestvo SShA pod ideologicheskim pressom reaktsii" [Students in the U.S. Under the Ideological Pressure of the Reaction]. *Vestnik Vysshey Shkoly*, 12 (1968), 88–90.

Lisovsky, Vladimir, T. *Eskiz k portretu* [Study for a Portrait]. Moscow, 1969, 206 pp.

———, and V. Chervyakov. "Vo imya chego buntuyet molodezh' zapada?" [In the Name of What Does the Youth of the West Rebel?]. *Molodaya Gvardiya*, 7 (1968), 267–280.

Lomeyko, Vladimir, B. *Leveye istiny: Retsidiv detskoy bolezni "levachestva" v studencheskom dvizenii zapada* [Left of Truth: A Relapse into the Infantile Disorder of "Leftism" in the Student Movement in the West]. Moscow, 1970, 110 pp.

Lorints, L. "Nesostoyatel'nost' burzhuaznoy teorii 'depolitizatsii' obshchestva" [The Inconsistency of Bourgeois Theory of the "Depolitization" of Society]. *Sovetskoye Gosudarstvo i Pravo*, 3 (1972), 65–73.

Luk'yanova, L. "V ryadakh progressivkykh sil" [In the Ranks of the Progressive Forces]. *MEiMO,* 2 (1971), 114–118.

L'vov, Vladimir. "Fabrikanty chudes" [Manufacturers of Wonders]. *Neva,* 12 (1971), 152–164.

Makarov, Vadim, V. *Chem ty zhivesh, rovesnik? Zametki sotsiologa.* [What Are You Living for, Contemporary? Remarks of a Sociologist]. Volgograd, 1968, 110 pp.

Malinovsky, A. "Plata za tsivilizatsiyu" [The Price of Civilization]. *LG,* 42 (1972), 12. On short-sightedness.

Malygin, A. (Major General). "V bitve idey net kompromissov" [In the Struggle of Ideas There Are no Compromises]. *MK,* 1 (1969), 49–62. A warning about Western agents.

———. "Ne zabyvat' o bditel'nosti" [Don't Forget About Vigilance]. *MK,* 9 (1969), 32–38. A warning about Western ideological influences.

Mamut, L. S. "Kritika politicheskoy ideologii anarchizma" [Critique of the Political Ideology of Anarchism]. *Sovetskoye Gosudarstvo i Pravo,* 5 (1971), 42–52.

Marcuse, Herbert. *Soviet Marxism: A Critical Analysis.* New York, 1958. Quoted after the Vintage edition, 1961, 257 pp.

———. *An Essay on Liberation.* Boston, 1969, 91 pp.

———. *One-Dimensional Man.* Boston, 1964.

———. "Re-Examination of the Concept of Revolution" in R. Klibansky, ed., *Contemporary Philosophy: A Survey,* Florence, 1971, pp. 424–432.

———. *Counterrevolution and Revolt.* Boston, 1972, 138 pp.

Martynova, A. " 'Amerikanskiy ray' Erika Sigala" [The "American Paradise" of Eric Segal]. *LG,* 10 (1971), 15.

Masol, V. and Ye. Matsegora. "Nauchno-tekhnicheskiy progress i kul'-turno-tekhnicheskiy uroven' trudyashchikhsya" [Scientific-Technical Progress and the Cultural-Technical Standard of Working People]. *K,* 7 (1972), 42–53.

Mayzel's, S. "Chto takoye 'obshchestvo vsedozvolennosti'?" [What is the "Permissive Society"?]. *IL,* 11 (1971), 215–218.

Mehnert, Klaus. *Peking and the New Left.* Berkeley, California, 1969, 156 pp.

Meleshchenko, Yu. "Kharakter i osobennosti nauchno-tekhnicheskoy revolyutsii" [Character and Features of the Scientific-Technical Revolution]. *VF,* 7 (1968), 13–28.

Mel'nikov, A. "Intelligentsiya SShA: Chislennost', sostav, sotsial'naya differentsyatsiya" [The Intelligentsia of the U.S.: numbers, composition, social differentiation]. *VF*, 7 (1968), 13–28. The beginning of a series on the scientific-technical revolution. This series continued for several months; see, for example, S. Kugel'.

———, and S. Sonov. "Rabochiy klass i ego soyuzniki" [The Working Class and its Allies]. *MEiMO*, 1 (1971), 2 (1971). The relevant sections are in 2 (1971), 70–78.

Mertner, E., and G. Maynush. "Pornografiya i fashizm" [Pornography and Fascism]. *LG*, 1 (1971), 13.

Meshcheryakova, V. "Partiya 'chernoy pantery'" [The "Black Panther" Party]. *KVS*, 12 (1971), 86–88.

———. "Molodezh' v bor'be protiv imperializma" [Youth in the Struggle against Imperialism]. *KVS*, 24 (1971), 80–82.

Mikhaylov, V. "Psikhoanaliz—novaya religiya? [Psychoanalysis—a New Religion?]. *LG*, 46 (1969), 13.

Mikul'sky, K. "Nauchno-tekhnicheskaya revolyutsiya v usloviyakh ekonomicheskogo sorevnovaniya dvukh sistem" [The Scientific-Technical Revolution in the Conditions of the Economic Competition of the Two Systems]. *K*, 10 (1972), 100–111.

Mileykovsky, A. "Burzhuaznyye i reformistskiye ideologi o sovremennom kapitalizme" [Bourgeois and Reformist Ideologists on Contemporary Capitalism]. *MEiMO*, 4 (1971), 41–52.

Mills, Charles Wright. "Letter to the New Left." *New Left Review*, September-October 1960.

Minayev, L. "Studencheskoye dvizheniye v stranakh kapitala" [The Student Movement in the Lands of Capital]. *K*, 2 (1970), 95–106.

Mis, G. "Fenomen? Net, zakonomernost'!" [Phenomenon? No, a Logical Pattern!]. *MK*, 1 (1972), 65–72. On Communism and Youth in West Germany.

Mitin, D. "S chetyrekh koles—na dva" [From Four Wheels to Two!]. *LG*, 32 (1972), 13. On the bicycle trend in the U.S.

Mitin, M. "O tak nazyvayemykh 'novykh variantakh' Marksizma" [On the So-called "New Variants" of Marxism]. *IL*, 3 (1969), 220–226.

Mitkevich, G. "Problemy Albanskoy molodezhi" [Problems of Albanian Youth]. *MK*, 2 (1972), 96–102.

Mlechina, I. "Narkoz i skalpel Gyuntera Grassa" [Anesthesia and Scalpel of Günter Grass]. *LG*, 47 (1969), 15.

———. "Chto trevozhit Martina Val'zera" [What Troubles Martin

Walser]. *LG*, 43 (1970), 15. A positive comment on Martin Walser.

Modrzhinskaya, Ye. "Amerikanskaya intelligentsiya ishchet novyye puti" [The American Intelligentsia Seeks New Paths]. *MEiMO*, 11 (1966), 117–122.

Mokhnachev, M. "Molodezhnoye dvizheniya v stranakh Latinskoy Ameriki" [The Youth Movement in the Nations of Latin America]. *MK*, 3 (1960), 106–113.

Molchanov, N. "Plata za strakh" [Wage for Fears]. *LG*, 27 (1968), 14.

———. "Studenty na zapade buntuyut" [Students in the West Rebel]. *LG*, 45 (1968), 13.

———. "Frantsiya mezhdu proshlym i budushchim" [France Between the Past and the Future]. *LG*, 22 (1969), 9, 14 ff.

———. "Zapadnaya intelligentsiya" [The Western Intelligentsia]. *LG*, 1 (1970), 13.

Moskvichyev, L. "Anti-Communism Under the Guise of 'De-Ideologization'." *International Affairs*, 10 (1972), 41–47.

Moykin, N. "Pereval gryaznykh vetrov" [Shift in the Dirty Winds]. *IL*, 11 (1971), 212–214.

Mozhnyagun, S. "Gerbert Markuze v neskol'kikh izmereniyakh" [Herbert Marcuse in Several Dimensions]. *LG*, 15 (1969), 13.

———. "'Banka s chervyami' Marshalla Maklyuyena" [The "Bowl of Worms" of Marshall McLuhan]. *LG*, 50 (1972), 15.

Mukimov, Yu. "Dve zhizni, odna sud'ba" [Two Lives, One Fate]. *LG*, 31 (1972), 12. On the court trial of two young muggers in the USSR.

Murphy, R. "Kanadskaya molodezh' segodnya" [Canadian Youth Today]. *MK*, 3 (1963), 95–102.

Myalo, Kh. G. "Sotsial'naya dinamika mayskogo dvizheniya" [The Social Dynamics of the May Movement]. *VF*, 6 (1969), 47–58. France during 1968.

———. "Problema 'tret'ego mira' v levoekstremistskom soznanii" [The Problem of the "Third World" in the Left-Extremist Consciousness]. *VF*, 1 (1972), 81–93.

Nadel', S. N. "Sovremennyy kapitalizm i nauchno-tekhnicheskaya intelligentsiya" [Contemporary Capitalism and the Scientific-Technical Intelligentsia]. *K*, 1 (1970), 109–121.

———. *Nauchno-tekhnicheskaya intelligentsiya v sovremennom burzhuaznom obshchestve* [The Scientific-Technical Intelligentsia in Contemporary Bourgeois Society]. Moscow, 1971, 192 pp.

Narodnoye Khozyaystvo SSSR [Statistical Yearbook of the USSR]. Moscow, annually.

Newfield, Jack, *A Prophetic Minority: The American New Left*. New York, 1967, 158 pp.

Nikitina, L. "Gerbert Markuze 'perevooruzhayetsya'" [Herbert Marcuse "Rearms"]. *LG*, 38 (1972), 15.

Nikolayev, V. "Gryadet li novyi Gulliver?" [Is a New Gulliver Coming?]. *LG*, 21 (1969), 122. On acceleration among youth.

Nikolayevskaya, A. "Semyuel Bekett ili mir bez lyudey" [Samuel Beckett, or the World Without People]. *LG*, 2 (1873), 13.

Nikolyukin, A. "Dukhovnyy shirpotreb" [Spiritual Mass Consumption]. *LG*, 25 (1971), 15. On crime and sex in Western mass literature.

Novikov, N. "Sotsial'noye soderzhaniye sovremennogo levogo radikalizma v SShA" [The Social Content of Contemporary Left Radicalism in the U.S.]. *MEiMO*, 5 (1970), 101–111.

———. "'Revolyutisiya' s pomoshch'yu soznaniya" ["Revolution" with the Help of Consciousness]. *IL*, 9 (1971), 248–252. On Charles Reich's *Greening of America*.

Novinskaya, M. "Molodezh' zapada—ot apatii k bor'be" [The Youth of the West—from Apathy to Struggle]. *LG*, 11 (1969), 13.

Novinskaya, M. I. "'Studencheskaya revolyutisiya' v SShA i krizis burzhuaznykh tsennostey" [The "Student Revolution" in the U.S. and the Crisis of Bourgeois Values]. *VF*, 12 (1972), 89–101.

Novinskaya, M. N. "Molodezh v usloviyakh sovremennogo kapitalizma" [Youth Under the Conditions of Modern Capitalism]. *VF*, 11 (1969), 72–81. Was to have been the beginning of a series "On Youth and Social Progress." The series was not continued.

Novopashin, Yu. "S bol'noy golovy na zdorovuyu." [Giving a Headache to the Healthy]. *MK*, 7 (1972), 100–105.

Nun'yes, Mercedes. "Zapiski zaklyuchennoy" [Stories of a Woman Inmate]. *MK*, 3 (1969), 107–113.

Ognev, S. "Kto takie sovremennyye Trotskisty" [Who are the Contemporary Trotskyists?]. *Agitator*, 12 (1971), 59–61.

Oldridzh, Dzheyms. See Aldridge, James.

Ono, Ichiro. "Studenty Yaponii: za mir, protiv imperializma i militarizma" [The Students of Japan: For Peace, Against Imperialism and Militarism]. *MK*, 10 (1960), 121–126.

Onyshchuk, I. "Universitety i studenchestvo v razvytykh kapitalistiche-skikh stranakh" [The Universities and Students in the Developed Capitalist Nations]. *MEiMO*, 3 (1970), 106–116.

———. "Universitet segodnya" [The University Today]. *MEiMO*, 4 (1972), 119–127.

Orlov, V. S. *Podrostok i prestupleniye* [Adolescent and Crime]. Moscow, 1969, 201 pp.

Orlova, P. "Molodyye levyye" [The Young Lefts]. *Novyy Mir*, 6 (1967), 229–234. No quotation marks yet.

Ostrovityanov, Yu. "Mir absurda i mir razuma" [The World of the Absurd and the World of Reason]. *LG*, 1 (1969), 12.

———. " 'Novaya atlantida' Deniela Bella" [The "New Atlantis" of Daniel Bell]. *LG*, 17 (1969), 12 f.

———. " 'Postindustrial'naya tsivilizatsiya', ili kapitalizm v 2000 godu?" [Postindustrial Civilization, or Capitalism in the Year 2000?]. *VF*, 7 (1969), 30–41.

Panyukov, V. "Vash nachal'nik" [Your Boss]. *LG*, 2 (1970), 10. On management in the USSR.

Parsons, Howard, L. "Zhiznennaya filosofiya Amerikantsa i 'novyye levyye' " [The Philosophy of Life of Americans and the "New Lefts"]. *VF*, 6 (1968), 99–110.

———. *Ethics in the Soviet Union Today*. New York, American Institute for Marxist Studies (no date), 23 pp.

Pavlov, L. " 'Fabrika' modernizma Endi Uorkhola" [The "Factory" of Modernism of Andy Warhol]. *LG*, 24 (1972), 14. About and against Andy Warhol.

Pekelis, V. "Sovetchik v lyubvi?" [Counselor in Matters of Love?]. *LG*, 43 (1969), 12 ff.

Perevedentsev, F. "Speshit'li zamuzh?" [Hurry into Marriage?]. *LG*, 35 (1972), 12. Do people in the USSR get married too late?

Peschansky, V. "Universitet i 'isteblishment' " [University and "Establishment"]. *MEiMO*, 2 (1971), 107–113. About England.

Petrov, G. "Peshchernoye ocharovaniye" [Cave Magic]. *MK*, 3 (1966), 104–107. About sex in the U.S.

Petrovsky, A. "Okh, uzh eti paradoksy" [Oh, these Paradoxes]. *LG*, 43 (1972), 12 ff. An answer to K. Dombrovsky's "These Talented . . .".

Pisareva, L. "Ostraya sotsial'naya problema sovremennogo burzhuaznogo mira: O roste prestupnosti sredi molodezhi v FRG" [The Acute Social Problem of the Contemporary Bourgeois World: On the Rise in Criminality among the Youth of the FRG]. *Sovetskaya Yustitsiya,* 21 (1968), 28–30.

Polyakov, Yu. "Proletarskaya citadel'" [A Proletarian Citadel]. *MK,* 8 (1972), 96–102. About the Renault Works in Paris.

Ponomarev, B. "Aktual'naya zadacha ideyno-politicheskoy bor'ba. Trotskizm: orudiye antikommunisma" [The Acute Task of the Ideological-Political Struggle. Trotskyism: a Weapon of Anti-Communism]. *K,* 18 (1971), 14–34.

Popov, S. "'Teorii' vne nauki" ["Theories" Outside of Science]. *MK,* 7 (1970), 34–41.

Popov, Yu. "O prirode melkoburzhuaznoy ideologii v strankakh Afriki" [The Essence of Petty Bourgeois Ideology in the Nations of Africa]. *Narody Azii i Afriki,* 5 (1971), 37–44.

Prazsky, Jan. "Whose Axe Does Extremism Grind?" *World Marxist Review,* 6 (1972), 127–133.

Proffer, Carl, R. (ed.). *Soviet Criticism of American Literature in the Sixties: An Anthology.* Ann Arbor, Michigan, 1973, 213 pp.

Pumpyansky, A. "Troye v dzhinsakh" [A Trio in Jeans]. *MK,* 8 (1966), 98–103.

——. "Nuzhno li bombit' universitety?" [Must One Bomb the Universities?]. *IL,* 4 (1969), 239–243. A critique of the "New Left."

P'yuzo, Mario. "Vlast' mafii" [The Power of the Mafia]. *LG,* 22 (1970), 13. Excerpts from *The Godfather.*

Rakhovetsky, G., and L. Korshikov. "Boyevoy avangard yaponskoy molodezhi" [The Fighting Advance Guard of Japanese Youth]. *MK,* 10 (1961), 114–118.

Reich, Charles. *The Greening of America,* New York, 1970.

——. "Poiski 'novogo soznaniya'" [The Search for a "New Consciousness"]. *LG,* 41 (1971), 13. Excerpts from Reich's *The Greening of America.*

——. "Molodaya Amerika" [Young America]. *MEiMO,* 10 (1971), 113–120. *Excerpts from The Greening of America.* See E. Arab-Ogly's, "Youth and the Future of America."

Renold, Alice. "Frantsiya: Student, 68" [France: Student, 68]. *Koms. pr.,* May 22, 1928, p. 3.

Reshetov, P. "'Otkrytoye' pokoleniye" [The "Open" Generation]. *MK,* 3 (1967), 18–22.

――――. "Proroki ukhodyat v otstavku" [The Prophets Retire]. *MK*, 6 (1972), 90–95.

――――. "Put' k istine" [The Way to Truth]. *Molodaya Gvardiya*, 1 (1970), 272–281.

Reutova, S. "Demokraticheskoye studencheskoye dvizheniye v FRG i v zapadnom Berline" [The Democratic Student Movement in the FRG and West Berlin]. *MEiMO*, 6 (1970), 118–123.

Rigan, Simon. "Bog vozvrashchayetsya?" [Is God Returning?]. *LG*, 37 (1971), 13. On religion in the West.

Rodari, D. "Prinimayu, potomy chto ponimayu" [I Accept Because I Understand]. *MK*, 5 (1968), 101–103. On methods used in Italy to win young people over to Communism.

Romanzov, Yuri. "America's New Politics Movement." *NT*, 38 (1967), 34, 10 ff. On a short-lived anti-Vietnam War organization.

Ross, D. "Dvizheniye amerikanskoy molodezhi" [The American Youth Movement]. *MK*, 1 (1961), 97–103. A summary of an article in *Political Affairs*, a journal of the Communist party of the U.S.

Rostow, W. W. *The Stages of Economic Growth: A Non-Marxist Manifesto*. Cambridge [Engl.], 1960, 178 pp.

Roszak, Theodore. *The Making of a Counter Culture*. New York, 1969. Quotations are from the Anchor Books edition, 303 pp.

Rozental', E. "Khippi i drugiye" [Hippies and Others]. *Novyy Mir*, 7 (1971), 182–204.

Rubinov, A. "Koeffitsiyent Zabyvchivosti" [Coefficient of Forgetfulness]. *LG*, 40 (1971), 14. Shoplifting in the USSR.

――――. "Oskorbleniye podozreniyem" [The Insult of Suspicion]. *LG*, 44 (1972), 12. Also on shoplifting in the USSR.

Rubinsky, Yu. "Burya nad Frantisiyey" [Storm Over France]. *MEiMO*, 8 (1968), 97–103.

――――. "Frantsiya: Mezhdu 'preyemstvennots'yu' i 'dialogom'" [France: Between "Succession" and "Dialogue"]. *MEiMO*, 6 (1971), 97–105.

Rukhovich, S. "Mif burzhuaznoy propagandy o 'dukhovnom krizise' sovremennoy molodezhi" [The Bourgeois Propaganda Myth about the "Spiritual Crisis" of Contemporary Youth]. *MK*, 5 (1961), 102–109.

Rybakov, M. "Opyt, kotoryy nel'zya zabyvat'" [An Experience Which Should Not Be Forgotten]. *Oktyabr'*, 7 (1971), 206–211.

Sager, Peter. "Moskau und die extremistischen Studenten im Westen." *Zeitbild*, February 24, 1971, pp. 13–17.

Salychev, S. "Revolyutsionnoye dvizheniye nashikh dney" [The Revolutionary Movement of Our Day]. *MEiMO*, 4 (1971), 27–40. Pages 34–
40 are about youth.

———. *Politicheskiye bitvy v stranakh kapitala* [The Political Battles in
the Lands of Capital]. Moscow, 1971, 344 pp. The book contains some
passages on youth.

———. *"Novyee levyye: S kem i protiv kogo* ["The New Lefts": For
Whom and Against Whom?]. Moscow, 1972, 95 pp. Imprimatur November 18, 1972.

Salycheva, L. A. "Studencheskoye dvizheniye: 1960–1970" [The Student
Movement: 1960–1970]. *SShA*, 4 (1972), 24–31.

Sedin, L. "Student Revolt in the West." *NT*, 21 (1968), 10 ff.

Semenov, Vadim S. *Kapitalizm i klassy* [Capitalism and Classes]. Moscow, 1969, 399 pp.

Sevortyan, F. "Bunt—vo imya chego" [Revolt—in the Name of What].
MK, 2 (1971), 102–106.

Shakhnovich, M. "Sumerki magov" [The Dawn of the Magicians]. *LG*,
46 (1972), 15. On superstition in the West.

Sharikov, V. G. "Sud'ba *Doklada Skrentona*" [The Fate of the *Scranton
Report*]. *SShA*, 10 (1971), 59–62.

Shlapentokh, V. "Znakomstva i svad'by" [Acquaintances and Marriages].
LG, 24 (1971), 12 and 29 (1972), 10.

Shlikhter, A. "Burlyat universitety Kanady" [The Universities of Canada
Seethe]. *MEiMO*, 5 (1971), 117–122.

Shmeleva, T. "Pochemu buntuyut studenty SShA?" [Why are the Students in the USA Rebelling?]. *Agitator*, 20 (1968), 60 ff.

———. "Studencheskoye dvizheniye v stranakh kapitala" [The Student
Movement in the Nations of Capital]. *PS*, 3 (1969), 67–74.

Shreyder, Yu. "Lyubov' k orakulam" [Love for Oracles]. *LG*, 1 (1970),
12. Against match making by computer.

Silin, Y. "The Youth Movement in the Capitalist Countries." *International Affairs*, 5 (1970), 110–112.

Skvortsov, L. V. "Ideologicheskiye mify antikommunizma: evolyutsiya i
novyye tendentsii" [The Myths of Anti-Communism: Evolution and
New Tendencies]. *VF*, 9 (1972), 45–58.

Smith, Hedrick. "Top Soviet Critic Attacks 3 Plays." *New York Times*,
October 27, 1972.

———. " 'New Man' is the Hero on Leningrad Stages." *New York Times*,
December 31, 1972.

Snegireva, T. "Vremya byt' muzhchinoy" [It Is Time To Become a Man]. *LG*, 42 (1969), 11.

Solovev, E. "Ekzistentsializm: Istoriko-kriticheskiy ocherk" [Existentialism: An Historical-Critical Survey]. *VF*, 12 (1966), 76–88, and 1 (1967), 126–139.

Spiridonov, L. "V. I. Lenin o roli i meste studenchestva v revolyutsionnom dvizhenii" [V. I. Lenin on the Role and Place of Students in the Revolutionary Movement]. *MK*, 12 (1970), 40–45.

Spitsyn, G. " 'Angely' d'yavola" [The "Angels" of the Devil]. *MK*, 1 (1966), 101–104.

Steigerwald, R. "Critical Remarks on a 'Critical Theory'." *NT*, 24 (1970), 19–24.

———. *"Tretiy put' " Gerberta Markuze* ["The Third Way" of Herbert Marcuse]. Moscow, 1971, 339 pp. Translation from the German, after a review in *Novyy Mir*, 12 (1972), 267–274.

Stolpovsky, V. "Gerbert Markuze, postavshchik TsRU" [Herbert Marcuse, Caterer to the CIA]. *Trud*, August 2, 1969, p. 3.

Struchkov, N. A. "Izucheniye obstoyatel'stv, obuslovlivayushchikh prestupnost' v SSSR" [A Study of the Factors Causing Crime in the USSR]. *Sovetskoye Gosudarstvo i Pravo*, 12 (1971), 98–105.

Sturua, Melor. " 'Zemletryaseniye' v Garvarde" ["Earthquake" at Harvard]. *Molodaya Gvardiya*, 6 (1970), 245–265; 7 (1970), 234–251, and in "From the Editors," 251–253.

Stzhizhovsky, L. *Vstrechi na Reyne* [Meetings on the Rhine]. Moscow, 1971. After a review in *Oktyabr'*, 4 (1972), 222 ff.

Tareyev, Ye. "Tabletki v karmane: blago ili zlo?" [Pills in the Pocket: Good or Bad?]. *LG*, 12 (1973), 13.

Telliez, Robert. "A Year Unlike All Others." *NT*, 6 (1969), 7–9. Against ultra-revolutionaries in France.

Timofeyev, L. "Na sele i v gorode" [In the Village and in the City]. *LG*, 40 (1971), 10. On the flight from the countryside in the USSR.

Timofeyev, T. "Vedushchaya sila obshchestvennogo progressa" [The Guiding Force of Social Progress]. *Izvestiya*, October 5, 1972, p. 4. The "guiding force" is the proletariat.

Tochilovsky, V. "Sushchestvuyet li problema 'otchuzhdeniya'?" [Is There a Problem of "Alienation"?]. *Koms. Pr.*, May 30, 1968, p. 2.

Toffler, Alvin. "Oshlomlennyye budushchim" [Future Shock]. *LG*, 30 (1971), 13.

Tomin, V. (ed.). *Molodym nasledovat' mir* [The Young Will Inherit The World]. Moscow, 1968, 240 pp.

Trusov, B. "Kriminal'nyy sluchay" [A Criminal Case]. *LG,* 38 (1972), 16. Street crime in the USSR.

Tur, Ariadne and Pyotr. "Talking Points in Schwabing." *NT,* 17 (1967), 29 ff. On hippies.

Tur, Herbert. "Svet protiv t'my" [Light Against Darkness]. *MK,* 4 (1963), 100–104. About the FRG.

Tyazhel'nikov, E. "V avangarde demokraticheskoy molodezhi mira" [In the Advance Guard of the Democratic Youth of the World]. *MK,* 12 (1970), 33–39.

———. "Lenin i molodezh' " [Lenin and Youth]. *VF,* 1 (1970), 12–23.

Uayner, Bernard. " 'Tikhiy' protsess v Sietle" [The "Quiet" Trial in Seattle]. *Za Rubezhom,* 4 (1971), 16–18.

Ulle, Dieter. "Kriticheskiye zametki k sotsial'noy filosofi Gerberta Markuze" [Is Herbert Marcuse's "Critical Theory of Society" Really Critical?] [Critical Comments on the Social Philosophy of Herbert Marcuse]. *VF,* 9 (1968), 77–86. From East Berlin.

Urlanis, B. "Bezotsovshchina" [Fatherlessness]. *LG,* 2 (1970), 12.

———. "V sem'ye odin rebenok" [One Child in the Family]. *LG,* 39 1972), 13. Concerns the number of children in a family. There is a letter to the editors responding to this article in *LG,* 46 (1972), 13.

Usov, G. "Frants Fanon i ego revolyutsiya otchayaniya" [Franz Fanon and his Revolution of Despair]. *MEiMO,* 10 (1969), 133–142. A critique of Fanon's book *The Wretched of the Earth.*

Valyuzhenich, A. V. "Gimn supermeny" [Superman's Hymn]. *SShA,* 2 (1970), 84 ff. About Marcuse.

Varlamov, K. "Lenin protiv melkoburzhuaznogo revolyutsionarizma" [Lenin Against Petty Bourgeois Revolutionarism]. *MK,* 8 (1969), 44–56.

Vasilenko, V. "Sovetskaya molodezh' i mezhdunarodnyye organizatsii" [Soviet Youth and International Organizations]. *MK,* 11 (1969), 85–89.

Velikovich, L. "Myatezhnyye katoliki" [Protesting Catholics]. *MK,* 8 (1970), 98–103.

Velikovsky, S. "Intelligentsiya v sovremennoy klassovoy bor'be" [The Intelligentsia in the Contemporary Class Struggle]. *MEiMO,* 11 (1971), 109–117.

————. "Bastuyushchaya intelligentsiya" [The Striking Intelligentsia]. *IL*, 7 (1971), 238–247.

Verchenko, Yu., and A. Chubar'yan. "Ismyshleniya Ral'fa Fishera i pravda istorii" [The Inventions of Ralph Fischer and the Truth of History]. *MK*, 1 (1961), 98–104. Review of Fischer's book, *Pattern for Soviet Youth*.

Vergani, Guido. "Eskalatsiya poroka" [The Escalation of Vice]. *LG*, 1 (1971), 13.

Vinter, Rol'f. "Strana nasiliya" [The Land of Violence]. *Za Rubezhom*, 35 (1970), 16–19. About the U.S.

Vishnevsky, S. N. "Delo sud'i Duglasa" [The Case of Judge Douglas]. *SShA*, 9 (1970), 91–96.

Vlastovsky, V. "Eti vzroslyye, vzroslyye deti" [These Grown-ups are Grown-up Children]. *LG*, 38 (1972), 12.

Volkov, V., and V. Vessensky. "Svet i teni nad Kordil'erami" [Light and Shadows Over the Cordillera]. *MK*, 2 (1969), 109–114.

Volodin, A. "Ty tozhe gde-nibud' odin" [You too Are Somewhere Alone]. *LG*, 8 (1970), 13. Loneliness in the USSR, and computers.

Volzhsky, V. "Chetyre goda avantyur" [Four Year Adventure]. *LG*, 14 (1972), 15.

Vul'f, V. "Vokrug Vudstokskogo festivalya" [Around the Woodstock Festival]. *Teatr*, 8 (1970), 147–156.

Vyalykh, L. (Major). "Molodezh' zapada v bor'be za luchsheye budushcheye" [The Youth of the West in the Struggle for a Better Future]. *KVS*, 10 (1972), 83–87.

Yakovlev, A. "Protiv antiistorizma" [Against Anti-Historicism]. *LG*, 46 (1972), 4.

Yakovlev, B. "Marks i molodezh' " [Marx and Youth]. *Yunost'*, 5 (1968), 58–65.

Yanayev, G. "Molodezh stran kapitala v bor'be za demokratiyu i mir" [The Youth of the Lands of Capital in the Struggle for Democracy and Peace]. *KVS*, 19 (1968), 81–86.

————. "Molodezh' mira muzhayet v bor'be" [The Youth of the World Grows in Struggle]. *MK*, 11 (1968), 2–8.

Yaropolov, Ye. "Vremya pod' 'yema, vremya ispytaniy: Molodezhnoye dvizheniye v Italii i deyatel'nost' ital'yanskoy federatsii kommunisticheskoy molodezhi" [A Time of Advance, A Time of Trial: The

Youth Movement in Italy and the Activities of the Italian Federation of Communist Youth]. *MK*, 2 (1970), 99–105.

———. "Avanti popolo . . . !" [Avanti Popolo . . . !] *MK*, 9 (1972), 101–107.

Yaroshevsky, B. " 'Vzryvayushcheyesya Pokoleniye' " [The "Exploding Generation"]. *MK*, 7 (1961), 108–112.

Yefimov, P. "Trudovaya Frantsiya boretsya" [Working France Struggles]. *Agitator*, 12 (1968), 16–19.

Yelistratova, A. "Uil'yam Golding i ego roman 'Shpil' " [William Golding and his Book *"Shpil"*]. *IL*, 10 (1968), 211–218. A review of W. Golding's books.

Yemelyanov, T. "Loskutnyye znamena 'novykh levykh' " [The Ragged Flags of the "New Left"]. *LG*, 43 (1970), 14 ff.

Yevtushenko, Ye. Speech at the Fifth Writers' Congress. *LG*, 28 (1971), 11.

"Youth of the World at the Walls of the Winter Palace." *Yunost'*, 11 (1967), 77–78. A short report on the Leningrad Convocation on "Youth and October" for the 50th Anniversary of the October Revolution.

Yulina, N. S. "Buntuyushchaya molodezh'v poiskakh ideologii" [Rebellious Youth in Search of an Ideology]. *SShA*, 9 (1971), 53–63.

Yurin, Yu. V. "Marksistskiy analiz 'novogo levego' dvizheniya" [A Marxist Analysis of the "New Left" Movement]. *SShA*, 9 (1972), 81 ff. A very positive review of Gil Green's book, *The New Radicalism*.

Zakharova, M. N. "G. Toro: Ot neprotivleniya k soprotivleniyu" [H. Thoreau: From Non-resistance to Resistance]. *SShA*, 11 (1971), 37–45. About Henry David Thoreau's essay "On the Duty of Civil Disobedience."

Zalustskaya, W. V. (ed.). *Otets v sem'ye* [The Father in the Family]. Moscow, 1970, 254 pp.

Zamoshkin, Yu., and N. V. Motroshilova. "Kritichna li 'kriticheskaya teoria obshchestva' Gerberta Markuze" [Is Herbert Marcuse's "Critical Theory of Society" Really Critical?]. *VF*, 10 (1968), 66–77.

———. " 'Novyye levyye': ikh mysli i nastroyeniya" [The "New Lefts": Their Thought and Feelings]. *VF*, 4 (1971), 43–48.

Zasursky, Ya. "Studenty atakuyut 'isteblishment' " [The Students Attack the "Establishment"]. *LG*, 46 (1969), 15.

——, and O. Prudkov. "Sorok vtoraya ulitsa" [Forty-Second Street]. *LG*, 4 (1971), 15.

Zenushkina, I. S. "Biznes i molodezhnoye dvizheniye" [Business and the Youth Movement]. *SShA*, 2 (1972), 88–92.

Zetkin, Klara. *My Recollections of Lenin*. Moscow, 1956, 93 pp.

Zhemanov, O. N. "Kritika kontsepsii 'oburzhuazivaniya' rabochego klassa" [Critique of the Concept of the "Embourgeoisement" of the Working Class]. *VF*, 12 (1970), 3–13.

Zhilin, Yu. "Nekotorye problemy bor'by protiv revizionizma na sovremennom etape" [Some Problems of the Struggle Against Revisionism at the Present Stage]. *MEiMO*, 8 (1970), 4–15 and 9 (1970), 3–18. The relevant sections in 9 (1970) are pp. 4–6.

Zhil'nikov, Ye. "Rasprava nad 'panterami' [Dealing with the "Panthers"]. *MK*, 10 (1970), 113–118.

Zhil'tsova, T. "Pod znakom zodiaka?" [Under a Sign of the Zodiac?]. *LG*, 41 (1972), 13.

Zhukhovitsky, L. "Vokrug tantsploshchadki" [Around the Dance Floor]. *LG*, 44 (1972), 12. On boredom of young people in the USSR.

Zhukov, Yu. "Oborotni" [Werewolves]. *Pravda*, May 30, 1968, p. 4.

——. "Zloba dnya: K itogam parizhskogo literaturnogo sezona" [News of the Day: On the Events of the Paris Literary Season]. *IL*, 8 (1968), 190–213.

Zubin, L. " 'Bol'noye obshchestvo' " [The "Sick Society"]. *KVS*, 22 (1968), 81–84.

INDEX

INDEX

This index includes the *names* of all persons who figure prominently in the book. Of the *subjects,* those appearing all too frequently have been omitted in the Index, such as: America (U.S.), anarchism, bourgeoisie (bourgeois), capitalism, Communism (Communist, Communist Party, Soviet Communism), Kremlin, left ("left," New Left, ultra-left), Marx (Marxist), Moscow, party, proletariat, radical (extremist), revolution (rebel, revolutionary, revolts), schools, socialism, Soviet Union (Russia, USSR), student, university (campus), youth.